THE
EVERYTHING
GLUTEN-FREE SLOW COOKER COOKBOOK

Dear Reader,

I wrote this book to help make your gluten-free life a little easier! Many people struggle with making a healthy dinner every night, but for those with celiac disease, gluten sensitivity, or food allergies, it can be a huge challenge.

I've been gluten-free since 2007 when I learned I was severely intolerant to gluten. At first, I struggled making dinner because I couldn't rely on wheat-based staples such as pasta or frozen meals. Several years later I realized that by using my slow cookers I could make multiple gluten-free meals at once, freezing some for later. This was a huge revelation to me. So I started using my slow cookers several nights a week. Slow cooking made me excited about gluten-free cooking again!

I've made a special effort to include gluten-free baked goods in this cookbook, such as sandwich bread and chocolate cake. These are foods that are often most missed when first starting a gluten-free diet. I hope this cookbook will encourage you to dust off that slow cooker to make healthy and delicious gluten-free meals for your entire family!

Sincerely,

Carrie S. Forbes

Welcome to the EVERYTHING® Series!

These handy, accessible books give you all you need to tackle a difficult project, gain a new hobby, comprehend a fascinating topic, prepare for an exam, or even brush up on something you learned back in school but have since forgotten.

You can choose to read an Everything® book from cover to cover or just pick out the information you want from our four useful boxes: e-questions, e-facts, e-alerts, and e-ssentials.

We give you everything you need to know on the subject, but throw in a lot of fun stuff along the way, too.

We now have more than 400 Everything® books in print, spanning such wide-ranging categories as weddings, pregnancy, cooking, music instruction, foreign language, crafts, pets, New Age, and so much more. When you're done reading them all, you can finally say you know Everything®!

QUESTION

Answers to common questions

FACT

Important snippets of information

ALERT

Urgent warnings

ESSENTIAL

Quick handy tips

PUBLISHER Karen Cooper

MANAGING EDITOR, EVERYTHING® SERIES Lisa Laing

COPY CHIEF Casey Ebert

ASSISTANT PRODUCTION EDITOR Melanie Cordova

ACQUISITIONS EDITOR Lisa Laing

DEVELOPMENT EDITOR Brett Palana-Shanahan

EDITORIAL ASSISTANT Matthew Kane

EVERYTHING® SERIES COVER DESIGNER Erin Alexander

LAYOUT DESIGNERS Erin Dawson, Michelle Roy Kelly, Elisabeth Lariviere

Visit the entire Everything® series at *www.everything.com*

THE
EVERYTHING®
Gluten-Free
Slow Cooker
Cookbook

Carrie S. Forbes

Avon, Massachusetts

TO MY DAD.
Thank you for making countless batches of chocolate chip cookies; cheesy omelets for a picky girl on Sunday mornings; and never growing tired of reading Dr. Seuss's Green Eggs and Ham. *I love you more than you'll ever know.*

An Everything® Series Book.
Everything® and everything.com® are registered trademarks of F+W Media, Inc.

Published by Adams Media, a division of F+W Media, Inc.
57 Littlefield Street, Avon, MA 02322 U.S.A.
www.adamsmedia.com

ISBN 10: 1-4405-3366-0
ISBN 13: 978-1-4405-3366-2
eISBN 10: 1-4405-3528-0
eISBN 13: 978-1-4405-3528-4

Printed in the United States of America.

10 9

Library of Congress Cataloging-in-Publication Data

Forbes, Carrie S.
   The everything gluten-free slow cooker cookbook / Carrie S. Forbes.
      p. cm.
   Includes bibliographical references and index.
   ISBN 978-1-4405-3366-2 (pbk. : alk. paper) – ISBN 1-4405-3366-0 (pbk.
: alk. paper) – ISBN 978-1-4405-3528-4 (ebook : alk. paper) – ISBN
1-4405-3528-0 (ebook : alk. paper)
   1. Gluten-free diet–Recipes. 2. Electric cooking, Slow. I. Title.
   RM237.86.F67 2012
   641.5'884–dc23

                                    2012014512

Always follow safety and commonsense cooking protocol while using kitchen utensils, operating ovens and stoves, and handling uncooked food. If children are assisting in the preparation of any recipe, they should always be supervised by an adult.

Many of the designations used by manufacturers and sellers to distinguish their products are claimed as trademarks. Where those designations appear in this book and Adams Media was aware of a trademark claim, the designations have been printed with initial capital letters.

Nutritional stats by Nicole Cormier, RD.

This book is available at quantity discounts for bulk purchases.
For information, please call 1-800-289-0963.

Contents

Acknowledgments

First and foremost, thank you to my amazing husband Michael. Michael, without your love, patience, brainstorming, and encouragement over all these years of writing a food blog, I could not have written this book. Thank you for being a willing guinea pig, washing endless amounts of dishes, and for always loving me just because. To the faithful readers of my blog "Gingerlemongirl.com," I cannot thank you enough. To Clara Ogren, for inspiring me and being my allergen-free partner in crime. To Amy Adamchak, for pushing me when I needed it! To Jennifer Yandle for always listening and being as excited as I was about this project. To Cheryl Harris: thank you for coming into my life when I most needed your guidance, compassion, and encouragement. Your coaching through this experience has been simply invaluable.

To the blog readers who assisted me in testing the recipes in this book, THANK YOU! Because of your suggestions, tips, and constructive criticism these recipes are outstanding! Also many thanks to my neighbors for taste-testing and filling your refrigerators with abundant amounts of gluten-free slow cooker leftovers! Lastly, a huge thanks to the people at Adams Media who made this cookbook possible, and especially to my editor Lisa Laing for believing in me and providing excellent guidance and support through this process.

Introduction

WHEN YOU GO GLUTEN-FREE, many people assume that you are doomed to a life of bland, tasteless food. This is a common misconception. By using everyday ingredients such as meat, vegetables, herbs, and spices, it is possible to create simple, delicious, and naturally gluten-free meals. Using a slow cooker to create these meals makes the process even easier.

Suddenly learning that you have to follow a gluten-free diet due to health problems can be an extremely overwhelming diagnosis. Yet, because of the increased awareness of celiac disease and wheat allergies in recent years, more and more gluten-free foods are becoming readily available. A growing number of chain restaurants now offer gluten-free menus, and it's become common practice for grocery stores to add gluten-free labels to safe foods on their store shelves.

However, the high cost of specialty gluten-free food items, both in restaurants and stores, can become a huge financial burden for families. By making your own gluten-free meals, you will not only be saving money, but you will also be feeding your family much healthier meals. You will have more control over the ingredients in your foods, along with making sure the foods are safe by preventing cross-contamination in your home kitchen.

Hopefully, you will use this cookbook as a guide for learning the basics of gluten-free cooking. It will provide you with an abundance of gluten-free main dishes, side dishes, breads, desserts, holiday recipes, and even kid-friendly favorites to make sure there is something for everyone—even when you're on a limited budget.

The fundamental recipes in this book should be used as templates for creating meals that you and your family will love. I have also included tips and hints in each section for ideas on shopping, eating out, and keeping your kitchen safe from cross-contamination.

Many of the recipes include foods that are fresh and inherently gluten-free, such as poultry, meat, vegetables, fruits, eggs, and dairy. Additionally, numerous recipes offer substitution suggestions for other food intolerances so that you can easily make meals that are also dairy/casein-free or soy-free.

While these recipes mostly contain common gluten-free ingredients, you will need to purchase a few different types of specific gluten-free flours for some of the recipes. See Appendix A for suggestions on where to purchase specific gluten-free flours and other cooking ingredients. Alternately, in some recipes, you can use your favorite gluten-free all-purpose baking mix (such as Gluten-Free Bisquick) instead of the various gluten-free flours listed. Often it's cheaper to buy several types of gluten-free flours to make homemade gluten-free mixes; but for those with limited cabinet space, prepared gluten-free baking mixes can be a helpful solution.

The best part about all of these recipes? You get to make them using the convenience of a slow cooker. Being gluten-free is a challenge on the best of days, but by making use of a slow cooker to do the work for you, it not only makes life easier, but also gives you peace of mind that you can follow this diet and do it well. This cookbook uses several different sizes of slow cookers and it's recommended that you have a large slow cooker and a small/medium-sized slow cooker to be able to make all the dishes.

The goal of this book is to not only teach you the basics of a gluten-free diet, but to help you create tasty and nutritious foods every single day with the help of your slow cooker.

CHAPTER 1

Why Gluten-Free?

Gluten-free has become a hot phrase these days. More and more people are being diagnosed with celiac disease, wheat or gluten sensitivity, and food allergies. Many people even use the diet for nonmedical treatment of autism spectrum disorders. And still others feel that removing gluten from their diet improves their health and increases their energy. This chapter will teach you how to find naturally gluten-free foods, how to spend less on your grocery bill for gluten-free foods, and how to prevent cross-contamination in your home kitchen.

Gluten Defined

Gluten is the term used for several types of proteins found in wheat, barley, and rye. The proteins gliadin and glutelin are found in these grains and together form a substance called gluten. Gluten is a "storage protein," which means that it holds the key ingredients for these grains to continue proliferating.

Gluten is primarily found in foods like bread, pasta, cakes, muffins, crackers, and pizza dough. Wheat, barley, and rye are used in many baked goods because the gluten in these grains provides excellent elasticity, structure, and texture. Gluten is what causes pizza to have a chewy, stretchy texture. It gives French bread its soft white center and chewy crust. Gluten makes cinnamon rolls stretchy, soft, and light. It helps give structure to bread dough when rising, so that the bread becomes tall and stays tall after baking and cooling.

FACT

There are no "typical" signs and symptoms of celiac disease, according to the Mayo Clinic. Celiac patients often report having a wide range of symptoms that can be anything from well-known signs such as diarrhea, constipation, or malabsorption of nutrients, to migraine headaches, "brain fog," loss of memory, joint pain, irritability, depression, neuropathy, infertility, and osteoporosis.

Avoiding gluten can be difficult for several reasons. The biggest reason is that ingredients containing gluten are not required by law to be listed on food labels. However, by law, the top eight food allergens must be listed on every food label in the United States, and wheat (which is a primary source of gluten) is one of them. So although you may not see "gluten" in the ingredients list, you can look for food allergen information, for example, "contains wheat."

When you are removing gluten from your diet, you will also need to avoid these foods (most are derivatives of wheat), which also contain gluten:

- Barley
- Rye
- Triticale (a cross between rye and wheat)

- Bulgur
- Durum flour
- Farina
- Graham flour
- Kamut
- Semolina
- Spelt
- Couscous

As a matter of fact, it's often a good idea (especially when you first receive a diagnosis of celiac disease) to *only* eat foods that are either naturally gluten-free, or actually are labeled "gluten-free" until you have a better understanding of how to read food and nutrition labels.

Celiac Disease . . . Gluten Sensitivity . . . What's the Big Deal?

Celiac disease (also known as celiac sprue or gluten-sensitive enteropathy) is an auto-immune and digestive disorder that occurs in about one in 100 people in the United States. For people with this disorder, gluten can cause serious damage to their intestine if it is ingested. If you have celiac disease or gluten sensitivity, gluten damages the "villi" in your intestines. Since the villi (finger-like projections that contain most of the enzymes needed for digestion) are damaged for those with celiac disease, their bodies have enormous difficulty ingesting the healthy nutrients their bodies need such as fat, calcium, iron, and folate.

Some of the symptoms of celiac disease and gluten sensitivity include:

- Digestive problems such as bloating, vomiting, excess gas and/or pain, severe and/or chronic diarrhea, irritable bowel, weight loss, weight gain, etc.
- Constant and/or severe headaches or migraines
- Low levels of iron (anemia)
- Skin rashes (also known as *dermatitis herpetiformis*)
- Bone or joint pain

- Depression and/or anxiety
- Seizures
- Infertility
- Unexplained fatigue
- Failure to thrive (often seen in children with celiac disease)

Most people have a healthy immune system that prevents the body from being harmed by gluten, but for those with celiac disease the only effective treatment is avoiding foods with gluten altogether.

To get tested for celiac disease and/or gluten sensitivity you need to visit your family doctor or a gastroenterologist, who will do a blood test to check for high levels of a certain types of antibodies. If your blood test comes back with positive results for celiac disease, your doctor may then choose to do a biopsy of your small intestine to check for damage to the villi. A diagnosis is usually given using a combination of these diagnostic tests. Gluten sensitivity (as opposed to celiac disease) is sometimes diagnosed if a patient tests negatively for the disorder, yet his or her body reacts with symptoms that are similar to those with celiac disease.

Planning for a Gluten-Free Lifestyle

If you've been diagnosed with celiac disease, the first thing you will want to do is gather all the information you can. Ask your doctor to recommend a nutritionist or registered dietitian who can give you a better understanding of what going gluten-free really means. A nutritionist may also request that your doctor order tests to help you discover if you have any additional food sensitivities or nutritional deficiencies. These tests may include a bone scan or tests of vitamin D, calcium, iron, zinc, B_{12}, folate, or thyroid levels. Once your doctor and nutritionist have a better picture of what's going on in your body, they can help you to determine the best plan of action and what gluten-free foods will be the most nutritious choices for your body.

Research Online

Do some online research to find local grocery stores that have gluten-free foods, along with local restaurants with gluten-free items on their menus.

There are countless websites available that can help you find local gluten-free resources such as community support groups, books to help educate yourself and your family, gluten-free recipes and menus, and even gluten-free shopping guides. Your community may even have a gluten-free bakery that offers baked goods like pizza, sandwich bread, cakes, and cookies.

ALERT

Every time you visit a restaurant make sure to assess the knowledge of the wait staff and kitchen staff. Ask your server for a gluten-free menu. Ask about the steps taken in the kitchen area to prevent cross-contamination. If a waiter or chef doesn't understand what gluten-free means, it may be a sign that gluten-free options are not available. Never be afraid to ask specific questions—your health is important!

Community Resources

The best place to find out about the basics of a gluten-free diet (and businesses in your community that are understanding of the gluten-free diet) is your local library. You can check out gluten-free cookbooks and guidebooks, do research on the public access computers, and get help from a reference librarian. Make sure to check out any local community bulletin boards to learn about gluten-free support groups that may meet in the library, local restaurants, or local church facilities. (This is also a good way to find out about churches in your area that may provide the option of gluten-free Communion or Eucharist services.)

Another great source of information is your Community or County Extension Agency. There will generally be an agent who specializes in the food resources and support groups in the community. This is also a great organization to contact if you would like to find out about regional farms that sell fresh organic produce and meats, which are usually gluten-free. These farms may also make and sell hygiene products like goat's milk soap and lotions. Often if these products are organic they typically will not contain gluten, although you will have to ask to be sure.

ESSENTIAL

Children who have celiac disease can become sick from using Play-Doh, a common modeling compound made from wheat flour. Because children often put their fingers in their mouths during and after play, they can become sick from accidentally ingesting the gluten on their hands. Other alternatives include Moon Dough, which is hypoallergenic and wheat-free, and Aroma Dough, made from gluten-free flours.

Gluten Is Not Just in Food

Other products that can contain gluten are medications and vitamins, which may use gluten as a binder or filler. Shampoos, conditioners, toothpaste, lipsticks, lip balms, as well as face and hand creams, can contain gluten. You will have to do your research either online or by calling companies specifically to find out which products contain gluten and which ones are safe. Gluten can't get through your skin into your bloodstream, but if you are showering, bathing, or brushing your teeth with products that contain gluten, there is a slight possibility that it could enter your mouth and your digestive system.

The Basics of a Gluten-Free Diet

The best part about following a basic gluten-free diet is that you'll be eating more fresh, natural, and unprocessed foods. Which means you will not only be following a gluten-free diet, but a nutritionally balanced and healthy one.

It's often recommended when starting a gluten-free diet to start with naturally gluten-free foods. These foods include:

- Fruits
- Vegetables
- Beans
- Rice
- Nuts and seeds
- Unseasoned fresh meats
- Unseasoned fresh chicken

- Fish
- Milk, cheese, and plain yogurt
- Eggs

Most of these foods (except for the beans and rice) are located around the perimeter of your grocery store, where most of the fresh foods are. Most naturally gluten-free foods will not come in a bag or box. Other than canned fruits or vegetables, rice, beans, and nuts, you can find most gluten-free foods in their natural state in the produce, meat, and dairy sections.

Pantry Makeover

The thought of having to change your entire diet due to celiac disease or gluten sensitivity can feel completely overwhelming. No more bread? No pasta, pizza, doughnuts, or cookies?

While this may have been true even five years ago (at least as far as purchasing these items in a local grocery store or restaurant), the gluten-free food industry has come a long way. There are many companies that produce high quality and readily available gluten-free products like sandwich breads, pastas, flours, cookies, and snacks. Most large grocery stores now have a gluten-free section, where you can find substitutions for many of your gluten-rich favorite foods.

But before you jump into buying a whole bunch of gluten-free processed foods, take a look at your kitchen. You may already have a fair amount of food that is already gluten-free. You will also need to identify foods that contain gluten, which you will need to avoid.

Here is a list of naturally gluten-free foods you can keep:

- Baking ingredients such as baking powder, baking soda, salt, individual herbs and spices (not seasoning blends, which may contain gluten), oils, and sugar
- Canned, frozen, and jarred foods such as plain vegetables, beans, dried beans, fruits, peanut butter (and other nut butters), plain jams, jellies, and honey
- Canned tuna and chicken
- Plain rice (not seasoned rice mixes, which usually contain gluten)

- Fresh and frozen fruits and vegetables of all types
- Fresh and frozen unseasoned meats, chicken, and fish
- Eggs
- Natural cheeses ("cheese foods" often contain wheat)
- Milk and nondairy milk substitutions
- Unseasoned nuts

Other foods in your pantry should be moved to a designated "gluten section" or removed entirely. This includes any food that lists "flour" as an ingredient on the label. This will include most "cream of" soups, noodle soups, baking mixes, pancake mixes, all-purpose and self-rising flours, and even some nonstick baking sprays. And of course, breads, bagels, frozen pancakes, waffles, cookies, and crackers. Also off-limits are opened condiments in your fridge that family members have placed knives or spoons in (because they may have been contaminated by gluten).

Buying gluten-free specialty items can be very expensive. Gluten-free foods often cost as much as 400 percent more than their traditional wheat counterparts. For example, a loaf of regular bread may cost about $1.50, while a generally much smaller loaf of gluten-free bread can easily cost over $6.00. Because specialty gluten-free foods can be so expensive, it's cost-effective for families to eat as many naturally gluten-free foods as they can. Buying fruits and vegetables in season can help with food costs, along with purchasing canned or frozen versions during the winter months.

Another great way to save money on a gluten-free diet is to make most of your meals and snacks from scratch. You can make many of these foods at home using your slow cooker; even breads and other baked goods. Initially it might be expensive to buy gluten-free ingredients to make homemade baked goods, but they will still be cheaper than gluten-free store-bought products.

Gluten-Free Flours and Baking Ingredients

When you're following a gluten-free diet, you not only have to learn to cook gluten-free foods, but you also need to learn how to bake without gluten. Birthday parties need cake! Big breakfasts need biscuits, or pancakes, or toast. Sandwiches need bread to hold them together.

You can actually make gluten-free baked goods right in your slow cooker. To make these foods you will need a few special ingredients such as gluten-free flours. The gluten-free flours used in this book are brown rice flour, sorghum flour, millet flour, cornstarch, and arrowroot starch. Generally you will only need three of those flours per baking recipe. Sorghum flour and millet flour can be used interchangeably in these recipes. So if you prefer millet flour over sorghum flour, feel free to substitute.

Sometimes either blanched almond flour or garbanzo bean flour are added to bread recipes, usually for sandwich-type breads. These are very high-protein flours that will help the bread structurally to rise and keep its shape after baking. Many breads need yeast to help the bread rise. The best yeast to use in slow-cooker baking is a fast-acting yeast that doesn't need to be mixed with water to become activated. This type of yeast is usually called "rapid rise," "instant," or "bread machine yeast." This yeast will be mixed with the dry gluten-free ingredients when making the bread.

QUESTION

Why are so many different flours used in gluten-free baking recipes?
Wheat flour has been preferred for centuries because of the special properties of gluten. Since gluten-free flours don't contain the unique elastic properties of wheat flour, they don't have the same ability to produce baked goods that are light, yet sturdy. So gluten-free baked goods often have a much better texture and taste when you combine a variety of flours that have different properties.

Lastly, when baking gluten-free recipes, you need a binder, which helps replace the action of gluten in baked goods. The most commonly used binder in gluten-free baking is xanthan gum. This is a powder made from a strain of bacteria that is grown on corn. When xanthan gum is introduced to a liquid, the mixture becomes thick and sticky. This quality helps give structure to gluten-free baked goods. If you're allergic to corn products, you can use guar gum in place of the xanthan gum.

Preventing Cross-Contamination

People with celiac disease (and often those who are gluten intolerant) will experience major symptoms if the tiniest bit of gluten comes into contact with something they ingest. The smallest amount of gluten can cause gastrointestinal distress and pain, including severe bloating, diarrhea, vomiting, constipation, stomach pain, and headaches. And these physical symptoms can last for days. Therefore, learning to keep your kitchen safe for you or your loved ones is imperative. There are many different methods you can use to prevent cross-contamination in your home.

The easiest method of preventing cross-contamination is to simply become a gluten-free family. Using this method, there is simply no gluten in the home to worry about. All counters will be safe. You only need one toaster and one set of cooking utensils. You won't have to worry about separating foods or accidentally using the peanut butter that non-celiac family members were using to make sandwiches. However, this option is not always financially possible or it may be difficult to convince non-celiac family members to give up foods that do not cause them harm.

Also, children and adults alike will have to learn how to contend with a gluten-eating world when they leave home. Having celiac disease or gluten sensitivity means having to learn how to navigate in the world, whether you're at a grocery store, at work, or visiting a friend's house for dinner. So having a shared kitchen can come with the benefits of learning how to adequately keep your gluten-free foods safe.

FACT

It was once thought that only children suffered from celiac disease and only had certain symptoms such as diarrhea, stunted growth, and sometimes an enlarged stomach. In the 1950s and early 1960s doctors didn't know exactly what caused celiac disease, but they knew bananas and rice didn't seem to negatively affect the health of their patients. Children who were diagnosed with celiac disease during that time were sometimes called "Banana Babies" because bananas were so frequently prescribed by their doctors.

If your kitchen will contain both gluten-free and other foods, you'll need to set up a system to keep them apart. First, use separate cutting boards. Keep a gluten-free cutting board in a safe drawer on one side of the kitchen and keep another cutting board in another drawer. When preparing two types of meals, always prepare the gluten-free meals first, either on a clean surface or the gluten-free cutting board.

Use a color-coded or sticker system to differentiate gluten-free foods from gluten-containing foods. This method is especially helpful when you have children who aren't old enough to read yet. By placing large stickers of the same color on safe foods, it will be easy for them to tell the difference between safe and unsafe foods. Along with color-coding, teach your children and loved ones to place all gluten-free foods above gluten-containing foods in cabinets and on shelves. For example, if you have a shelf that contains regular baking ingredients, place all gluten-free baking ingredients on the shelf above the regular foods. This way you are preventing any chance of a crumb or bit of flour falling onto the gluten-free food.

When cooking gluten-free foods, you do not necessarily have to use specific pans, as long as it can be thoroughly scrubbed washed and sanitized in hot, soapy water. If a pan cannot be scrubbed (i.e. a nonstick pan), replace it. If you are worried about old crumbs being stuck on a particularly old pan, you can cover the pan in aluminum foil to protect the gluten-free foods from getting contaminated. However, you *will* need to use a designated gluten-free toaster. There is no way to completely protect yourself from all the crumbs that have been embedded in a toaster. Try to place the separate toasters as far away from each other as possible. And as with gluten-free foods, it would be helpful to color-code the gluten-free toaster with a sticker.

While you can continue to use metal cooking utensils for gluten-free foods, you cannot use wooden utensils that have come in contact with gluten-containing foods. Gluten can get embedded in tiny grains of wooden or bamboo utensils and bowls, and therefore they cannot be used for gluten-free foods, unless they are brand-new and only used for gluten-free preparations.

For your refrigerator, buy separate condiments and label them using the color-coding system. Remember if someone placed a knife that had been on regular bread in your gluten-free mayonnaise jar, it's cross-contaminated and can no longer be considered gluten-free. Therefore, it's important to keep a special gluten-free shelf in your refrigerator. Alternately, you can buy condiments that come in plastic squeeze jars so that they never come in contact with dirty knives or spoons.

Here are the main points to remember in helping prevent cross-contamination:

- Keep separate cutting boards in designated areas
- Prepare gluten-free foods and meals on a clean counter or cutting board before preparing gluten-containing foods
- Use a color-coded or sticker system to mark gluten-free items
- Make sure to wash all cooking pans thoroughly in hot, soapy water
- If in doubt, use foil to cover baking pans to keep foods safe
- Store gluten-free foods above gluten-containing foods in the pantry
- Have a separate color-coded area for gluten-free condiments in the refrigerator
- If you're concerned that gluten-free food has come in contact with gluten, stick with the adage, "If in doubt, throw it out."

CHAPTER 2

Slow Cooker Basics

Now that you have a better understanding of the foods that are safe for a gluten-free diet, it's time to learn how to cook them. This chapter will teach you how to use slow cookers in your everyday gluten-free meal planning. You will also learn what types of slow cookers will work best for your family, when to use the slow cooker, important slow cooker safety tips, and how to easily clean and store these super versatile kitchen appliances.

The Gluten-Free Diet and Your Slow Cooker

Now that you are removing gluten from your diet, you've probably realized you have to do a lot more food preparation than you may have done in the past. By using one or more slow cookers, you can allow the appliances to do the majority of the work for you. You won't have to stand by the stove stirring the pot every few minutes. Slow cookers give you the flexibility to do other things while you're cooking. With most cooking times ranging anywhere from two to eight hours, it will be a rare occurrence to have burned, unappetizing foods.

Many naturally gluten-free foods are a perfect fit for the slow cooker. Hearty beef roasts, whole chickens, and root vegetables like potatoes, carrots, and rutabagas will all cook beautifully in the slow cooker. One way to make gluten-free meals easier during the week is to use the slow cooker to prepare two to three larger meals on the weekend, which you can freeze to warm up in portions throughout the week. At first it will seem time-consuming to cook several meals, but you'll thank yourself later in the week as you enjoy home-cooked meals that only take a few minutes to reheat.

FACT

The West Bend company first created an electric cooker in the early 1960s for cooking beans. It was simply called The Beanery. It was meant to be an electric version of the popular stoneware Boston Bean Pot.

A really good reason to use slow cookers for gluten-free cooking is that going out to eat when you are on a restricted diet can be frustrating. You have to worry about whether or not the wait staff will understand what gluten-free means and if the kitchen staff understands how to prevent cross-contamination. By using your slow cooker you can prepare more meals easily and quickly at home. While the cooking periods may be longer than regular stovetop cooking, it often takes very little time to prepare the ingredients for a slow cooker meal.

If you're in a huge hurry, try a recipe from the "Five Ingredients or Fewer" chapter. If you have picky kids, let them choose and help you prepare a recipe from the "Kid-Friendly Meals" chapter. And slow cooker meals aren't just for the winter months. The slow cooker is actually a wonderful appliance to use during the late spring and summer months because you can cook a whole meal without heating up your kitchen. Slow cookers are also very frugal appliances; they generally use about the same amount of energy as an incandescent light bulb.

Choosing the Perfect Slow Cooker

Are you cooking for two, four, or ten? How often you plan on cooking and how many you are cooking for will help decide what size and type of slow cooker you will need. For most of the recipes in this book you will be able to use a 4-quart slow cooker. This is a medium-sized slow cooker and is helpful for cooking both smaller meals and meals that will have about six servings.

Original slow cookers of the 1970s were round and tall in shape. Today's newer and more modern slow cookers are usually oval in shape and offer a more wide and flat base. This wide base is extremely useful when cooking roasts and whole chickens, as well as cooking large pots of soup and stew. In this cookbook you will also learn how to bake gluten-free sandwich bread in a slow cooker; the wide base of a larger oval slow cooker is perfect for holding a loaf pan.

QUESTION

How hot does a slow cooker get?
Newer slow cookers generally are supposed to heat to 300°F on the high setting and 200°F on the low setting. Which means your food should stay somewhere between 170°F and 280°F.

Slow Cooker Size

While there are numerous sizes of slow cookers made by many different appliance companies, only a few sizes were used during the testing of this book. Primarily, a 4-quart oval slow cooker was used for most recipes yielding 4–6 servings. For smaller dishes, desserts, appetizers, and sauces, a small 2.5-quart oval slow cooker was used. For the occasional large roast, turkey breast, whole chicken, and the gluten-free sandwich bread, a large 6-quart oval slow cooker was used.

If you plan on primarily cooking larger amounts of food to save for meals throughout the week or if you have a big family you will probably want to have a 5–7-quart slow cooker. However, for smaller desserts, appetizers, and sauces, you may want a smaller 1.5–2.5-quart slow cooker. If you have limited storage or counter space, the best option for you may be a medium-sized 3–4-quart slow cooker.

You will need to note that if a recipe suggests using a 4-quart slow cooker and you only have a 6-quart slow cooker, you will need to significantly adjust the cooking times. The food can either cook much faster or much slower depending on the amount of food, the type of food, and the temperature characteristics of your individual slow cooker. The outcome of the recipe can also be quite different than its intended purpose. For example, if you prepared the Pear Clafoutis (Chapter 4) in a 6-quart slow cooker as opposed to the recommended 2.5-quart slow cooker, instead of having a cake-like dessert, you would end up with a delicious pancake that's ready in about an hour as opposed to the suggested cooking time of three hours.

FACT

You can now purchase heavy-duty removable plastic liners for slow cookers, which can make cleanup a breeze. They are manufactured by Reynolds and can be purchased at most grocery stores. To use them, you simply place the liner in the slow cooker and add the foods as directed by your recipe. When you have finished serving your food, you remove the liner and throw it away.

In some cases if you only have a larger 6–7-quart slow cooker you can cook a recipe that's meant for a smaller slow cooker by placing the ingredients in an oven-safe casserole dish that will fit inside the larger slow cooker. This method is especially effective for casserole dishes and some desserts such as the Blueberry Cobbler found in Chapter 14.

How Old Is That Slow Cooker?

All of the recipes in this cookbook were tested using newer slow cookers that were bought within the past five to six years. Slow cookers made since about 2005 cook hotter due to USDA food temperature safety regulations;

therefore foods in newer slow cookers will cook faster than in older models. As a general rule of thumb, most of the recipes in this book were finished cooking at three hours on high heat or six hours on low heat. This means that if you prefer your roast beef a little more on the rare side, you will have to check the internal temperature of the roast sooner than the suggested cooking time.

Planning Gluten-Free Meals Around Your Slow Cooker

When deciding how and when to use your slow cooker, it's helpful to have a weekly menu plan in place. This can help you determine if you need to cook a meal in advance using the slow cooker and how to use your leftovers for meals throughout the week. For instance, you may choose to roast a chicken on Sunday night. After the meal, you could use the bones to make chicken stock, which could be used to cook rice or potatoes or could be added to a casserole later in the week.

ESSENTIAL

Some grocery stores have all of their specialty gluten-free products in a designated section or aisle. Newer grocery stores have started to incorporate gluten-free foods throughout the entire store with similar gluten-containing foods. For example, at Harris Teeter, a higher-end grocery store in southeastern United States, you can find frozen gluten-free pizzas located next to the regular wheat-based frozen pizzas.

Recipes using boneless, skinless cuts such as chicken breasts, thighs, and boneless pork loin will cook faster than recipes calling for bone-in cuts. Therefore, many of the recipes in this book could even be made for dinner in the evening because they will be fully cooked in two hours on high heat. This is perfect for weeknight meals. If you have errands to run, you can stop by home first, toss the ingredients in the slow cooker, and when you come back home your meal will be ready.

If you have recipes that need to be cooked for longer periods of time, they can easily be cooked overnight. A few examples of foods that can be cooked over long periods are dried beans, chicken stock, beef stock, or some soups. Some types of pork roasts can also withstand very long cooking periods.

If you work full-time and don't have a lot of time during the week to use your slow cooker, the weekends are the perfect time to take advantage of cooking meals for the week ahead. If you have several slow cookers you can put them all to use on Saturday or Sunday and prepare two to three meals, which can be divided up into portions and refrigerated for two days or frozen for up to three months. Freezing slow-cooked foods can be especially helpful if you happen to have an abundance of naturally gluten-free foods (often from stocking up on a sale at the grocery store or extra food from generous neighbors) and don't want them to go out of date. You can slow cook the extra food and freeze it in individual portions or in 2–3 cup amounts for casseroles or soups.

High Versus Low

Because newer slow cookers cook at higher temperatures it can be easy to overcook lean cuts of meat like chicken breasts or pork loin. If you are concerned about whether or not meats (or chicken in particular) have been cooked enough, check the temperature with a food thermometer. These handy devices can be purchased at any big box department store or specialty kitchen store.

In general, foods should reach these temperatures to be considered safe for consumption:

▼   SAFE MINIMUM COOKING TEMPERATURES

CATEGORY	FOOD	MINIMUM TEMPERATURE
Ground Meats	Beef, Pork, Veal, Lamb	160°F
Beef, Lamb	Steaks, Roasts, Chops	145°F
Poultry	Chicken, Turkey, Cornish Hen	165°F
Pork, Ham	Fresh Pork and Ham (raw)	145°F

From FoodSafety.Gov

If your slow cooker has a tendency to cook too quickly, it might be a good idea to set a kitchen timer or the general timer on your microwave or oven to help you remember when to remove foods from the slow cooker.

If your slow cooker seems to be undercooking foods, it may be time to purchase a new one, as it would be very unsafe to consume foods (especially meats) that are not cooked properly. In general you do not want to use your slow cooker to reheat foods, since the food could be sitting for an extended period of time at too low of a temperature, allowing bacteria to thrive.

FACT

Did you know that slow cookers may take longer to cook foods at higher altitudes? You may need to adjust your cooking times if you live in an elevated area. This will be particularly important to remember when making gluten-free baked goods. For example, if you are making bread, you may need to bake it for an additional 45 minutes to an hour longer than the recipe suggests.

However, for some cooked foods, such as mashed potatoes, dips, soups, or stew, the slow cooker can be ideal for keeping these foods safely warm for extended periods of time. A good example of using the slow cooker for this purpose would be to keep these foods warm for a holiday or family buffet.

Cleaning Tips and Slow Cooker Safety

Some people don't like using slow cookers because they assume they are hard to clean. While this can be true in some cases, generally slow cooker inserts are incredibly easy to clean. Most modern slow cookers are made with a glazed stoneware insert. Some older-style slow cookers did not have removable inserts, which did make them very hard to clean since they could not be immersed in water.

Many of the recipes in this book recommend using nonstick cooking spray or olive oil to grease the slow cooker before use. Greasing the slow cooker before each use helps food to not stick to the inside surface of the cooker even during long cooking periods. If you choose not to grease your slow cooker, it's recommended to clean the slow cooker insert as soon as it's cool enough to handle. As long as the slow cooker is still slightly warm, sticky food residue should still release easily from the glazed stoneware with hot, soapy water.

However, if you happen to forget to grease the slow cooker and then don't have time to wash it as soon as it's cooled down enough to handle, there are a few tricks you can use to better clean your stoneware.

- Add hot soapy water to the slow cooker, as high up as the food was while cooking. Allow it to soak on the counter for several hours before washing.
- Use a nonabrasive nylon brush or sponge to scrub hard-to-clean areas of your slow cooker.
- Use nonabrasive cleaners such as a glass top stove cream cleaner for stubborn, stuck-on food.
- Make sure *not* to leave your slow cooker insert soaking in water in the sink. Due to the unglazed bottom surface area, the slow cooker can soak up water and then later crack while cooking.
- Vinegar is a great nonchemical option for cleaning water spots or stains in your slow cooker insert.

Don't forget the outside of your slow cooker also needs to be cleaned. Make sure the base is unplugged and then wipe down the outside and inside of the slow cooker with a washcloth and hot, soapy water. Dry it afterward thoroughly with a clean towel. Never immerse the base in water.

It's also extremely important to follow several safety tips while using your slow cooker. First, make sure the slow cooker is on a sturdy surface and that the cord is safely tucked away. For instance, you do not want to have a hot slow cooker sitting on a table that may be close to a high-traffic area where children are playing or running in and out of the room. Someone could trip over the cord, or accidentally pull it out of the wall and get hurt either by the cord, the hot contents of the slow cooker, or the hot base of the slow cooker itself.

ALERT

Make sure to refrigerate leftover cooked food as soon as possible when you've finished serving your meal. Foods left to cool on the counter are ideal candidates for bacterial growth that can cause food poisoning. FoodSafety.gov suggests not leaving perishable foods out for more than two hours, to prevent the occurrence of illness-causing bacteria. Perishable foods include meat, fish, poultry, dairy, eggs, and leftovers.

Secondly, it's always important to unplug your slow cooker after you've finished cooking your meal. This is especially important if you have a slow cooker that does not have an indicator light telling you that it's on, or an electric timer that automatically switches the temperature to warm. It's best to use slow cookers (without these safety features) only when you are home so that you can keep an eye on them.

It's also highly recommended to defrost all meats and chicken in the refrigerator before cooking them, as using them frozen may lower the overall temperature of the food to unsafe levels during the beginning of slow cooking a meal.

CHAPTER 3

Slow Cooker 101: Recipes

Chicken Broth

When you remove the meat from the bones, save the dark meat for use in a casserole and the white meat for chicken salad. (To keep the chicken moist, return it to the strained broth and let it cool overnight in the refrigerator before you chop it for the salad.)

INGREDIENTS | YIELDS 4 CUPS

3 pounds bone-in chicken pieces
1 large onion, peeled and quartered
2 large carrots, scrubbed
2 stalks of celery
1 teaspoon salt
½ teaspoon freshly ground black pepper
4½ cups water

Schmaltz

The chicken fat that will rise to the top of the broth and harden overnight in the refrigerator is known as schmaltz. You can save that fat and use it instead of butter for sautéing vegetables.

1. Add the chicken pieces and onion to a 4–6-quart slow cooker.

2. Slice the carrots and cut the celery into pieces that will fit in the slow cooker and add them. Add the salt, pepper, and water. Cover and cook on low for 6–8 hours. (Cooking time will depend on the size of the chicken pieces.) Allow to cool to room temperature.

3. Strain, discarding the cooked vegetables. Remove any meat from the chicken bones and save for another use. Refrigerate the (cooled) broth overnight. Remove and discard the hardened fat. The resulting concentrated broth can be kept for 1 week in the refrigerator or frozen for up to 3 months.

PER SERVING (1 CUP) | Calories: 98 | Fat: 3.5 g | Protein: 4.5 g | Sodium: 898 mg | Fiber: 0 g | Carbohydrates: 11 g | Sugar: 0 g

Roast Chicken

One of the easiest and most affordable gluten-free meals you can make is a roasted chicken.

INGREDIENTS | SERVES 6

3–4 medium white potatoes, quartered
1 small onion, quartered
2 carrots, sliced
1 large stalk celery, sliced
1 (3–4 pound) whole chicken
2 tablespoons olive oil
1 teaspoon salt
½ teaspoon ground pepper
½ teaspoon dried thyme
¼ teaspoon dried rosemary

1. Add potatoes, onion, carrots, and celery to the bottom of a greased 4-quart slow cooker.

2. Rinse off whole chicken, pat dry with a paper towel, and place on top of the vegetables.

3. Drizzle chicken with olive oil. Sprinkle salt, pepper, and herbs evenly over chicken.

4. Cover and cook on high for 3½ hours or on low for 6 hours.

PER SERVING | Calories: 264 | Fat: 8 g | Protein: 25 g | Sodium: 504 mg | Fiber: 3.5 g | Carbohydrates: 20 g | Sugar: 3 g

"Precooked" Chicken

Make this chicken on the weekends and you'll have cooked chicken ready to use for a quick dinner on busy weeknights. Instead of chicken breasts you can also use a whole chicken that has been cut into quarters.

INGREDIENTS | SERVES 4

4 large skinless, boneless chicken breasts
½ cup gluten-free chicken broth or water

Easy Weeknight Meals

Use this chicken for quick weeknight stir-fries or chicken salad. It can also be added to pasta dishes or served with baked potatoes and steamed broccoli.

1. Place chicken breasts in a greased 4-quart slow cooker. Pour chicken broth or water over the chicken.

2. Cook on high for 3–4 hours or on low for 6–7 hours.

3. Place chicken and broth in the refrigerator for up to 3 days until needed. Do not cut chicken until it's completely cooled, to help retain its moisture. If not used within 3 days, freeze for up to a month.

PER SERVING | Calories: 281 | Fat: 6.5 g | Protein: 38 g | Sodium: 404.5 mg | Fiber: 0 g | Carbohydrates: 1.5 g | Sugar: 0 g

Dijon Beef Roast

Dijon mustard gives this roast a delicious tangy flavor. This recipe is perfect for roast beef sandwiches or for a traditional Sunday meal with mashed potatoes and gravy.

INGREDIENTS | SERVES 6

1 large onion, thickly sliced

1 (3–4 pound) beef round roast

3–4 tablespoons Dijon mustard

½ teaspoon salt

½ teaspoon ground pepper

1 tablespoon olive oil

½ cup gluten-free beef broth, or water

1. Place the onion slices in a greased 4-quart slow cooker.

2. Rub the beef roast with the Dijon mustard. Place on top of sliced onions.

3. Sprinkle salt and pepper on top of beef roast and drizzle with olive oil and beef broth.

4. Cover and cook on high for 2½–3 hours or on low for 5–6 hours. Cooking time will vary depending on your preference of doneness (either rare/medium/or well-done). For a more rare roast, check the internal temperature (should be around 145°F) after cooking for 1½ hours on high or 3 hours on low. Serve roast with the cooked onions and au jus drizzled on top.

PER SERVING | Calories: 499 | Fat: 24 g | Protein: 54 g | Sodium: 346 mg | Fiber: 1 g | Carbohydrates: 3 g | Sugar: 1 g

Beef Broth

Unlike chicken or turkey broth, beef broth requires a larger ratio of meat to the amount of bones used to make it. This method makes a concentrated broth. As a general rule, for regular beef broth you can usually mix ½ cup of this broth with ½ cup water.

INGREDIENTS | YIELDS ABOUT 4 CUPS

1 (2-pound) bone-in chuck roast
1 pound beef bones
1 large onion, peeled and quartered
2 large carrots, scrubbed
2 stalks of celery
1 teaspoon salt
½ teaspoon freshly ground black pepper
4½ cups water

Boiling Broth

You don't want to let broth come to a boil during the initial cooking process because fat will render from the meat, incorporate into the broth, and make it cloudy. However, after you have strained the broth and removed the fat, you can keep it in the refrigerator longer if you bring it to a boil every other day; cool it and return it to the refrigerator until needed.

1. Add the chuck roast, beef bones, and onion to a 4-quart or larger slow cooker. Slice the carrots and cut the celery into pieces that will fit in the slow cooker and add them. Add the salt, pepper, and water. Cover and cook on low for 8 hours.

2. Use a slotted spoon to remove the roast and beef bones. Reserve the roast and the meat removed from the bones for another use; discard the bones.

3. Once the broth has cooled enough to make it easier to handle, strain it; discard the cooked vegetables. Refrigerate the (cooled) broth overnight. Remove and discard the hardened fat. The resulting concentrated broth can be kept for 1 week in the refrigerator or frozen for up to 3 months.

PER SERVING (1 CUP) | Calories: 16 | Fat: 0.5 g | Protein: 2.5 g | Sodium: 782 g | Fiber: 0 g | Carbohydrates: 0 g | Sugar: 0 g

Ham Broth

In the same way that adding a ham bone to the cooking liquid for ham and bean soup improves the soup's flavor, ¼ cup of ham broth for every ¾ cup of chicken broth can give a boost to potato soup, too.

INGREDIENTS | YIELDS ABOUT 4 CUPS

1 (3-pound) bone-in ham or 3 pounds of ham bones

1 large onion, peeled and quartered

12 baby carrots

2 stalks celery, cut in half

4½ cups water

1. Add all ingredients to a 4–6-quart slow cooker. Cover and cook on low for 6 hours or until the ham pulls away from the bone.

2. Strain; discard the celery and onion. Reserve any ham removed from the bones and the carrots for another use.

3. Once cooled, cover and refrigerate the broth overnight. Remove and discard any hardened fat. The broth can be kept for 1 week in the refrigerator or frozen up to 3 months.

PER SERVING (1 CUP) | Calories: 18 | Fat: 0.5 g | Protein: 2.5 g | Sodium: 659 mg | Fiber: 0 g | Carbohydrates: 0 g | Sugar: 0 g

Fish Stock

Use fish stock in any fish or seafood dish instead of water or chicken stock.

INGREDIENTS | YIELDS 3 QUARTS

3 quarts water

2 onions, quartered

Head and bones from 3 whole fish, any type

2 stalks celery, chopped

2 tablespoons peppercorns

1 bunch parsley

1. Place all ingredients into a 4–6-quart slow cooker. Cook on low for 8–10 hours.

2. Strain out all of the solids. Refrigerate overnight. The next day skim off any foam that has floated to the top. You can use the stock immediately or refrigerate or freeze it for later use. Stock will stay fresh in the fridge for up to 1 week and up to 6 months in the freezer.

PER SERVING (1 CUP) | Calories: 39 | Fat: 1.5 g | Protein: 5 g | Sodium: 50 mg | Fiber: 0 g | Carbohydrates: 0 g | Sugar: 0 g

Herbed Tilapia Stew

Any type of white fish filets (such as haddock or cod) will also work in this recipe. Fish cooks very, very quickly even on the low setting in a slow cooker, so this is one recipe you will need to set a timer for.

INGREDIENTS | SERVES 6

2 pounds frozen boneless tilapia filets

4 tablespoons butter

1 (14.5-ounce) can diced tomatoes, with juice

4 cloves garlic, minced

½ cup sliced green onions

2 teaspoons Thai fish sauce

2 tablespoons fresh thyme, chopped or 1 teaspoon dried thyme

1. Grease a 4-quart slow cooker with nonstick cooking spray. Place all ingredients in the slow cooker.

2. Cover and cook on high for 1½–2 hours or on low for 2½–3 hours. Watch the cooking time. If your fish filets are very thin you may need to reduce the cooking time.

3. When fish is cooked through, filets will easily separate and flake with a fork. Break the fish up into the tomatoes and cooking liquids. Serve stew over cooked rice or gluten-free pasta.

PER SERVING | Calories: 208 | Fat: 9 g | Protein: 27 g | Sodium: 180 mg | Fiber: 1 g | Carbohydrates: 4 g | Sugar: 2 g

Roasted Winter Vegetables

This is a perfect side dish to roast chicken or roast beef. To make sure all the vegetables cook evenly, cut into small cubes that are similar in size. If you find the vegetables are becoming too dry, add in about ½ cup vegetable broth a little at a time until they are as moist as you would like them to be.

INGREDIENTS | SERVES 4

5–6 cups cubed root vegetables

2 tablespoons olive oil

½ teaspoon salt

1 teaspoon freshly ground pepper

Winter Root Vegetables

Use a variety of your favorite root vegetables such as carrots, turnips, sweet potatoes, white potatoes, parsnips, or onions. If using turnips, rutabagas, or sweet potatoes, make sure to peel the tough skin off before adding to the other vegetables.

1. Place cubed vegetables in a greased 4-quart slow cooker.

2. Drizzle with olive oil and sprinkle with salt and pepper.

3. Cover and cook on high for 3½–4 hours or on low for 7–8 hours until vegetables are fork tender. Stir vegetables every hour or so to prevent them from overbrowning on the bottom.

PER SERVING | Calories: 167 | Fat: 7 g | Protein: 3 g | Sodium: 341 mg | Fiber: 5 g | Carbohydrates: 25 g | Sugar: 7 g

Vegetable Stock

This is a great recipe for using up leftover vegetables and peelings. Vegetable stock is a healthy ingredient to keep in the fridge to make quick soups or to cook gluten-free starches such as rice and potatoes.

INGREDIENTS | YIELDS 6 CUPS

2 carrots, roughly chopped

1 onion, quartered

3 cloves garlic

2 stalks celery, roughly chopped

2 red potatoes, quartered, peeled or unpeeled

6 cups water

1 teaspoon salt

1 teaspoon ground pepper

1. Place chopped vegetables in a 4–6 quart slow cooker.

2. Pour water over the vegetables and add salt and pepper.

3. Cover and cook on high for 4–6 hours or on low for 8–10 hours.

4. Allow broth to cool slightly and then strain out vegetables. Pour stock into clean glass jars and refrigerate for up to a week or freeze for several months until needed. If you plan to freeze the stock either store in zip-top bags or leave 2 inches of room in each glass jar to allow liquids to expand.

PER SERVING (1 CUP) | Calories: 11 | Fat: 0 g | Protein: 0 g | Sodium: 896 mg | Fiber: 0 g | Carbohydrates: 3 g | Sugar: 2 g

Reducing Stocks

A simple way to add more flavor to your stock is to simply cook it down (reduce it by half) in a pot on the stove. Reduced stocks have a great depth of flavor and can be used as a sauce, gravy, or as the liquid to cook rice, potatoes, or gluten-free pasta.

Slow Cooker Baked Potatoes

Here's a great way to keep your kitchen cool on a warm summer day. Serve these baked potatoes with grilled steaks or salmon.

INGREDIENTS | SERVES 4–6

4–6 medium-sized baking potatoes
1 tablespoon butter, per potato
¼ teaspoon salt, per potato
¼ teaspoon ground pepper, per potato

1. Wrap potatoes in aluminum foil and place in a 4-quart or larger slow cooker.

2. Cover and cook on high for 4 hours or on low for 8 hours until potatoes are fork tender.

3. When ready to serve, remove potatoes from cooker, remove foil, cut potatoes in half. Add butter, salt, and pepper for each serving.

PER SERVING | Calories: 258 | Fat: 12 g | Protein: 4 g | Sodium: 604.5 mg | Fiber: 5.5 g | Carbohydrates: 35.5 g | Sugar: 2.5 g

Basic Bean Soup

A hearty vegetarian bean soup that serves a crowd.

INGREDIENTS | SERVES 8

1 (16-ounce) bag of dried mixed beans or 2¼ cups of cooked beans
1 (14.5-ounce) can diced tomatoes, with juice
6 cups (48-ounces) gluten-free vegetable broth
2 cups carrots, finely diced
1½ cups celery, finely diced
1 cup onions, finely chopped
2 tablespoons gluten-free ketchup or tomato paste
1 teaspoon Italian seasoning
½ teaspoon ground pepper
1 teaspoon salt

1. Soak beans according to package directions. Rinse beans (soaked or precooked) and place in a 4.5-quart or larger slow cooker.

2. Add diced tomatoes with juice, broth, and all vegetables and seasonings to the slow cooker.

3. Cover and cook on high for 5–6 hours or on low for 10–12 hours until beans are tender.

PER SERVING | Calories: 220 | Fat: 1 g | Protein: 15.5 g | Sodium: 889.5 mg | Fiber: 15 g | Carbohydrates: 39 g | Sugar: 5.5 g

Boston Baked Beans

This comfort food is made with nutritious northern beans and smoked bacon and simmered in a tangy homemade barbecue sauce. If you don't have time to precook the northern beans simply use 3 (15-ounce) cans of northern beans that have been drained and well rinsed.

INGREDIENTS | SERVES 8

6 cups precooked northern beans (see sidebar)

½ pound raw bacon, diced

1 onion, finely diced

3 tablespoons molasses

1½ teaspoons ground pepper

½ teaspoon dry mustard

½ cup gluten-free ketchup

1 tablespoon gluten-free Worcestershire sauce

¼ cup brown sugar

1. Layer cooked northern beans, bacon, and onions in a greased 4-quart slow cooker.

2. In a bowl or glass measuring cup whisk together the molasses, ground pepper, dry mustard, ketchup, Worcestershire sauce, and brown sugar.

3. Pour sauce over the layered beans. Cover and cook on high for 4–5 hours or on low for 8–10 hours.

PER SERVING | Calories: 362 | Fat: 14 g | Protein: 14 g | Sodium: 444 mg | Fiber: 10.5 g | Carbohydrates: 46.5 g | Sugar: 19 g

Preparing Great Northern Beans

Presoaking beans removes the enzymes that make them difficult for some people to digest. Rinse and drain the amount of beans called for in the recipe and then add them to a bowl or saucepan. Add enough water to cover the beans by 2 inches. Cover and let soak overnight or for 8 hours. Drain the beans, then rinse and drain again. Add the beans to a saucepan with enough water to cover the beans by 2 inches. Bring to a boil over high heat, and then reduce the heat and simmer the beans for 40 minutes to 1 hour or until they just begin to become tender. Drain, and add to the slow cooker according to the recipe instructions.

Steamed Spaghetti Squash

People are often intimidated by cooking spaghetti squash, but by using your slow cooker it's an incredibly easy process. Serve this freshly cooked squash instead of pasta for a healthy gluten-free main dish.

INGREDIENTS | SERVES 4

1 large spaghetti squash

¾ cup water

Safely Cutting Winter Squashes

You can cook any type of winter squash (such as acorn squash, butternut squash, or pumpkins) using this method with the slow cooker. Because these squashes are rock hard when fresh, they can be extremely hard to cut, even with a very sharp knife. The possibility of cutting yourself once they are soft after being cooked is much less likely.

1. Place whole spaghetti squash and water in a 4-quart or larger greased slow cooker.

2. Cook on high for 4 hours or on low for 8 hours until squash is fork tender or a knife can be inserted in the center easily.

3. Remove the squash carefully from the slow cooker. Allow to cool for several minutes. With a sharp knife cut top and bottom off of squash, then cut in half lengthwise. Scoop seeds out of the center of the squash and use a fork to remove the noodle-like threads of the spaghetti squash.

4. Serve as a side dish topped with butter, salt, and pepper or as the base of a gluten-free meal in place of pasta.

PER SERVING | Calories: 13 | Fat: 0 g | Protein: 1 g | Sodium: 3 mg | Fiber: 1 g | Carbohydrates: 3 g | Sugar: 2 g

Fresh Corn on the Cob

Cooking corn on the cob using the slow cooker means you don't have to worry about babysitting it on the stove. It will be hot and ready as soon as it's time to eat.

INGREDIENTS | SERVES 4

4–5 cups water
4 ears corn, shucked and cleaned
½ teaspoon salt
2 tablespoons butter

1. Place water in a 4-quart slow cooker. Add ears of corn and salt.

2. Cover and cook on high for 2–3 hours until corn is tender enough to eat. Corn can also be cooked on low for 4–5 hours and will not be overcooked.

3. Remove corn carefully from slow cooker using tongs and rub with butter. Serve immediately while hot.

PER SERVING | Calories: 173 | Fat: 7 g | Protein: 4 g | Sodium: 310.5 mg | Fiber: 3.5 g | Carbohydrates: 29.5 g | Sugar: 5 g

Caramelized Onions

Caramelized onions are a great addition to roasts, dips, and sandwiches.

INGREDIENTS | YIELDS 1 QUART

4 pounds Vidalia or other sweet onions
3 tablespoons butter
1 tablespoon balsamic vinegar

Storing Caramelized Onions

Store the onions in an airtight container. They will keep up to 2 weeks refrigerated or up to 6 months frozen. If frozen, defrost overnight in the refrigerator before using.

1. Peel and slice the onions in ¼" slices. Separate them into rings. Thinly slice the butter.

2. Place the onions into a 4-quart slow cooker. Scatter the butter slices over the top of the onions and drizzle with balsamic vinegar. At this point, the slow cooker may look full but the onions will quickly reduce. Cover and cook on low for 10 hours.

3. If after 10 hours the onions are wet, turn the slow cooker up to high and cook uncovered for an additional 30 minutes or until the liquid evaporates.

PER SERVING (½ CUP) | Calories: 129.5 | Fat: 4.5 g | Protein: 2.5 g | Sodium: 10 mg | Fiber: 4 g | Carbohydrates: 21 g | Sugar: 10 g

Gluten-Free Millet Bread

Many people who are sensitive to gluten are also sensitive to other grains such as corn. This bread is free of gluten, corn, yeast, dairy/casein, soy, and rice and is a perfect alternative for those with multiple food sensitivities.

INGREDIENTS | SERVES 12

⅓ cup sorghum flour
⅓ cup arrowroot starch
1 cup millet flour
1 teaspoon xanthan gum
1 teaspoon baking soda
¼ teaspoon salt
3 tablespoons sugar
3 tablespoons oil
2 eggs
1 cup almond milk
1 tablespoon lemon juice or apple cider vinegar

Use Recycled Cans for Slow Cooker Baking

When using recycled aluminum cans for baking, make sure to carefully cut away sharp edges with wire cutters so that you do not chance cutting your fingers when filling or emptying the cans. Clean cans carefully between each use with a baby bottle cleaner.

1. In a large bowl whisk together sorghum flour, arrowroot starch, and millet flour. Add xanthan gum, baking soda, salt, and sugar. Mix together thoroughly.

2. In a smaller bowl mix together the oil, eggs, almond milk, and lemon juice or apple cider vinegar.

3. Mix wet ingredients into dry ingredients with a fork, until you have a thick batter.

4. Grease 3 emptied and cleaned (15-ounce) aluminum cans and place ⅓ of the bread batter into each can. The cans will be about half full.

5. Place the cans in a 4-quart slow cooker. Pour ½ cup of water around the cans.

6. Cover the slow cooker and vent the lid with a chopstick. Cook on high for 3–3½ hours or on low for 6–7 hours. Bread should rise and double in size and become golden brown on top when done.

7. Remove cans of bread carefully from slow cooker and allow the bread to cool before removing from cans. Slice each loaf into 4 round pieces of bread. Serve warm.

PER SERVING | Calories: 126.5 | Fat: 5 g | Protein: 3.5 g | Sodium: 178 mg | Fiber: 1.5 g | Carbohydrates: 36 g | Sugar: 4.5 g

Gluten-Free Corn Bread

When you're gluten-free, one of the hardest foods to replace can be bread. This easy recipe for gluten-free cornbread is baked right in your slow cooker. Perfect as a side for weeknight meals or to use in stuffing for the holidays!

INGREDIENTS | SERVES 12

⅓ cup brown rice flour

⅔ cup arrowroot starch

⅔ cup gluten-free cornmeal

1 teaspoon xanthan gum

2 teaspoons baking powder

½ teaspoon salt

3 tablespoons sugar

¼ cup oil

2 eggs

1 cup milk or dairy-free substitute

Gluten-Free Cornmeal

Many companies that process cornmeal also make mixes that include wheat flour. It's important to find a company that makes cornmeal that has been tested to have less than 20 ppm (parts per million) of gluten. This recipe was tested using Bob's Red Mill brand gluten-free cornmeal.

1. In a large bowl whisk together brown rice flour, arrowroot starch, and cornmeal. Add xanthan gum, baking powder, salt, and sugar. Mix together thoroughly.

2. In a smaller bowl mix together the oil, eggs, and milk.

3. Mix wet ingredients into dry ingredients with a fork, until you have a thick batter.

4. Grease 3 emptied and cleaned (15-ounce) aluminum cans and place ⅓ of the cornbread batter into each can. The cans will be about half full.

5. Place the cans in a 4-quart slow cooker. Pour ½ cup of water around the cans.

6. Cover the slow cooker and vent the lid with a chopstick. Cook on high for 3–3½ hours or on low for 6–7 hours. Bread should rise and double in size and become golden brown on top when done.

7. Remove cans of bread carefully from slow cooker and allow bread to cool before removing from cans. Slice each loaf into 4 round pieces of bread. Serve warm.

PER SERVING | Calories: 147 | Fat: 6 g | Protein: 2.5 g | Sodium: 203.5 mg | Fiber: 1 g | Carbohydrates: 20.5 g | Sugar: 4.5 g

Gluten-Free Breakfast Granola

Finding gluten-free granola can be a challenge in most grocery stores, but it's super easy to make your own in the slow cooker. Make sure to stir the ingredients about every 30 minutes to prevent uneven cooking or overbrowning.

INGREDIENTS | SERVES 10

2½ cups gluten-free rolled oats

¼ cup ground flaxseeds

½ cup unsweetened shredded coconut

½ cup pumpkin seeds

½ cup walnuts, chopped

½ cup sliced almonds

1 cup dried cranberries

¾ cup brown sugar

⅓ cup coconut oil

¼ cup honey

½ teaspoon salt

1 teaspoon ground cinnamon

Change It Up

Don't like pumpkin seeds, walnuts, or dried cranberries? Use the seeds, nuts, and dried fruit that you prefer in your own granola. Use raisins, sunflower seeds, cocoa nibs, dried cranberries, or even dried bananas. The different variations are endless. You can even add chocolate chips if you'd like, but only after the granola has been cooked and cooled!

1. Mix all ingredients together and place in a greased 4-quart slow cooker.

2. Cover slow cooker and vent with a wooden spoon handle or a chopstick. Cook on high for 4 hours, or on low for 8 hours, stirring every hour or so.

3. When granola is toasty and done, pour it onto a cookie sheet that has been lined with parchment paper. Spread the granola out evenly over the entire sheet of parchment paper. Allow granola to cool and dry for several hours.

4. Once cooled, break granola up and place in an airtight container or a tightly sealed glass jar and store in pantry for up to 1 month. For longer storage keep granola in freezer for up to 6 months.

PER SERVING | Calories: 400 | Fat: 20.5 g | Protein: 7.5 g | Sodium: 126 mg | Fiber: 5.5 g | Carbohydrates: 51 g | Sugar: 32 g

Chunky Applesauce

Apples are so versatile in the slow cooker. Use whatever type of apples you prefer for this recipe. When you make your own applesauce you can control the amount of sugar (if any) that you would like to add.

INGREDIENTS | SERVES 6

3–5 pounds apples
2 tablespoons lemon juice

Need Some Sugar?

Apples are more or less sweet depending on their variety. If you'd like to sweeten your applesauce start by adding ¼ cup of your favorite sweetener as soon as the apples have finished cooking: sugar, honey, agave nectar, concentrated fruit juice or apple cider, or even molasses.

1. Peel, core, and roughly dice apples. You should have about 10 cups of uncooked, diced apples.

2. Place apples and lemon juice in a greased 2.5-quart or 4-quart slow cooker.

3. Cook on high for 4 hours or on low for 7–8 hours.

4. Apples will be done when they are easily mashed with a fork. Mash cooked apples in the slow cooker until they are a chunky consistency. Cool for 30 minutes and then refrigerate in an airtight container.

5. Serve as a side dish to pork, chicken, or beef or just as a snack paired with a handful of your favorite nuts or seeds.

PER SERVING | Calories: 180 | Fat: 0.5 g | Protein: 1 g | Sodium: 1 mg | Fiber: 5 g | Carbohydrates: 48 g | Sugar: 38 g

CHAPTER 4

Breakfasts

Blueberry French Toast Casserole

Store-bought gluten-free bread is too expensive to waste if it becomes stale. This recipe shows you how to make a frugal but delicious breakfast or dessert using leftover or stale gluten-free bread.

INGREDIENTS | SERVES 6

7 cups gluten-free bread, cubed
1⅓ cups almond milk
5 eggs, whisked
1 tablespoon vanilla
1 tablespoon maple syrup
½ teaspoon salt
2 tablespoons butter (melted) or coconut oil
2 teaspoons cinnamon
3 tablespoons sugar
1½ cups blueberries, fresh or frozen

1. In a large bowl mix together the cubed gluten-free bread, almond milk, whisked eggs, vanilla, maple syrup, and salt.

2. Pour mixture into a greased 4-quart slow cooker.

3. Drizzle melted butter or coconut oil over the casserole. Sprinkle cinnamon and sugar evenly over the bread. Top with blueberries.

4. Cover slow cooker and vent with a wooden spoon handle or chopstick. Cook on high for 2½–3 hours or on low for 5–6 hours.

5. Remove lid and allow liquids to evaporate the last 20 minutes of cooking. Serve warm.

PER SERVING | Calories: 468 | Fat: 10 g | Protein: 18 g | Sodium: 920 mg | Fiber: 4 g | Carbohydrates: 73 g | Sugar: 17 g

Ham and Cheese Slow Cooker Omelet

Eggs are one of the most affordable proteins available and they are naturally gluten-free. If you make a large family-sized omelet like this on Sunday evening you'll have ready-made breakfasts for the rest of the week.

INGREDIENTS | SERVES 5

10 eggs
½ teaspoon ground mustard
½ teaspoon salt
½ teaspoon paprika
½ teaspoon ground pepper
½ teaspoon dill weed
1½ cups ham, diced
1½ cups shredded Cheddar cheese
½ cup chopped green onions

How to Store Fresh Green Onions

Green onions have small white bulbs and long green stalks. Both parts of the onion can be eaten. They are also referred to as spring onions and scallions. Either way, they will often go bad if left in the fridge. The best way to preserve them is to buy two or three bunches, slice them all up and place them in the freezer in a zip-top bag from which the air has been removed. They will stay fresh and can be used right from the freezer.

1. Whisk eggs in a large bowl. Add in ground mustard, salt, paprika, ground pepper, and dill weed. Stir in diced ham.

2. Pour egg mixture into a greased 2.5-quart slow cooker.

3. Sprinkle cheese and scallions over the top of the egg mixture.

4. Cover and cook on high for 1½–2 hours or on low for 2½–3 hours.

PER SERVING | Calories: 352 | Fat: 25 g | Protein: 29 g | Sodium: 1,130.5 mg | Fiber: 0.5 g | Carbohydrates: 3 g | Sugar: 1.5 g

Eastern North Carolina Cheesy Grits Casserole

Cheesy grits is a favorite dish to bring church potlucks and luncheons. This recipe combines eggs, bacon, and cheesy grits all in one pot.

INGREDIENTS | SERVES 8

1½ cups gluten-free Bob's Red Mill regular yellow grits (also known as "polenta style"; not quick-cooking)

4¼ cups water

1 teaspoon salt

½ teaspoon ground pepper

4 tablespoons butter, divided

6 eggs

1 pound bacon, cooked and crumbled

1 cup Cheddar cheese, shredded

1. Pour grits, water, salt, pepper, and 2 tablespoons of butter into a greased 4-quart slow cooker.

2. Cover and cook on high for 3 hours or on low for 6 hours.

3. 30 minutes before serving, whisk eggs together and cook them in a saucepan over medium heat in the remaining 2 tablespoons of butter for 4–5 minutes until eggs are cooked through. Fold scrambled eggs into the cooked grits in the slow cooker. Add crumbled bacon and cheese.

4. Cook on high an additional 30 minutes to melt cheese and heat bacon through.

PER SERVING | Calories: 525 | Fat: 40 g | Protein: 17.5 g | Sodium: 906.5 mg | Fiber: 1.5 g | Carbohydrates: 25.5 g | Sugar: 0.5 g

Breakfast Spanish Tortilla

Traditionally served as tapas or an appetizer in Spanish restaurants and bars, this version of the Spanish tortilla removes a lot of the fat and makes a healthy breakfast casserole. Conventionally it does not contain cheese, but feel free to sprinkle some on top in the last 30 minutes of cooking.

INGREDIENTS | SERVES 6

2 small onions, finely diced

3 tablespoons olive oil

10 eggs

1 teaspoon salt

1 teaspoon ground pepper

3 large baking potatoes, peeled and thinly sliced

1. In a skillet over medium heat slowly cook onions in olive oil until lightly brown and caramelized, about 5–6 minutes.

2. In a large bowl whisk together the eggs, salt, and pepper.

3. Layer half of the potatoes and fried onions in a greased 4-quart slow cooker. Pour half the eggs over the layers. Repeat layers ending with the last of the whisked eggs.

4. Cover and cook on low for 6–7 hours or on high for 3½–4 hours.

PER SERVING | Calories: 316 | Fat: 15 g | Protein: 14 g | Sodium: 522 mg | Fiber: 5 g | Carbohydrates: 32 g | Sugar: 4 g

Breakfast Burrito Filling

Serve in a large gluten-free brown rice tortilla or corn tortilla with your favorite breakfast burrito toppings, such as diced avocados, sour cream, or salsa.

INGREDIENTS | SERVES 4

1¼ pounds lean boneless pork, cubed

12 ounces diced tomatoes with green chiles (or plain diced tomatoes if you prefer a less spicy filling)

1 small onion, diced

1 jalapeño, seeded and diced

½ teaspoon ground chipotle

¼ teaspoon cayenne pepper

2 cloves garlic, peeled and minced

Place all ingredients into a greased 2.5-quart slow cooker. Stir together. Cover and cook on low for 8 hours. Stir before serving.

PER SERVING | Calories: 203.5 | Fat: 5 g | Protein: 32.5 g | Sodium: 74 mg | Fiber: 1.5 g | Carbohydrates: 5.5 g | Sugar: 3 g

Crustless Quiche Lorraine

Ham is often already salty, so take that into consideration when deciding how much salt you add to the egg mixture. The gluten-free bread "crust" in this recipe is also optional; the quiche is just as delicious without it.

INGREDIENTS | SERVES 4

4 slices gluten-free bread, toasted
4 teaspoons butter
2 cups Swiss cheese, grated
½ pound cooked ham, cut into cubes
6 large eggs
1 tablespoon mayonnaise
½ teaspoon Dijon mustard
1 cup heavy cream
½ teaspoon salt
½ teaspoon freshly ground pepper
Dash of cayenne pepper

1. Grease a 4-quart slow cooker with nonstick spray. If desired, remove the crusts from the gluten-free toast. Butter each slice with 1 teaspoon of butter, tear the toast into pieces, and arrange the toast pieces butter-side down in the slow cooker.

2. Spread half of the cheese over the toast pieces, and then spread the ham over the cheese, and top the ham layer with the remaining cheese.

3. In a bowl, beat the eggs together with the mayonnaise, mustard, cream, salt, black pepper, and cayenne pepper. Pour the egg mixture into the slow cooker.

4. Cover and cook on high for 1½–2 hours or on low for 3–4 hours until the eggs are set.

PER SERVING | Calories: 764 | Fat: 56 g | Protein: 41.5 g | Sodium: 1,237.5 mg | Fiber: 1 g | Carbohydrates: 24 g | Sugar: 2 g

Eggs Florentine

Freshly ground black pepper goes well in this dish. You can use up to a teaspoon in the recipe. If you prefer to go lighter on the seasoning to accommodate individual tastes, be sure to have a pepper grinder at the table for those who want to add more.

INGREDIENTS | SERVES 4

9 ounces (2 cups) Cheddar cheese, grated, divided

1 (10-ounce) package frozen spinach, thawed

1 (8-ounce) can sliced mushrooms, drained

1 small onion, peeled and diced

6 large eggs

1 cup heavy cream

½ teaspoon Italian seasoning

½ teaspoon garlic powder

½ teaspoon freshly ground black pepper

Make It Dairy-Free

To make egg casseroles dairy-free, replace the cream with full-fat coconut milk. For the Cheddar cheese, there are many dairy-free alternatives available now; one in particular called Daiya is sold in shreds and melts beautifully in dishes like this.

1. Grease a 4-quart slow cooker with nonstick spray. Spread 1 cup of the grated cheese over the bottom of the slow cooker.

2. Drain the spinach and squeeze out any access moisture; add in a layer on top of the cheese. Next add the drained mushrooms in a layer and then top them with the onion.

3. In a small bowl beat together the eggs, cream, Italian seasoning, garlic powder, and pepper. Pour over the layers in the slow cooker. Top with the remaining cup of cheese.

4. Cover and cook on high for 2 hours or until eggs are set.

PER SERVING | Calories: 605.5 | Fat: 51 g | Protein: 30 g | Sodium: 712 mg | Fiber: 3 g | Carbohydrates: 10 g | Sugar: 3 g

Sausage and Cheese Casserole

A big bowl of freshly prepared fruit salad would be the perfect accompaniment to this savory casserole.

INGREDIENTS | SERVES 8

1 tablespoon extra-virgin olive oil or vegetable oil

1 large onion, peeled and diced

1 green pepper, seeded and diced

1 pound ground sausage

4 cups frozen gluten-free hash brown potatoes, thawed and drained of all liquid

8 large eggs

¼ cup water

½ teaspoon salt

½ teaspoon freshly ground pepper

½ pound Cheddar cheese, grated

Feeding a Crowd

You can stretch this recipe to even more servings by increasing the amount of chopped peppers you sauté with the onion. In fact, a mixture of red, green, and yellow peppers makes for a delicious combo.

1. Preheat a deep 3½-quart nonstick sauté pan over medium-high heat and add the oil. Once the oil is heated, add the onion and pepper and sauté until the onion is transparent, or about 5 minutes.

2. Add the sausage, browning (and crumbling) and cook for 5 minutes. Remove any excess fat, if necessary, by carefully dabbing the pan with a paper towel.

3. Stir the hash browns into the sausage mixture, and then transfer the mixture to a 4-quart slow cooker treated with nonstick spray.

4. In a medium bowl, whisk together the eggs, water, salt, and pepper. Pour over the sausage–hash brown mixture in the slow cooker. Cover and cook on low for 4 hours.

5. Turn the cooker to warm. About 45 minutes before you'll be serving the casserole, sprinkle the cheese over the cooked mixture in the slow cooker. After 30 minutes, uncover the casserole and let stand for 15 minutes before serving.

PER SERVING | Calories: 466.5 | Fat: 31.5 g | Protein: 24.5 g | Sodium: 772 mg | Fiber: 2 g | Carbohydrates: 22 g | Sugar: 2 g

Breakfast Quinoa with Fruit

Take a break from oatmeal and try this fruity quinoa instead!

INGREDIENTS | SERVES 4

1 cup quinoa

2 cups water

½ cup dried mixed berries

1 pear, thinly sliced and peeled if desired

½ cup dark brown sugar

½ teaspoon ground ginger

¼ teaspoon cinnamon

⅛ teaspoon cloves

⅛ teaspoon nutmeg

Place all ingredients into a 4-quart slow cooker. Stir. Cook for 2½ hours on high or around 4 hours on low or until the quinoa has absorbed most of the liquid and is light and fluffy.

PER SERVING | Calories: 297 | Fat: 3 g | Protein: 6.5 g | Sodium: 14 mg | Fiber: 5 g | Carbohydrates: 64 g | Sugar: 32.5 g

What Is Quinoa?

Pronounced "keen-wah," this crop is grown as a grain, although it's actually a seed. It's become very popular in recent years, being touted as a health food. The grain itself has been used for thousands of years in South America. It's a perfect addition to the gluten-free diet because of its high nutritional content.

Breakfast Risotto

Serve this as you would cooked oatmeal: topped with additional brown sugar, raisins or other dried fruit, and milk.

INGREDIENTS | SERVES 6

¼ cup butter, melted

1½ cups Arborio rice

3 small apples, peeled, cored, and sliced

1½ teaspoons ground cinnamon

⅛ teaspoon freshly ground nutmeg

⅛ teaspoon ground cloves

⅛ teaspoon salt

⅓ cup brown sugar

1 cup apple juice

3 cups whole milk

1. Add the butter and rice to a greased 4-quart slow cooker; stir to coat the rice in the butter.

2. Add the remaining ingredients and stir to combine. Cover and cook on low for 6–7 hours or on high for 2–3 hours until the rice is cooked through and is firm, but not mushy.

PER SERVING | Calories: 420 | Fat: 12 g | Protein: 7.5 g | Sodium: 108.5 mg | Fiber: 3 g | Carbohydrates: 71 g | Sugar: 29 g

Arborio Rice

Arborio rice is a short-grain rice used in risotto because it has a creamy texture when cooked. Other varieties used in risotto are Vialone Nano and Carnaroli rice.

Baked Oatmeal

A regional dish from Lancaster, Pennsylvania, this simple baked oatmeal is sweet and hearty. Serve cut in squares and drizzled with maple syrup for breakfast, or for a unique dessert serve warm with ice cream.

INGREDIENTS | SERVES 6

3 cups gluten-free rolled oats
2 teaspoons baking powder
1 teaspoon salt
2 eggs, gently whisked
¼ cup butter, melted
¾ cup brown sugar
1½ cups milk

Room for Interpretation

As is, this simple oatmeal cake tastes like warm salty butter and brown sugar. Yet you can make endless flavor variations with this dish. By adding any combination of raisins, chocolate chips, sliced almonds, pecans, chopped walnuts, diced apples, dried cherries, dried cranberries, several tablespoons of cocoa, vanilla, cinnamon, or freshly grated nutmeg, you can create your own unique favorite adaptation.

1. In a large bowl mix together the oatmeal, baking powder, and salt.

2. Make a well in the center of the dry ingredients and add the eggs, melted butter, brown sugar, and milk. Mix together thoroughly.

3. Lightly grease a 4-quart slow cooker. Pour oatmeal batter into the slow cooker.

4. Cover slow cooker and vent lid with a wooden spoon handle or a chopstick. Cook on high for 3½–4 hours or on low for 6–7 hours. Make sure to keep an eye on the dish in the last hour of cooking to be sure it doesn't burn.

5. The baked oatmeal is finished when the edges are golden brown and a toothpick inserted in the middle comes out clean. This oatmeal is almost like a cake or brownie in texture; if you want a more creamy-textured oatmeal, add an additional cup of milk to the batter before cooking.

PER SERVING | Calories: 387 | Fat: 14 g | Protein: 9.5 g | Sodium: 616 mg | Fiber: 4 g | Carbohydrates: 58 g | Sugar: 30.5 g

Pull-Apart Cinnamon Raisin Biscuits

Who ever thought you could make gluten-free biscuits in the slow cooker? Well you can and they turn out light and soft with a perfect crumb! To prevent the biscuits on the edge from browning too quickly you can line the slow cooker with parchment paper.

INGREDIENTS | SERVES 9

1 cup brown rice flour
1 cup arrowroot starch
1 tablespoon baking powder
1 teaspoon xanthan gum
½ teaspoon salt
⅓ cup sugar
½ teaspoon ground cinnamon
⅓ cup vegetable shortening
2 eggs
¾ cup whole milk
½ cup raisins

Quick Vanilla Glaze

Impress your family by making a quick powdered sugar glaze for these lightly sweetened biscuits/buns. Mix together 1 cup of powdered sugar with 1½ tablespoons of water or milk and ½ teaspoon of vanilla extract. Drizzle artistically over warm buns and serve immediately.

1. In a large bowl whisk together the brown rice flour, arrowroot starch, baking powder, xanthan gum, salt, sugar, and cinnamon.

2. Cut in the vegetable shortening using a fork and knife, until it resembles small peas within the gluten-free flour mixture.

3. In a small bowl whisk together eggs and milk. Pour into the flour mixture and mix with a fork to combine, until the dough is like a very thick, sticky cake batter. Fold in the raisins.

4. Grease a 4-quart slow cooker and/or line with parchment paper.

5. Drop biscuit dough in balls about the size of a golf ball into the bottom of the greased slow cooker. The biscuits will touch each other and may fit quite snugly.

6. Cover slow cooker and vent lid with the handle of a wooden spoon or a chopstick. Cook biscuits on high for about 2–2½ hours or on low for around 4–4½ hours. Biscuits around the edge of the slow cooker will be more brown than those in the center. The biscuits should have doubled in size during cooking. The biscuits are done when a toothpick inserted in the center of the middle biscuit comes out clean.

7. Turn the slow cooker off and remove the insert to a heat-safe surface such as the stovetop or on top of potholders. Allow the biscuits to cool for several minutes before removing from slow cooker insert. They will "pull-apart" individually.

PER SERVING | Calories: 267 | Fat: 9.5 g | Protein: 3.5 g | Sodium: 323 mg | Fiber: 1.5 g | Carbohydrates: 42 g | Sugar: 13.5 g

Millet Porridge with Apples and Pecans

Millet, like quinoa, is a small seed cereal crop that is perfect for the gluten-free diet. It's very easy to digest and makes a healthy hot breakfast.

INGREDIENTS | SERVES 4

4 cups almond milk

1 cup dried millet

1 apple, diced (and peeled if preferred)

2 teaspoons cinnamon

½ cup honey

½ cup chopped pecans

¼ teaspoon salt

A Note on Millet

Millet is particularly high in magnesium, which is a common deficiency in many with celiac disease. It also seems to help lower triglycerides and C-reactive protein (an inflammatory marker important in assessing cardiovascular risk). For more information on millet, see Cheryl Harris, RD's website: *www.harriswholehealth.com*.

1. Grease a 2.5-quart slow cooker with nonstick cooking spray.

2. Pour in almond milk, millet, the diced apple, cinnamon, honey, chopped pecans, and salt. Stir to combine.

3. Cook on high for 2½–3 hours or on low for 5–6 hours or until all of the liquid has been absorbed into the millet. Try not to overcook as it can become mushy.

PER SERVING | Calories: 388.5 | Fat: 12 g | Protein: 15 g | Sodium: 253 mg | Fiber: 7 g | Carbohydrates: 56.5 g | Sugar: 17 g

Pear Clafoutis

Clafoutis is a soft pancake-like breakfast with cinnamon and pears. If you choose to use a larger slow cooker than the specified 2.5-quart, you will need to reduce the cooking time. When the sides are golden brown and a toothpick stuck in the middle comes out clean the clafoutis is done.

INGREDIENTS | SERVES 4

2 pears, stem and seeds removed, cut into chunks, and peeled if preferred

½ cup brown rice flour

½ cup arrowroot starch

2 teaspoons baking powder

½ teaspoon xanthan gum

¼ teaspoon salt

⅓ cup sugar

1 teaspoon ground cinnamon

2 tablespoons vegetable shortening, melted

2 eggs

¾ cup whole milk

1 tablespoon vanilla

Gluten-Free Baking Shortcut

Don't want to mix up all these ingredients? You can replace the brown rice flour, arrowroot starch, baking powder, and xanthan gum with 1 cup of Bob's Red Mill Gluten-Free Pancake Mix, or your favorite gluten-free pancake mix.

1. Place cut-up pears into a greased 2.5-quart slow cooker.

2. In a large bowl whisk together the brown rice flour, arrowroot starch, baking powder, xanthan gum, salt, sugar, and cinnamon.

3. Make a well in the center of the dry ingredients and add melted shortening, eggs, milk, and vanilla. Stir to combine wet with dry ingredients.

4. Pour batter over pears. Cover slow cooker and vent lid with a chopstick or the handle of a wooden spoon.

5. Cook on high for 2½–3 hours or on low for 5–6 hours. Serve warm or cold drizzled with maple syrup.

PER SERVING | Calories: 377 | Fat: 11 g | Protein: 6 g | Sodium: 451.5 mg | Fiber: 4 g | Carbohydrates: 64 g | Sugar: 28 g

Cheesy Hash Brown Casserole

This is a perfect slow cooker recipe that is easy to put together the night before. Place it in the fridge and it can be slow cooked for a little over 2 hours on high in the morning.

INGREDIENTS | SERVES 4

1 package shredded hash browns, squeezed dry of all water

2 eggs

2 cups shredded Cheddar cheese, divided

1 cup mayonnaise

¼ cup chopped onion

½ cup melted butter or margarine, divided

1½ cups gluten-free Rice Chex cereal, crushed

1. Grease a 2.5- or 4-quart slow cooker.

2. In a large bowl, mix together the drained hash browns, eggs, 1½ cups cheese, mayonnaise, chopped onions, and ¼ cup melted butter. Pour into greased slow cooker.

3. In small bowl stir together crushed Rice Chex, remaining melted butter, and remaining cheese. Spread topping evenly over hash browns. Cover slow cooker and vent the lid with a chopstick or the handle of a wooden spoon.

4. Cook on high for 2½ hours or on low for 4 hours until casserole is cooked through and is firm and cheese has melted on the top.

PER SERVING | Calories: 954 | Fat: 72 g | Protein: 22 g | Sodium: 669 mg | Fiber: 2.5 g | Carbohydrates: 40 g | Sugar: 1 g

Almond and Dried Cherry Granola

This variation of breakfast granola focuses more on gluten-free whole grains and has less sugar in the overall recipe than most granolas.

INGREDIENTS | SERVES 24

5 cups old-fashioned gluten-free rolled oats

1 cup slivered almonds

¼ cup mild honey

¼ cup canola oil

1 teaspoon vanilla

½ cup dried tart cherries, raisins, or dried cranberries

¼ cup unsweetened flaked coconut

½ cup sunflower seeds

1. Place the oats and almonds into a 4-quart slow cooker. Drizzle with honey, oil, and vanilla. Stir the mixture to distribute the syrup evenly. Cook on high, uncovered, for 1½ hours, stirring every 30 minutes.

2. Add the cherries, coconut, and sunflower seeds. Reduce heat to low. Cook for 4 hours, uncovered, stirring every 30 minutes.

3. Allow the granola to cool fully, and then store it in an airtight container for up to 1 month in the pantry.

PER SERVING | Calories: 117.5 | Fat: 4.5 g | Protein: 4 g | Sodium: 1.5 mg | Fiber: 2.5 g | Carbohydrates: 16.5 g | Sugar: 4 g

"Baked" Apples

Serve these lightly spiced apples as a simple dessert or a breakfast treat.

INGREDIENTS | SERVES 6

6 baking apples, peeled, and thickly sliced

½ cup water

1 cinnamon stick

1" knob peeled fresh ginger

1 vanilla bean

1. Place the apples in a single layer on the bottom of a 4- or 6-quart slow cooker. Add the water, cinnamon stick, ginger, and vanilla bean. Cook on low for 6–8 hours or until the apples are tender and easily pierced with a fork.

2. Use a slotted spoon to remove the apples from the slow cooker. Discard the cinnamon stick, ginger, vanilla bean, and water. Serve hot.

PER SERVING | Calories: 77 | Fat: 0 g | Protein: 0.5 g | Sodium: 0.5 mg | Fiber: 2 g | Carbohydrates: 20.5 g | Sugar: 15 g

Baking with Apples

When baking, choose apples with firm flesh such as Granny Smith, Jonathan, McIntosh, Cortland, Pink Lady, Pippin, or Winesap. They will be able to hold up to long cooking times without turning to mush. Leaving the skin on adds fiber.

Amish Apple Butter

Traditionally flavored with warm spices and sweetened with honey, this condiment is called a "butter" due to its thick consistency and soft texture. Since apple butter needs a long, unhurried cooking period to caramelize the fruit and deepen the flavors, the slow cooker is the most suitable modern cooking appliance to make it.

INGREDIENTS | YIELDS 8 CUPS

10 cups (about 5 pounds) Gala apples, peeled, cored, and quartered

1 cup honey

3 tablespoons lemon juice or apple cider vinegar

1½ teaspoons ground cinnamon

½ teaspoon ground cloves

½ teaspoon allspice

Old-Fashioned Apple Butter Making

Apple butter used to be made in large copper pots while simmering over a hot fire all day long. It was often done by a church group, or a large family who could share the responsibility of stirring the pot throughout the long day to prevent it from burning. Once finished, the apple butter would be canned and sold to raise money for a good cause or shared among all who helped make it.

1. Place apples in a greased 4-quart slow cooker.

2. Pour honey and lemon juice over apples and add cinnamon, cloves, and allspice. Stir to coat apples.

3. Cover and cook on low for 14–16 hours (yes, 14–16 *hours*), until the apple butter is a deep, dark brown and is richly flavored.

4. Ladle into pint jars and store in the refrigerator for up to 6 weeks. You can also process and can the apple butter if you prefer.

PER SERVING (2 TABLESPOONS) | Calories: 25 | Fat: 0 g | Protein: 0 g | Sodium: 0 mg | Fiber: 0 g | Carbohydrates: 6.5 g | Sugar: 6 g

Apple and Pear Spread

Make the most of in-season apples and pears in this easy alternative to apple or pear butter.

INGREDIENTS | YIELDS 1 QUART

4 Winesap apples, cored, sliced, and peeled

4 Bartlett pears, cored, sliced, and peeled

1 cup water or pear cider

¼ cup brown sugar

¼ cup sugar

¼ teaspoon ginger

¼ teaspoon cinnamon

¼ teaspoon nutmeg

¼ teaspoon allspice

1. Place all ingredients into a 4-quart slow cooker. Cook on low for 10–12 hours.

2. Uncover and cook on low for an additional 1–2 hours or until thick and most of the liquid has evaporated.

3. Allow to cool completely then pour into the food processor and purée. Pour into clean glass jars. Refrigerate up to 6 weeks.

PER SERVING (2 TABLESPOONS) | Calories: 11.5 | Fat: 0 g | Protein: 0.5 g | Sodium: 0.5 mg | Fiber: 0.5 g | Carbohydrates: 3 g | Sugar: 2.5 g

Do-It-Yourself Brown Sugar

Brown sugar is simply white sugar that has been mixed with molasses. Make brown sugar by combining 1 cup granulated sugar with ¼ cup molasses. Store in an airtight container.

Blackberry Jam

This easy low-sugar jam does not need to be canned; it will keep up to a month in the refrigerator.

INGREDIENTS | YIELDS ABOUT 1 QUART

3 cups fresh blackberries

1¾ ounces low-sugar/no-sugar pectin

½ cup sugar

¾ cup water

1. Place all ingredients in a 2-quart slow cooker. Stir.

2. Cook on high, uncovered, for 5 hours. Using a fork or potato masher, smash the berries a bit until they are the texture you prefer. Pour jam into an airtight container.

3. Refrigerate overnight before using.

PER SERVING | Calories: 32 | Fat: 0 g | Protein: 0 g | Sodium: 2 mg | Fiber: 1 g | Carbohydrates: 9 g | Sugar: 7 g

Peach Marmalade

You can spread this on toast or gluten-free biscuits. It can also be used to turn an ordinary gluten-free cracker (Glutino is a wonderful brand) into a delicious snack or appetizer.

INGREDIENTS | YIELDS ABOUT 8 CUPS

2 pounds peaches, peeled, pitted, and chopped

½ cup (about 6 ounces) dried apricots, chopped

1 (20-ounce) can pineapple tidbits in unsweetened juice, undrained

2 medium oranges

1 small lemon

2½ cups granulated cane sugar

2 (3-inch) sticks cinnamon

Innovative Peach Marmalade Uses

By keeping this marmalade the consistency of applesauce you have the added versatility of using it as a condiment to top cooked chicken breasts, easily mixing it together with barbecue or chili sauce to create a sweet and savory dipping sauce, or using it to replace applesauce in many different recipes.

1. Add peaches to a food processor or blender along with the apricots and pineapple (with juice).

2. Remove the zest from the oranges and lemon. Add to the food processor or blender. Cut the oranges and the lemon into quarters and remove any seeds, then add to the food processor or blender. Pulse until entire fruit mixture is pulverized. Pour into a greased 4–6-quart slow cooker.

3. Add the sugar to the slow cooker and stir to combine with the fruit mixture. Add the cinnamon sticks. Cover and, stirring occasionally, cook on low for 4 hours or until the mixture reaches the consistency of applesauce. When finished cooking remove cinnamon sticks.

4. Unless you process and seal the marmalade into sterilized jars, store in covered glass jars in the refrigerator for up to 3–4 weeks. The marmalade can also be frozen for up to 6 months.

PER SERVING (2 TABLESPOONS) | Calories: 40 | Fat: 0.5 g | Protein: 0 g | Sodium: 0 mg | Fiber: 0.5 g | Carbohydrates: 10 g | Sugar: 10 g

CHAPTER 5

Appetizers and Sauces

Parmesan Artichoke Dip

For a more savory dip, reduce the amount of mayonnaise to 2 cups and stir in 2 cups of room-temperature sour cream immediately before serving. For fewer servings, cut the recipe in half and reduce the cooking time.

INGREDIENTS | SERVES 24

2 (13½-ounce) jars of marinated artichoke hearts

4 cups mayonnaise

2 (8-ounce) packages of cream cheese, cubed

12 ounces (3 cups) freshly grated Parmesan cheese

4 cloves of garlic, peeled and minced

1 teaspoon dried dill

½ teaspoon freshly ground black pepper

Instead of . . .

Instead of using artichokes, you can use fresh or frozen spinach (drained of all liquids). For a more hearty dip add 1 pound of fresh lump crabmeat and ½ teaspoon of Old Bay Seasoning.

1. Drain and chop the artichoke hearts. Add to a 2.5-quart slow cooker along with the mayonnaise, cream cheese, Parmesan cheese, garlic, dill, and pepper. Stir to combine. Cover and cook on low for 1 hour; uncover and stir well.

2. Re-cover and cook on low for an additional 1–1½ hours or until the cheese is melted completely and the dip is heated through. To serve, reduce the heat setting of the slow cooker to warm. Serve with gluten-free tortillas, rice crackers, or gluten-free toast points.

PER SERVING | Calories: 344 | Fat: 35 g | Protein: 6 g | Sodium: 456 mg | Fiber: 0 g | Carbohydrates: 2 g | Sugar: 0.5 g

Tex-Mex Taco Dip

This is a super easy gluten-free taco dip made with everyday pantry ingredients.

INGREDIENTS | SERVES 6

1 (8-ounce) package cream cheese

1 (14.5-ounce) can diced tomatoes, drained, reserving 4 tablespoons juice

½ cup refried beans

1 package gluten-free taco seasoning

¼ cup black olives, sliced

Make Your Own Taco Seasoning

You can create your own taco seasoning to keep on hand by mixing together: 1 tablespoon chili powder, ¼ teaspoon garlic powder, ¼ teaspoon onion powder, ¼ teaspoon dried oregano, ½ teaspoon paprika, 1½ teaspoons cumin, 1 tablespoon sugar, ½ teaspoon salt, and ½ teaspoon ground pepper. Store in an airtight container and use when a recipe calls for taco seasoning.

1. Grease a 1.5-quart slow cooker with nonstick cooking spray.

2. Add cream cheese, drained diced tomatoes, reserved tomato juice, refried beans, and taco seasoning. Mix together, cover, and cook on low for 4–5 hours or on high for 2–2½ hours.

3. Right before serving, sprinkle sliced black olives on top of dip. Serve with gluten-free corn chips, rice chips, or gluten-free toast points.

PER SERVING | Calories: 78 | Fat: 6 g | Protein: 2 g | Sodium: 228.5 mg | Fiber: 1.5 g | Carbohydrates: 5 g | Sugar: 1.5 g

Spicy Cheddar Hamburger Dip

A hearty dip with ground beef and garlic, this dish could also be served over cooked rice for a Mexican-inspired gluten-free meal.

INGREDIENTS | SERVES 6

1 pound ground beef
½ cup finely chopped onion
4 cloves garlic, peeled and crushed
½ jalapeño pepper, seeded and minced
¼ teaspoon salt
1 (15-ounce) can tomato sauce
½ teaspoon oregano
1 (8-ounce) package cream cheese
1 cup Cheddar cheese, shredded
1 teaspoon chili powder

Handling Hot Peppers

Make sure to wear gloves when deseeding and mincing hot peppers such as jalapeños. Those with sensitive skin can actually get a chemical burn from touching the seeds and/or the membrane surrounding the seeds.

1. Brown ground beef in a skillet with the onion, garlic, and jalapeño. Pour browned ground beef mixture into a greased 2.5-quart slow cooker.

2. Add salt, tomato sauce, oregano, cream cheese, Cheddar cheese, and chili powder.

3. Cover and cook on high for 2–3 hours or on low for 5–6 hours.

4. Serve with gluten-free corn tacos or rice chips.

PER SERVING | Calories: 282 | Fat: 19 g | Protein: 22 g | Sodium: 678 mg | Fiber: 1.5 g | Carbohydrates: 7 g | Sugar: 4 g

Swedish Meatballs with Gravy

No one will ever guess these uniquely spiced meatballs simmering in a savory gravy are gluten-free. To easily make them dairy-free use almond milk in place of the milk called for and coconut oil in place of the butter.

INGREDIENTS | SERVES 4

1 slice gluten-free bread
4 tablespoons whole milk, divided
¼ cup finely diced onion
2 tablespoons butter, divided
1 pound ground beef
1 egg
¼ teaspoon ground pepper
¼ teaspoon ground allspice
¼ teaspoon ground nutmeg
2 tablespoons brown rice flour
1 cup gluten-free beef broth

1. In a small bowl crumble up the bread and add 2 tablespoons milk to soften it. Set aside. In a small skillet soften the onions in 1 tablespoon of butter for about 3–5 minutes until softened and translucent.

2. In a large bowl mix together the softened bread, onions cooked in butter, ground beef, egg, pepper, allspice, and nutmeg. Mix together thoroughly and roll tablespoons of the meat mixture into small meatballs.

3. Brown meatballs (in small batches) in a nonstick skillet and then transfer them to a greased 4-quart slow cooker.

4. In the same skillet you browned the meatballs in whisk together the remaining tablespoon of butter and the brown rice flour. Whisk for 1–2 minutes to toast the flour. Slowly pour in the beef broth, whisking constantly. Cook for 3–5 additional minutes until you have a thickened gravy. Whisk in remaining 2 tablespoons of milk.

5. Pour gravy over the meatballs in the slow cooker. Cover and cook on high for 3–4 hours or on low for 6–8 hours.

PER SERVING | Calories: 326 | Fat: 19 g | Protein: 26.5 g | Sodium: 347 mg | Fiber: 0.5 g | Carbohydrates: 10.5 g | Sugar: 1.5 g

Sweet and Sour Mini Hot Dog Snackers

Sometimes it can be difficult to make sure certain brands of sandwich meats and hot dogs are gluten-free. To make it easier, instead of searching high and low for mini gluten-free hot dogs, simply use a brand of regular gluten-free hot dogs you trust and cut them into bite-sized pieces.

INGREDIENTS | SERVES 4

1 package gluten-free hot dogs, cut into bite-sized pieces

½ cup grape jelly

½ cup gluten-free barbecue sauce

2 tablespoons orange juice

½ teaspoon ground white pepper

1 tablespoon gluten-free Worcestershire sauce

½ teaspoon ground mustard

1. Place cut-up hot dogs into a greased 2.5-quart slow cooker.

2. In a bowl mix together the jelly, barbecue sauce, orange juice, pepper, Worcestershire sauce, and mustard. Pour over the hot dogs in the slow cooker.

3. Cover and cook on high for 3–4 hours or on low for 6–8 hours.

PER SERVING | Calories: 260 | Fat: 6 g | Protein: 2.5 g | Sodium: 647.5 mg | Fiber: 1 g | Carbohydrates: 41 g | Sugar: 29 g

Hot Chicken Buffalo Bites

Love buffalo wings? Then you will love these chicken bites even more; they are made with juicy chicken breasts so you won't have to worry about bones. They are super easy and much less messy!

INGREDIENTS | SERVES 6

3 large chicken breasts, cut into 2-inch strips

2 tablespoons brown rice flour

¼ cup melted butter

3 cloves garlic, peeled and minced

⅓ cup Frank's Red Hot sauce

¼ cup gluten-free ranch dressing

Fresh Garlic Versus Garlic Powder

In a pinch use 1½ teaspoons garlic powder in this recipe. The garlic flavor won't be quite as pungent and rich as it is when you use fresh garlic, but it will still be easy and enjoyable.

1. Place chicken pieces into a greased 2.5-quart slow cooker.

2. In a saucepan whisk together the brown rice flour and melted butter for 2–3 minutes to toast the flour.

3. Slowly whisk in the garlic and Frank's Red Hot sauce. Pour sauce over chicken in the slow cooker.

4. Cover and cook on high for 3 hours or on low for 6 hours. Serve with ranch dressing to dip in. If using a larger slow cooker, make sure to reduce cooking time by about half.

PER SERVING | Calories: 227 | Fat: 15 g | Protein: 18 g | Sodium: 511.5 mg | Fiber: 0 g | Carbohydrates: 4 g | Sugar: 0.5 g

Mango Pork Morsels

In this recipe, the mango provides natural sweetness and a tropical flair. Plate and pierce each morsel with a toothpick.

INGREDIENTS | SERVES 10

1½ pounds lean pork loin, cubed

2 mangoes, cubed (see sidebar)

3 cloves garlic, minced

1 jalapeño, seeded and minced

1 tablespoon salsa

¼ teaspoon salt

¼ teaspoon freshly ground black pepper

2 teaspoons ground chipotle

1 teaspoon New Mexican chili powder

½ teaspoon oregano

2 tablespoons orange juice

2 tablespoons lime juice

How to Cut Up a Mango

Slice the mango vertically on either side of the large flat pit. Then, using the tip of a knife, cut vertical lines into the flesh without piercing the skin. Make horizontal lines in the flesh to form cubes. Use a spoon to scoop out the cubes. Repeat for the other side.

1. Quickly brown the pork in a nonstick skillet. Add the browned pork and cubed mango to a 4-quart slow cooker.

2. In a small bowl, whisk together the garlic, jalapeño, salsa, salt, pepper, chipotle, chili powder, oregano, and the orange and lime juices. Pour over the mango and pork. Stir.

3. Cook on low for 6 hours; remove the cover and cook on high for 30 minutes. Stir before serving.

PER SERVING | Calories: 32 | Fat: 0 g | Protein: 0.5 g | Sodium: 73 mg | Fiber: 1 g | Carbohydrates: 8 g | Sugar: 6.5 g

Gluten-Free "Shake It and Bake It" Drumsticks

Remember that wonderful chicken seasoning from your childhood? You can now make it gluten-free for crispy chicken drumsticks right in your slow cooker!

Make It and Shake It for Later

Double or triple the batch of the seasoned coating ingredients so in the future you can prepare this delicious gluten-free appetizer or light meal in snap.

1. In a heavy-duty gallon-sized zip-top bag mix together the seasoning ingredients: crushed tortilla chips, olive oil, salt, paprika, celery seeds, pepper, garlic powder, onion flakes, basil, parsley, and oregano.

2. To prepare the slow cooker either wrap 4–5 small potatoes in foil and place them in the bottom of a greased 4-quart slow cooker, or make 4–5 foil balls about the size of a small potato and place them in the bottom of the slow cooker. (This will help the chicken to get a little bit crispy in the slow cooker instead of cooking in its juices.)

3. Place 2 drumsticks in the bag with the seasoning mix, seal it tightly, and shake the bag to coat the chicken. Place coated chicken drumsticks on top of the foil balls. Repeat with remaining drumsticks, 2 at a time.

4. Cover slow cooker and vent the lid with a chopstick to help release extra moisture. Cook on high for 4 hours or on low for 8 hours.

PER SERVING | Calories: 149 | Fat: 10 g | Protein: 14 g | Sodium: 257.5 mg | Fiber: 0 g | Carbohydrates: 0.5 g | Sugar: 0 g

Pineapple Teriyaki Drumsticks

Serve this crowd-pleasing favorite as a hearty appetizer. Pair leftovers with steamed rice for a great lunch.

INGREDIENTS | SERVES 12

12 chicken drumsticks

8 ounces canned pineapple slices in juice

¼ cup gluten-free teriyaki sauce or gluten-free soy sauce

1 teaspoon ground ginger

¼ cup gluten-free hoisin sauce

1. Arrange the drumsticks in a single layer on a broiling pan. Broil for 10 minutes on high, flipping the drumsticks once halfway through the cooking time.
2. Drain the juice from the pineapple into a 4–6-quart slow cooker. Add the teriyaki sauce, ginger, and hoisin sauce. Stir to combine.
3. Cut the pineapple rings in half. Add them to the slow cooker.
4. Add the drumsticks to the slow cooker and stir to combine. Cover and cook on low for 4–6 hours or on high for 2–3 hours.

PER SERVING | Calories: 146 | Fat: 6.5 g | Protein: 15 g | Sodium: 377 mg | Fiber: 0.5 g | Carbohydrates: 6 g | Sugar: 5 g

Hot Cinnamon Chili Peanuts

These seasoned peanuts are a surprising hit with chili powder and cinnamon and just a hint of sweetness with honey and brown sugar.

INGREDIENTS | YIELDS 1½ CUPS

1½ cups peanuts

¼ cup brown sugar

2 teaspoons cinnamon

1½ teaspoons chili powder

¼ teaspoon salt

2 teaspoons honey

2 teaspoons oil

1. Combine all ingredients and place in a greased 2.5-quart slow cooker.
2. Cover slow cooker and vent lid with a chopstick or the handle of a wooden spoon. Cook on high for 2 hours or on low for 4 hours. If using a larger slow cooker, you will probably need to reduce the cooking time to only 1 hour on high or 2 hours on low.
3. Pour peanut mixture out onto a baking sheet lined with parchment paper. Allow to cool and dry and then transfer to a container with an airtight lid. Store in the pantry for up to 2 weeks.

PER SERVING (¼ CUP) | Calories: 266 | Fat: 19.5 g | Protein: 9.5 g | Sodium: 114 mg | Fiber: 4 g | Carbohydrates: 18 g | Sugar: 12 g

Balsamic Almonds

These sweet and sour almonds are a great addition to a cheese platter or appetizer plate.

INGREDIENTS | SERVES 15

2 cups whole almonds
½ cup dark brown sugar
½ cup balsamic vinegar
½ teaspoon kosher salt

Healthy Almonds

Botanically speaking, almonds are a seed, not a nut. They are an excellent source of vitamin E and have high levels of monoun-saturated fat, one of the two "good" fats responsible for lowering LDL cholesterol.

1. Place all ingredients into a 4-quart slow cooker. Cook uncovered on high for 4 hours, stirring every 15 minutes or until all the liquid has evaporated. The almonds will have a syrupy coating.

2. Line 2 cookie sheets with parchment paper. Pour the almonds in a single layer on the baking sheets to cool completely. Store in an airtight container in the pantry for up to 2 weeks.

PER SERVING | Calories: 108 | Fat: 6 g | Protein: 3 g | Sodium: 83 mg | Fiber: 1.5 g | Carbohydrates: 11 g | Sugar: 9 g

Cinnamon and Sugar Pecans

Not only a tasty snack, these chopped sweet pecans are also delicious sprinkled over French toast.

INGREDIENTS | SERVES 12

3 cups pecan halves
3 tablespoons butter, melted
2 teaspoons vanilla
½ cup sugar
1 teaspoon cinnamon
½ teaspoon salt

1. Add all ingredients to a 4-quart slow cooker. Stir to coat the nuts evenly. Cover and cook on low for 4–5 hours or on high for 2 hours, stirring occasionally.

2. Uncover and continue to cook on low for another hour, stirring occasionally, to dry the nuts. Next, evenly spread the nuts on a baking sheet lined with parchment paper or aluminum foil until completely cooled. Store in an airtight container in the pantry for up to 2 weeks.

PER SERVING | Calories: 249 | Fat: 22.5 g | Protein: 2.5 g | Sodium: 98 mg | Fiber: 3 g | Carbohydrates: 12.5 g | Sugar: 9.5 g

Slow Cooker Snack Mix

Making a snack mix with gluten-free Chex cereal is a breeze in the slow cooker. Unlike the oven method, there is virtually no risk of burning and little attention or hands-on time is needed.

INGREDIENTS | SERVES 20

2 tablespoons melted butter

1 teaspoon garlic powder

1 teaspoon onion powder

1 teaspoon paprika

1 teaspoon dried thyme

1 teaspoon dill weed

1 teaspoon chili powder

1 teaspoon gluten-free Worcestershire sauce

2¼ cups gluten-free Corn Chex cereal

2¼ cups gluten-free Rice Chex cereal

1 cup gluten-free Glutino pretzels

1 cup roasted peanuts or almonds

1. Pour the butter, spices, and Worcestershire sauce into the bottom of a 6-quart slow cooker. Stir.

2. Add the cereal, pretzels, and nuts. Cook uncovered on low for 2–3 hours, stirring every 30 minutes.

3. Pour onto a baking sheet and allow to cool. Store in an airtight container in the pantry for up to 2 weeks.

PER SERVING | Calories: 93 | Fat: 5 g | Protein: 3 g | Sodium: 75 mg | Fiber: 1 g | Carbohydrates: 10 g | Sugar: 0.5 g

Snack Mix Variations

Mexican: substitute 1 teaspoon each cayenne pepper, ground chipotle, hot New Mexico chili powder, and oregano for the thyme, dill weed, and Worcestershire sauce. Japanese: substitute 1 teaspoon each sesame seeds, gluten-free soy sauce, ground ginger, and white pepper for the paprika, thyme, dill weed, and Worcestershire sauce.

Low-Carb Snack Mix

For this recipe, use raw almonds, cashews, pecans, shelled pumpkin seeds, shelled sunflower seeds, walnuts, and raw or dry-roasted peanuts. The amounts you use of each kind of nut is up to you, although because of their size, ideally the recipe shouldn't have more than 1 cup of sunflower seeds.

INGREDIENTS | SERVES 24

4 tablespoons butter, melted

3 tablespoons gluten-free Worcestershire sauce

1½ teaspoons garlic powder

2 teaspoons onion powder

½ teaspoon sea salt

8 cups raw nuts

Toasted Pepitas

Raw pumpkin seeds are also known as "pepitas" when sold in Latino food markets. Toasted pepitas make a healthy and crispy topping for salads, casseroles, and stir fries. Simply add ½ cup of pepitas to a hot, heavy-bottomed skillet. Drizzle with 2 tablespoons olive oil and ⅛ teaspoon of salt and stir for about 5 minutes until lightly toasted.

1. Add all ingredients to a 4-quart slow cooker. Stir to coat the nuts evenly. Cover and cook on low for 6 hours, stirring occasionally.

2. Uncover and continue to cook on low for another hour to dry the nuts and seeds, stirring occasionally, and then evenly spread them on a baking sheet lined with aluminum foil or parchment paper until completely cooled. Store in an airtight container in the pantry for up to 2 weeks.

PER SERVING | Calories: 276 | Fat: 27 g | Protein: 6 g | Sodium: 71.5 mg | Fiber: 2.5 g | Carbohydrates: 6 g | Sugar: 1 g

Marinara Sauce

Marinara sauce is full of authentic Italian flavor. This method proves you don't need a laundry list of ingredients for great flavor. Serve this sauce over steamed spaghetti squash or cooked gluten-free pasta.

INGREDIENTS | SERVES 6

2 teaspoons olive oil

2–3 cloves garlic, crushed

1 sweet onion, finely diced

1 (28-ounce) can whole, peeled Roma tomatoes with basil

Simmering Sauces All Day

Simple sauces like this can be simmered for long periods of time on low heat. The longer the sauce cooks the better the flavor will be once it's time to eat.

1. In a medium-sized skillet, heat oil. Add garlic and onion and sauté for 3–5 minutes until golden and soft.

2. Pour sautéed onion and garlic into a 4-quart slow cooker. Add tomatoes. Using a fork or a potato masher, break up the tomatoes into the sauce. They will be a little bit chunky. If you prefer, use an immersion blender to blend until smooth.

3. Cover and cook on high for 4–5 hours or on low for 8–10 hours.

PER SERVING | Calories: 36 | Fat: 2 g | Protein: 1.5 g | Sodium: 7.5 mg | Fiber: 2 g | Carbohydrates: 7 g | Sugar: 4 g

Hearty Bolognese Sauce

Try this warm and comforting meaty tomato sauce with cooked gluten-free pasta, spaghetti squash, or even cooked brown rice.

INGREDIENTS | SERVES 6

1 small onion, finely diced
1 carrot, peeled and finely diced
1 celery stalk, finely diced
2 tablespoons olive oil
¼ cup (2–3 slices) uncooked bacon, diced
1 pound ground beef
1 (28-ounce) can crushed tomatoes
1 cup red wine
1 cup gluten-free beef stock
½ teaspoon salt
½ teaspoon ground black pepper

Ragu Style Bolognese Sauce versus Marinara Sauce

In many Italian recipes the meat sauce (Bolognese) is usually seasoned with aromatic vegetables like onions, carrots, and celery instead of the traditional spices like oregano, garlic, or basil. Those spices are often in simple meatless tomato sauces such as marinara.

1. In a skillet brown the onion, carrot, and celery in olive oil until tender, about 6–8 minutes. Add the bacon and cook until it has rendered fat into the pan, about 3–4 minutes. Add the ground beef and cook until browned, about 5 minutes. If the ground beef renders a lot of fat, drain before adding to the slow cooker.

2. Transfer the cooked vegetables and meat into a 4-quart slow cooker.

3. Add the tomatoes, wine, and broth to the slow cooker. Stir all ingredients together.

4. Cover and cook on high for 4–5 hours or on low for 8–10 hours. Season with salt and pepper before serving.

PER SERVING | Calories: 26 | Fat: 17 g | Protein: 18.5 g | Sodium: 442 mg | Fiber: 2 g | Carbohydrates: 9 g | Sugar: 5 g

Homemade Ketchup

Condiments such as ketchup are generally gluten-free, but you always have to read the label and check with the manufacturer to make sure. Instead of worrying, you can make your own and know exactly what ingredients are in your specially made ketchup!

INGREDIENTS | YIELDS ABOUT 2½ CUPS

1 (15-ounce) can no-salt-added tomato sauce
2 teaspoons water
½ teaspoon onion powder
¾ cup sugar
⅓ cup cider vinegar
¼ teaspoon sea salt
¼ teaspoon ground cinnamon
⅛ teaspoon ground cloves
Pinch ground allspice
Pinch nutmeg
Pinch freshly ground pepper
⅔ teaspoon sweet paprika

1. Add all ingredients to a 2.5 quart slow cooker. Cover and, stirring occasionally, cook for 2–4 hours on low or until ketchup reaches desired consistency.

2. Turn off the slow cooker or remove the insert from the slow cooker. Allow mixture to cool, then put in a covered container (such as a recycled ketchup bottle). Store in the refrigerator for up to a month.

PER SERVING | Calories: 22 | Fat: 0 g | Protein: 0 g | Sodium: 87.5 mg | Fiber: 0 g | Carbohydrates: 5.5 g | Sugar: 5 g

Ketchup with a Kick

If you like zesty ketchup, you can add crushed red peppers, Mrs. Dash Extra Spicy Seasoning Blend, or salt-free chili powder along with, or instead of, the cinnamon and other seasonings. Another alternative is to use hot paprika rather than sweet paprika.

Puttanesca Sauce

Don't be afraid of the anchovies, they simply melt away and add a complex flavor to this spicy, salty, garlicky sauce.

INGREDIENTS | SERVES 6

4 anchovies in oil
1 tablespoon olive oil
4 cloves garlic, minced
1 onion, diced
1 cup sliced black olives
28 ounces crushed tomatoes
15 ounces diced tomatoes
1 tablespoon crushed red pepper
2 tablespoons drained nonpareil-sized capers
1 tablespoon sugar

What Is Sautéing?

Sautéing is a method of cooking that uses a small amount of fat to cook food in a shallow pan over medium-high heat. The goal is to brown the food while preserving its color, moisture, and flavor.

1. Pat the anchovies with a paper towel to remove any excess oil.

2. Heat the olive oil in a large, nonstick skillet and add the anchovies, garlic, and onion. Sauté until the anchovies mostly disappear into the onion and garlic and the onions are soft, about 3–5 minutes.

3. Place the onions, anchovies, and garlic into a 4-quart slow cooker. Add the remaining ingredients. Stir to distribute the ingredients evenly. Cook on low for 10–12 hours.

4. If the sauce looks very wet at the end of the cooking time, remove the lid and cook on high for 15–30 minutes before serving.

PER SERVING | Calories: 109 | Fat: 5.5 g | Protein: 3 g | Sodium: 389.5 mg | Fiber: 4 g | Carbohydrates: 14 g | Sugar: 8 g

Red Wine Sauce

Once you've had this elegant sauce with filet mignon, prime rib, or even a fancy hamburger, you'll make it often. You can also serve it over gluten-free noodles or rice.

INGREDIENTS | YIELDS 2 CUPS

4 shallots, peeled and chopped finely

2 cloves garlic, minced

2 tablespoons butter

2 tablespoons olive oil

1 cup sliced mushrooms (brown, white button, or exotic)

2 tablespoons brown rice flour

1 cup beef broth, heated

1 cup dry red wine such as Burgundy or Merlot

1 tablespoon gluten-free Worcestershire sauce

½ teaspoon salt

½ teaspoon pepper

1. Sauté the shallots and garlic in butter and oil in a large saucepan over low heat, for about 3–5 minutes until softened. Add the mushrooms and toss them till they are coated in the butter and oil.

2. Whisk in the flour and simmer for 3–4 minutes. Transfer sauce to a greased 2.5-quart slow cooker.

3. Whisk in the broth, red wine, Worcestershire, salt, and pepper. Cover and cook on high for 2–3 hours or on low for 4–5 hours.

PER SERVING (½ CUP) | Calories: 213 | Fat: 13 g | Protein: 2.5 g | Sodium: 540 mg | Fiber: 0.5 g | Carbohydrates: 12 g | Sugar: 1 g

Variations on a Theme

There are many, many different variations to this recipe. There is much to love about this very simple and basic sauce—that's why it's been popular for more than 200 years. Try different herbs such as parsley, rosemary, or basil. You can add heat using a few drops of hot pepper sauce such as Tabasco. Capers, chopped olives, or green peppercorns also can add a nice touch.

Welsh Rarebit

Welsh Rarebit can be served as a party dip or spooned over gluten-free toast points and then dusted with paprika. It's also good served as part of a breakfast buffet to be spooned over scrambled eggs or egg-topped gluten-free English muffins.

INGREDIENTS | SERVES 8

2½ cups gluten-free beer such as Red Bridge, New Grist, or Bard's Tale, divided

2 tablespoons butter

¼ teaspoon hot sauce

½ teaspoon gluten-free Worcestershire sauce

2 pounds sharp Cheddar cheese, grated (about 4 cups)

2 tablespoons cornstarch or brown rice flour

2 teaspoons dry mustard

2 large eggs

⅛ teaspoon paprika

Leftover Welsh Rarebit

Refrigerate leftover Welsh Rarebit in a covered container for up to a week. Reheat slowly (so the cheese doesn't separate) and serve over steamed vegetables or as a baked potato topper.

1. Pour 2 cups of the beer, butter, hot sauce, and Worcestershire sauce into a 4-quart slow cooker. Cook uncovered on high for ½ hour.

2. Put half the cheese in a zip-top bag with the cornstarch or brown rice flour. Shake well to coat the cheese with flour. Add all of the cheese/flour mixture and remaining cheese to the slow cooker. Cover and cook on low for 1 hour until the cheese is melted.

3. In a small bowl add the mustard and eggs; whisk to combine.

4. Whisk the remaining ½ cup of gluten-free beer into the egg mixture and slowly stir the egg mixture into the slow cooker.

5. Cover and cook on low for half an hour. To serve, reduce the heat setting of the slow cooker to warm. Dust with paprika.

PER SERVING | Calories: 520 | Fat: 38 g | Protein: 30 g | Sodium: 738.5 mg | Fiber: 0 g | Carbohydrates: 6 g | Sugar: 1 g

Plum Sauce

Plum sauce is usually served with egg rolls, which are generally not gluten-free. But this delicious sauce is also wonderful brushed on chicken or pork ribs; doing so near the end of the grilling time will add a succulent glaze to the grilled meat.

INGREDIENTS | YIELDS 4 CUPS

8 cups (about 3 pounds) plums, pitted and cut in half

1 small sweet onion, finely diced

1 cup water

1 teaspoon fresh ginger, peeled and minced

1 clove garlic, peeled and minced

¾ cup sugar

½ cup rice vinegar or cider vinegar

1 teaspoon ground coriander

½ teaspoon salt

½ teaspoon cinnamon

¼ teaspoon cayenne pepper

¼ teaspoon ground cloves

1. Add plums, onion, water, ginger, and garlic to a 4-quart slow cooker. Cover and, stirring occasionally, cook on low for 4 hours or until plums and onions are tender.

2. Use an immersion blender to pulverize the contents of the slow cooker before straining it or press the cooked plum mixture through a sieve.

3. Return the liquefied and strained plum mixture to the slow cooker and stir in sugar, vinegar, coriander, salt, cinnamon, cayenne pepper, and cloves. Cover and, stirring occasionally, cook on low for 2 hours or until the sauce reaches the consistency of applesauce.

PER SERVING (¼ CUP) | Calories: 78 | Fat: 0.5 g | Protein: 0.5 g | Sodium: 74.5 mg | Fiber: 1.5 g | Carbohydrates: 19.5 g | Sugar: 20 g

Side Dishes and Bean Recipes

Fresh Artichokes

Preparing artichokes takes some work, but they're good served with an avocado salad and poached salmon.

INGREDIENTS | SERVES 4

2 large, fresh artichokes

6 cups hot water

1 lemon

¼ cup butter, melted

¼ teaspoon seasoned salt

1. Rinse the artichokes under cool running water. Use a sharp knife to slice about an inch off the top of each artichoke; cut off the stem near the base. Use kitchen shears to trim about ½ inch off the top of each leaf. Use the knife to cut each artichoke in half vertically. Use a spoon or melon baller to scoop out and discard the fuzzy center, or "choke."

2. Place the artichoke halves in a 2.5-quart slow cooker. Pour in the hot water.

3. Cut 4 thin slices from the center of the lemon and add to the slow cooker; reserve the remaining lemon. Cover and cook on high for 4 hours or until the artichoke hearts are tender when pierced with a knife. Use a slotted spoon to remove the artichoke halves from the slow cooker.

4. To prepare the butter sauce, add the melted butter to a bowl. Add the juice from the reserved portions of the lemon. Stir in seasoned salt. Evenly drizzle over the artichoke halves and serve immediately.

PER SERVING | Calories: 144 | Fat: 12 g | Protein: 3 g | Sodium: 236 mg | Fiber: 5 g | Carbohydrates: 10 g | Sugar: 1 g

Wild Rice Pilaf

Wild rice is a perfect side dish for the gluten-free diet. It's naturally gluten-free and is actually in the grass family of botanicals. Wild rice has a rustic earthy flavor that's a nice alternative to plain white rice.

INGREDIENTS | SERVES 6

2 cups wild rice, uncooked

2 tablespoons butter

½ cup finely chopped onion

½ teaspoon salt

½ teaspoon pepper

2 (14-ounce) cans gluten-free chicken broth

½ cup water

1 (4-ounce) can sliced mushrooms, undrained

1 teaspoon dried thyme

1 teaspoon dried oregano

1. Pour rice into a mesh colander and rinse.

2. Add butter to a frying pan and heat until sizzling. Add chopped onion and wild rice. Cook over medium-high heat for 3–4 minutes until rice has a slightly nutty, toasty aroma, and onions are translucent.

3. Grease a 4-quart slow cooker with nonstick cooking spray. Add toasted rice and onions to slow cooker. Add remaining ingredients and mix well.

4. Cover and cook on high for 3 hours or on low for 6 hours until rice has absorbed most of the liquid. If rice is not absorbing the liquids fast enough, vent the lid of the slow cooker with a chopstick or wooden spoon handle.

PER SERVING | Calories: 261 | Fat: 5.5 g | Protein: 10 g | Sodium: 480 mg | Fiber: 4 g | Carbohydrates: 45 g | Sugar: 2 g

Apple and Sweet Potato Casserole

This sweet side dish would be perfect for Thanksgiving or even as a dessert with a scoop of ice cream.

INGREDIENTS | SERVES 6

4 large sweet potatoes, peeled and sliced

1 (15-ounce) can gluten-free apple pie filling

2 tablespoons butter, melted

¼ teaspoon salt

Canned Shortcuts

Using apple pie filling in this recipe is an easy way to add apples, spices, and sugar without a lot of hassle. Most canned, prepared apple pie fillings are made with cornstarch instead of wheat, but always read the nutrition label to make sure. Apple pie filling is good not only with sweet potatoes, but also in oatmeal, in a cake, or as a topping for a cheesecake.

1. Grease a 4-quart slow cooker with nonstick cooking spray. Place sweet potatoes in the bottom of the slow cooker.

2. Add apple pie filling, butter, and salt. Cover and cook on high for 3–4 hours until sweet potatoes are fork tender.

PER SERVING | Calories: 142 | Fat: 4 g | Protein: 1.5 g | Sodium: 146 mg | Fiber: 3.5 g | Carbohydrates: 26 g | Sugar: 10.5 g

Carrot Nutmeg Pudding

Carrots are often served as a savory side dish. In this recipe the carrots have just a little bit of sugar added to bring out their natural sweetness.

INGREDIENTS | SERVES 4

4 large carrots, grated

2 tablespoons butter

½ teaspoon salt

½ teaspoon nutmeg, freshly grated

2 tablespoons sugar

1 teaspoon vanilla

1 cup milk

3 eggs, beaten

1. Add carrots and butter to a large glass, microwavable bowl. Cook on high for 3–4 minutes until carrots are slightly softened.

2. Stir in remaining ingredients and pour into a greased 2.5-quart slow cooker. Cook on high for 3 hours or on low for 6 hours. Serve hot or cold.

PER SERVING | Calories: 200 | Fat: 12 g | Protein: 7.5 g | Sodium: 424 mg | Fiber: 2 g | Carbohydrates: 17 g | Sugar: 13.5 g

Herb-Stuffed Tomatoes

Serve these Italian-influenced stuffed tomatoes with a simple salad for an easy, light meal.

INGREDIENTS | SERVES 4

4 large tomatoes

1 cup cooked quinoa

1 stalk celery, minced

1 tablespoon minced fresh garlic

2 tablespoons minced fresh oregano

2 tablespoons minced fresh Italian parsley

1 teaspoon dried chervil

1 teaspoon fennel seeds

¾ cup water

1. Cut out the core of each tomato and discard. Scoop out the seeds, leaving the walls of the tomato intact.

2. In a small bowl, stir together the quinoa, celery, garlic, and spices. Divide into 4 even portions, and stuff 1 portion into the center of each tomato.

3. Place the filled tomatoes in a single layer in an 4-quart slow cooker. Pour the water into the bottom of the slow cooker. Cook on low for 4 hours.

PER SERVING | Calories: 100 | Fat: 1.5 g | Protein: 4 g | Sodium: 24 mg | Fiber: 4.5 g | Carbohydrates: 19.5 g | Sugar: 5 g

Grandma's Green Beans

This recipe is easy to double if you need extra servings for a church social or buffet. Serve these green beans with meatloaf or any grilled meat.

INGREDIENTS | SERVES 6

1 (1-pound) bag frozen green beans, thawed

1 medium sweet onion, peeled and diced

6 medium red potatoes

1 teaspoon sugar

½ teaspoon salt

½ teaspoon freshly ground black pepper

6 strips of bacon

Fresh Green Beans

You can substitute a pound to a pound and a half of fresh washed, trimmed, and cut green beans for the frozen. Increase the cooking time to 6 hours if you do.

1. Add the green beans and onion to a 4-quart or larger slow cooker.

2. Depending on your preference, you can either scrub and dice the potatoes or peel and dice them. Add the potatoes to the slow cooker along with the sugar, salt, and pepper.

3. Dice the bacon and add ⅔ of it to the slow cooker. Stir to mix well.

4. Sprinkle the remaining bacon pieces over the top of the bean mixture. Cover and cook on low for 4 hours or until the potatoes are cooked through. Taste for seasoning and add additional salt and pepper if needed.

PER SERVING | Calories: 311 | Fat: 13 g | Protein: 9 g | Sodium: 448 mg | Fiber: 6 g | Carbohydrates: 42 g | Sugar: 6 g

Harvard Beets

Beets are richly flavored, beautiful vegetables to serve at the dinner table. For those unaccustomed to the taste of beets, this sweet and sour recipe is a good place to start.

INGREDIENTS | SERVES 6

½ cup sugar

1 tablespoon cornstarch

¼ cup water

¼ cup white vinegar

¼ teaspoon ground cloves

2 (14-ounce) cans sliced or whole beets, drained (or 4 cups peeled and sliced fresh beets)

1. Grease a 2.5-quart slow cooker with nonstick cooking spray.

2. Add sugar, cornstarch, water, vinegar, and cloves to slow cooker and whisk together. Add drained beets.

3. Cover and cook on high for 3 hours. Serve hot or cold.

PER SERVING | Calories: 100 | Fat: 0 g | Protein: 1 g | Sodium: 52 mg | Fiber: 2 g | Carbohydrates: 24 g | Sugar: 21 g

Beets and Football

The origins of Harvard Beets is uncertain, but beets cooked in a sugar and vinegar solution have been eaten for hundreds of years in many different countries. The addition of cornstarch as a thickening agent is unique to America, though; specifically the northeastern states. One theory behind the name "Harvard Beets" is that the beets shared a similar color to Harvard's football team jerseys.

Sweet Potato Gratin with Leeks and Onions

The combination of sweet and savory makes this a fascinating, unique, and delicious dish.

INGREDIENTS | SERVES 6

2 leeks, white part only, rinsed and chopped

2 large sweet onions such as Vidalias, peeled and finely chopped

2 stalks celery with tops, finely chopped

4 tablespoons olive oil

4 sweet potatoes, peeled and sliced thinly

1 teaspoon dried thyme

1 teaspoon salt

½ teaspoon ground black pepper

3 cups 1% milk

1½ cups gluten-free cornbread crumbs

2 tablespoons butter or margarine, cut in small pieces

Instead of . . .

Instead of gluten-free cornbread, you can also use crushed corn tortillas as a topping. Several brands such as Utz and Food Should Taste Good actually have "This is a gluten-free food" listed on some of their products. If you have any questions about a product, make sure to call the company to ask about their gluten cross-contamination prevention policies.

1. In a skillet over medium heat add the leeks, onions, celery, and olive oil and sauté for 3–5 minutes, until softened.

2. Grease a 4-quart slow cooker with nonstick cooking spray.

3. Layer the sweet potato slices in the slow cooker with the sautéed vegetables. Sprinkle thyme, salt, and pepper on each layer as you go along. Finish with a layer of potatoes.

4. Add the milk until it meets the top layer of potatoes. Then add the cornbread crumbs. Dot with butter or margarine.

5. Cover and cook on high for 4 hours or on low for 8 hours, until the potatoes are fork tender. In the last hour of cooking, vent the lid of the slow cooker with a chopstick or wooden spoon handle to allow excess condensation to escape.

PER SERVING | Calories: 405 | Fat: 18.5 g | Protein: 10 g | Sodium: 710 mg | Fiber: 5 g | Carbohydrates: 51 g | Sugar: 14.5 g

Scalloped Potatoes with Bacon

Scalloped potatoes is an ideal dish the for the slow cooker. Potatoes cooked slowly over low heat are extremely tender and delicious.

INGREDIENTS | SERVES 8

2 tablespoons cornstarch

1 teaspoon salt

½ teaspoon pepper

2 cups milk

4 cups potatoes, thinly sliced (about 6–8 medium potatoes)

½ pound bacon, cooked and crumbled

3 tablespoons butter, cut in small pieces

½ cup Cheddar cheese, shredded

½ cup scallions, sliced

Make It Dairy-Free

For a recipe like this you can easily make it dairy-free by using coconut oil or olive oil in place of the butter, coconut milk or almond milk in place of the dairy milk, and Daiya (soy-free, gluten-free, and dairy-free cheese product) in place of the dairy cheese.

1. Grease a 4-quart slow cooker with nonstick cooking spray.

2. In a small bowl mix together the cornstarch, salt, pepper, and milk.

3. Place ⅓ of the potatoes in the bottom of the slow cooker. Pour ⅓ of the milk mixture over the potatoes. Sprinkle ⅓ of the bacon over the milk. Continue to layer ingredients, finishing with potato slices.

4. Dot butter over potatoes. Cover slow cooker and cook on low for 6–8 hours until potatoes are tender.

5. Thirty minutes prior to serving sprinkle cheese and green onions on top of potatoes. Allow cheese to melt and then serve.

PER SERVING | Calories: 293 | Fat: 21 g | Protein: 8 g | Sodium: 604.5 mg | Fiber: 2 g | Carbohydrates: 17 g | Sugar: 4.5 g

Spinach with Baked Eggs and Cheese

This is an excellent brunch, lunch, or supper. Everyone loves it, and even after a tough day, it's easy to put together.

INGREDIENTS | SERVES 4

1½ cups gluten-free cornbread crumbs

3 (10-ounce) packages frozen spinach, thawed, moisture squeezed out

2 tablespoons butter or margarine, melted

½ cup shredded Swiss cheese

½ teaspoon nutmeg

1 teaspoon salt

½ teaspoon ground black pepper

1 cup heavy cream

8 eggs

Herbs and Spices

People often confuse herbs with spices. Herbs are green and are the leaves of plants—the only herb (in Western cooking) that is a flower is lavender. Frequently used herbs include parsley, basil, oregano, thyme, rosemary, cilantro, and mint. Spices are roots, tubers, barks, or berries. These include pepper, cinnamon, nutmeg, allspice, cumin, turmeric, ginger, cardamom, and coriander.

1. Grease a 4-quart slow cooker with nonstick cooking spray. Sprinkle cornbread crumbs on the bottom of the slow cooker.

2. In a medium bowl, mix the spinach, butter, cheese, nutmeg, salt, and pepper together. Stir in the cream. Spread the spinach-cheese mixture on top of the cornbread crumbs.

3. Using the back of a tablespoon, make 8 depressions in the spinach mixture. Break open the eggs and place one egg in each hole.

4. Cover and cook on low for 3 hours or on high for 1½–2 hours until the yolks are cooked through, but not hard. Serve with gluten-free toast and fresh fruit.

PER SERVING | Calories: 634 | Fat: 44 g | Protein: 25.5 g | Sodium: 1,127 mg | Fiber: 4 g | Carbohydrates: 35.5 g | Sugar: 4 g

Slow-Cooked Collard Greens

This is a Southern side dish staple that goes perfectly with barbecue chicken or ribs and Gluten-Free Corn Bread (see Chapter 3).

INGREDIENTS | SERVES 8

1 meaty smoked ham hock, rinsed

1 large carrot, chopped

1 large onion, chopped

1 (1-pound) package fresh chopped collard greens, with tough stems removed

1 teaspoon garlic, minced

½ teaspoon crushed red pepper

¼ teaspoon black pepper

6 cups gluten-free chicken broth

1 cup water

Make It Vegetarian

If you prefer, you can make these hearty greens without the ham hock. Simply leave the ham hock out of the recipe, use vegetable broth instead of chicken broth, and add 1 (15-ounce) can of diced tomatoes (or your favorite salsa) and a few tablespoons of olive oil. Cook as directed and serve with the vegetable broth ladled over each serving.

1. Place ham hock, carrot, and onion in a 6-quart slow cooker.

2. Add collard greens. Sprinkle greens with garlic, crushed red pepper, and black pepper.

3. Pour broth and water over collard greens.

4. Cover and cook on low for 8 hours. To serve, remove greens to a serving bowl. Remove meat from ham bone and discard fat and bones. Chop meat and add to greens. Ladle 1–2 cups broth over greens.

PER SERVING | Calories: 193 | Fat: 7.5 g | Protein: 17.5 g | Sodium: 1,580 mg | Fiber: 2.5 g | Carbohydrates: 14.5 g | Sugar: 1.2 g

Simple Peas and Pearl Onions

Garden peas have a naturally sweet flavor that pairs perfectly with pearl onions.

INGREDIENTS | SERVES 4

3 tablespoons butter

1½ cups pearl onions, skins removed

1 pound shelled peas, fresh or frozen

1 cup gluten-free chicken broth

½ teaspoon black pepper

½ teaspoon salt

1 teaspoon sugar

1. In a small pan, melt butter and sauté onions until they become softened, about 3–5 minutes.

2. Add cooked onions, peas, broth, pepper, salt, and sugar to a greased 4-quart slow cooker.

3. Cover and cook on low for 6–8 hours or on high for 4 hours until peas are the desired texture.

PER SERVING | Calories: 196 | Fat: 10 g | Protein: 7.5 g | Sodium: 563.5 mg | Fiber: 6 g | Carbohydrates: 20 g | Sugar: 7.5 g

Fresh Mint

Mint is an incredibly easy herb to grow in a home garden. It's drought tolerant and doesn't need much attention to thrive. Many different varieties of mint are available to grow such as lemon mint, pineapple mint, apple mint, and even chocolate mint! Adding 1–2 fresh chopped mint leaves to garden peas right before serving adds a fresh and bright flavor.

Red Beans and Rice

You can add an additional boost to the flavor of this dish by substituting spicy tomato-vegetable juice for the broth or water.

INGREDIENTS | SERVES 6

1 tablespoon olive oil

1 cup converted long-grain rice

1 (15-ounce) can red beans, rinsed and drained

1 (15-ounce) can pinto beans, rinsed and drained

½ teaspoon salt

1 teaspoon Italian seasoning

½ tablespoon dried onion flakes

1 (15-ounce) can diced tomatoes

1¼ cups gluten-free vegetable broth or water

1. Grease a 4-quart slow cooker with nonstick spray. Add the oil and rice; stir to coat the rice in the oil.

2. Add the red beans, pinto beans, salt, Italian seasoning, onion flakes, tomatoes, and vegetable broth or water to the slow cooker. Stir to combine. Cover and cook on low for 6 hours or until the rice is tender.

PER SERVING | Calories: 442 | Fat: 3.5 g | Protein: 21 g | Sodium: 421.5 mg | Fiber: 18 g | Carbohydrates: 82.5 g | Sugar: 8 g

Fingerling Potatoes with Herb Vinaigrette

Fingerling potatoes are small new potatoes. It's fun to use fingerling potatoes, because often they are small enough that they do not have to be chopped or diced. This dish is also delicious served cold as a potato salad.

INGREDIENTS | SERVES 4

2 pounds red or yellow fingerling potatoes, scrubbed

1 teaspoon salt

¼ cup lemon juice

⅓ cup extra-virgin olive oil

1 small shallot, minced (about 2 tablespoons)

1½ teaspoons minced fresh thyme leaves

1 tablespoon minced fresh basil leaves

1 tablespoon minced fresh oregano leaves

½ teaspoon Dijon mustard

1 teaspoon sugar

1. Place potatoes in a medium pot and cover with cold water. Bring to a boil and add salt to the water. Cook potatoes for 6–8 minutes until fork tender.

2. Drain potatoes and place in a greased 4-quart slow cooker.

3. In a small bowl whisk together lemon juice, olive oil, shallot, thyme, basil, oregano, mustard, and sugar. Drizzle vinaigrette over potatoes.

4. Cook on low for 4 hours or on high for 2 hours.

PER SERVING | Calories: 329 | Fat: 18 g | Protein: 4 g | Sodium: 615 mg | Fiber: 6 g | Carbohydrates: 39 g | Sugar: 4 g

Potato Frittata with Cheese and Herbs

Use both nonstick spray and butter in this recipe, or the starch in the potatoes will stick. You can experiment with different herbs and cheeses.

INGREDIENTS | SERVES 4

1 large Yukon gold potato, peeled
4 teaspoons butter, melted
6 eggs
½ cup grated Parmesan cheese
6 sage leaves, minced
½ teaspoon salt
½ teaspoon pepper
Fresh herbs, extra cheese, sour cream to garnish

An Untraditional Frittata

Usually frittatas are open omelets that are started in a heavy skillet on the stove and then finished by broiling in the oven. Using this slow cooker method you can put together the frittata the night before, then get up early, place it in the slow cooker and 2 hours later breakfast is hot and ready!

1. Using a mandolin, slice the potato as thinly as possible. Grease a 4-quart slow cooker with melted butter and with a spritz of nonstick cooking spray and place the potatoes on the bottom in a thin layer.

2. In a medium bowl, beat the eggs well. Add the cheese, sage, salt, and pepper; stir to combine. Pour over the potatoes.

3. Cover and cook on high for 2 hours or on low for 4 hours.

4. Cut into squares and serve at once. Add chopped fresh herbs, additional shredded cheese, or sour cream to garnish.

PER SERVING | Calories: 232 g | Fat: 15 g | Protein: 15 g | Sodium: 594.5 mg | Fiber: 1.5 g | Carbohydrates: 10 g | Sugar: 1 g

Colcannon

A traditional Irish potato and cabbage recipe, this side dish is an incredibly healthy way to include more vitamin-rich leafy green vegetables into your diet.

INGREDIENTS | SERVES 6

2½ pounds russet potatoes (about 4 large), peeled and cut into large chunks

1 teaspoon salt

6 tablespoons butter

3 cups chopped green cabbage (or kale, chard, or other leafy green)

1 cup whole milk

3 green onions, sliced

A Frugal Main Dish

Colcannon is often eaten with boiled ham or Irish bacon and is a staple in some Irish homes. The greens used for the dish are normally kale or cabbage, depending on what's available seasonally. Both of these greens are extremely affordable healthy food sources and can also be stretched in soups and stews. An old Irish holiday tradition was to serve colcannon with small gold coins hidden in it.

1. Add potatoes to a medium-sized pot on the stove. Cover with cold water and add salt. Bring to a boil. Cook potatoes until they are fork tender, about 10–15 minutes. Drain potatoes and add to a greased 4-quart slow cooker.

2. Add butter and chopped greens to slow cooker. Stir into potatoes.

3. Cover and cook on low for 4–5 hours or on high for 2½–3 hours.

4. An hour before serving, stir milk into the potatoes, and mash potatoes into the greens with a fork. Sprinkle with green onions.

PER SERVING | Calories: 266 | Fat: 13 g | Protein: 5 g | Sodium: 430.5 mg | Fiber: 5.5 g | Carbohydrates: 33.5 g | Sugar: 6 g

Butternut Squash with Walnuts and Vanilla

Butternut squash has a very mild and slightly sweet flavor. Often people who don't like sweet potatoes enjoy this alternative side dish. Many grocery stores now sell butternut squash that has been peeled and precut into cubes, which can make meal preparation a breeze.

INGREDIENTS | SERVES 4

1 butternut squash (about 2 pounds), peeled, seeds removed, and cut into 1" cubes

½ cup water

½ cup brown sugar

1 cup walnuts, chopped

1 teaspoon cinnamon

4 tablespoons butter

2 teaspoons grated ginger

1 teaspoon vanilla

1. Grease a 4-quart slow cooker with nonstick cooking spray. Add cubed butternut squash and water to slow cooker.

2. In a small bowl mix together brown sugar, walnuts, cinnamon, butter, ginger, and vanilla. Sprinkle this brown sugar mixture evenly over butternut squash.

3. Cook on high for 4 hours or on low for 6–8 hours, or until butternut squash is fork tender.

PER SERVING | Calories: 506 | Fat: 31 g | Protein: 7 g | Sodium: 20 mg | Fiber: 7 g | Carbohydrates: 58.5 g | Sugar: 32.5 g

"Roasted" Beets

Slice and eat these beets as a side dish or use in any recipe that calls for cooked beets.

INGREDIENTS | SERVES 8

2 pounds whole beets, stems and leaves removed

2 tablespoons lemon juice

¼ cup balsamic vinegar

Easy Pickled Beets

Making pickled beets can be a breeze. Simply slice 1 pound roasted beets. Place in a small saucepan and add ½ cup sugar, ½ cup white distilled vinegar, ¼ teaspoon cinnamon, and ½ small onion, peeled and sliced. Bring to a boil. Cool, and store in an airtight container overnight in the refrigerator before serving.

1. Place the beets in the bottom of a 4-quart slow cooker.

2. Pour the lemon juice and vinegar over the beets. Cook for 2 hours on low or until the beets are easily pierced with a fork.

3. Remove beets from the slow cooker. Allow to cool slightly. Wrap a beet in a paper towel and rub it to remove the skin. Repeat for the remaining beets. Discard cooking liquid.

PER SERVING | Calories: 65 | Fat: 0 g | Protein: 2 g | Sodium: 90 mg | Fiber: 3 g | Carbohydrates: 12 g | Sugar: 9 g

White Bean Cassoulet

The longer you cook this cassoulet, the creamier the beans become. Try serving this meal with toasted gluten-free croutons on top.

INGREDIENTS | SERVES 8

1 pound dried cannellini beans

2 cups boiling water

2 leeks, sliced

1 teaspoon canola oil

2 parsnips, diced

2 carrots, diced

2 stalks celery, diced

1 cup sliced baby bella mushrooms

½ teaspoon ground fennel

1 teaspoon crushed rosemary

1 teaspoon dried parsley

⅛ teaspoon ground cloves

¼ teaspoon salt

¼ teaspoon freshly ground black pepper

2 cups Vegetable Stock (see Chapter 3)

1. The night before making the soup, place the beans in a 4-quart slow cooker. Fill with water to 1" below the top of the insert. Soak overnight.

2. Drain the beans and return them to the slow cooker.

3. Slice only the white and light-green parts of the leek into ¼" rounds. Cut the rounds in half.

4. Heat the oil in a nonstick skillet. Add the parsnips, carrots, celery, mushrooms, and sliced leeks. Sauté for 1 minute, just until the color of the vegetables brightens. Add to the slow cooker along with the herbs and spices.

5. Cook on low for 8–10 hours.

PER SERVING | Calories: 229 | Fat: 1 g | Protein: 14 g | Sodium: 116 mg | Fiber: 16 g | Carbohydrates: 42 g | Sugar: 4 g

Slow-Cooked Southern Lima Beans with Ham

Lima beans are a Southern favorite and can withstand extremely long cooking periods without being mushy. In this traditional recipe, lima beans are flavored with bite-sized pieces of ham and simmered in a savory tomato-based sauce.

INGREDIENTS | SERVES 8

1 pound dry lima beans, soaked for 6–8 hours and rinsed with cold water

2 cups cooked ham, diced

1 sweet onion, chopped

1 teaspoon dry mustard

1 teaspoon salt

½ teaspoon freshly ground pepper

2 cups water

1 (15.5-ounce) can tomato sauce

1. Drain and rinse soaked lima beans. Add beans to a greased 4–6-quart slow cooker. Add all remaining ingredients. If needed add additional water to cover the beans by 1 inch.

2. Cook on high for 4 hours or on low for 8 hours. Serve over cooked rice or gluten-free pasta.

PER SERVING | Calories: 266 | Fat: 3 g | Protein: 20.5 g | Sodium: 1,083.5 mg | Fiber: 12 g | Carbohydrates: 40 g | Sugar: 7.5 g

Curried Lentils

Serve this Indian-style dish with freshly cooked rice. Aromatic varieties such as jasmine or basmati pair well with curry dishes.

INGREDIENTS | SERVES 6

2 teaspoons canola oil

1 large onion, thinly sliced

2 cloves garlic, minced

2 jalapeños, seeded and diced

½ teaspoon red pepper flakes

½ teaspoon ground cumin

1 pound yellow lentils

6 cups water

½ teaspoon salt

½ teaspoon ground turmeric

4 cups chopped fresh spinach

1. Heat the oil in a nonstick pan. Sauté the onion slices until they start to brown, about 8–10 minutes.

2. Add the garlic, jalapeños, red pepper flakes, and cumin. Sauté for 2–3 minutes. Add the onion mixture to a 4-quart slow cooker.

3. Sort through the lentils and discard any rocks or foreign matter. Add the lentils to the slow cooker.

4. Add the water, salt, and turmeric to the slow cooker and stir to combine. Cook on high for 2½ hours.

5. Add the spinach. Stir and cook on high for an additional 15 minutes.

PER SERVING | Calories: 293.5 | Fat: 2.5 g | Protein: 20 g | Sodium: 225 mg | Fiber: 24 g | Carbohydrates: 48 g | Sugar: 2.5 g

Easy "Refried" Beans

Some cooks like to mash the onion, jalapeño pepper, and garlic into the cooked beans; others prefer to discard them once the beans are cooked. (They've pretty much given up their flavors to the beans by this point anyhow.)

INGREDIENTS | SERVES 8

3 cups dried pinto beans

1 large onion, peeled and halved

½ fresh jalapeño pepper, seeded and chopped

6 cloves of garlic, peeled and minced

⅛ teaspoon ground cumin

9 cups water

1 teaspoon salt

½ teaspoon freshly ground black pepper

Reheating Refried Beans

Refried beans can be reheated in the microwave or using any other traditional method that you use to warm up leftovers. However, if you want to add a touch of authentic flavor (and fat) to them, melt some lard in a nonstick skillet over medium heat, stir in the beans and sauté until heated through.

1. Rinse and drain beans and place them in a bowl or saucepan. Add enough water to cover the beans by 2 inches. Cover and let soak overnight or for 8 hours. Drain the beans, then rinse and drain again.

2. Add the soaked beans, onion, jalapeño, garlic, and cumin to a 6-quart slow cooker. Pour in the water and stir to combine. Cover and, stirring occasionally and adding more water as needed, cook on high for 8 hours or until the beans are cooked through and tender. (If you have to add more than 1 cup of water during cooking, lower the temperature to low or simmer.)

3. Once the beans are cooked, strain them, reserving the liquid. Mash the beans with a potato masher, adding some of the reserved water as needed to attain desired consistency. Add salt and pepper.

PER SERVING | Calories: 260 | Fat: 1 g | Protein: 16 g | Sodium: 312.5 mg | Fiber: 11.5 g | Carbohydrates: 47.5 g | Sugar: 2 g

Betty's Beans Galore

You may know this dish as cowboy beans, ranch beans, or glorified baked beans—but I call them Betty's Beans for my dear friend who shared this recipe with me. The wonderful combination of spices, brown sugar, molasses, beans, and ground beef make for a filling and delicious one-pot meal.

INGREDIENTS | SERVES 8

½ pound bacon

1 pound ground beef

1 medium onion, chopped

¼ cup brown sugar

¼ cup white sugar

¼ cup gluten-free ketchup

¼ cup gluten-free barbecue sauce

1 teaspoon dry mustard

2 tablespoons molasses

½ teaspoon chili powder

½ teaspoon ground pepper

1 teaspoon salt

2 (15-ounce) cans pork and beans (do not drain)

1 (15-ounce) can red kidney beans (do not drain)

1 (15-ounce) can lima beans (do not drain)

1. Fry bacon in a skillet. Lay cooked bacon on paper towels to remove excess grease. Crumble bacon and add to a greased 4–6-quart slow cooker. Brown ground beef in skillet, drain of grease and add to slow cooker.

2. Add remaining ingredients to slow cooker. Cook on high for 4–6 hours or on low for 8–10 hours. Serve with Gluten-Free Corn Bread (see recipe in Chapter 3).

PER SERVING | Calories: 737 | Fat: 21 g | Protein: 50 g | Sodium: 797 mg | Fiber: 23.5 g | Carbohydrates: 88 g | Sugar: 26 g

Make It Healthier

Feel free to use half the sugar called for in this recipe. It's quite sweet as is, and the tangy flavor will not be compromised if you need to decrease the amount of sugar. Also, feel free to use turkey bacon and lean ground beef for an even healthier meal.

Ratatouille

Ratatouille, a rich and savory vegetable casserole, comes out surprisingly crisp-tender when made in the slow cooker.

INGREDIENTS | SERVES 6

1 onion, roughly chopped

1 unpeeled eggplant, sliced horizontally into ½" slices

2 zucchini, sliced into ½" rounds

1 green, red, or yellow pepper, seeded and sliced into thin strips

3 tomatoes, cut into wedges

2 tablespoons minced fresh basil

2 tablespoons minced fresh Italian parsley

¼ teaspoon salt

½ teaspoon freshly ground black pepper

3 ounces tomato paste

¼ cup water

1. Grease a 4-quart slow cooker with nonstick cooking spray. Place the onion, eggplant, zucchini, pepper, and tomatoes into the slow cooker. Sprinkle with basil, parsley, salt, and black pepper.

2. Whisk the tomato paste and water in a small bowl. Pour the mixture over the vegetables. Stir to combine.

3. Cook on low for 4 hours or until the eggplant and zucchini are fork tender.

PER SERVING | Calories: 68 | Fat: 0.5 g | Protein: 3.5 g | Sodium: 221.5 mg | Fiber: 6 g | Carbohydrates: 15 g | Sugar: 8 g

What Is Ratatouille?

Ratatouille is a traditional vegetable stew that originated in France in the city of Nice. The full name of the dish is *ratatouille niçoise*. The recipe has experienced a revival in the past few years after the success of a popular Disney movie of the same name. In the movie a rat named Remy makes the dish for a particularly picky French restaurant critic.

Vegetable Stew with Cornmeal Dumplings

The naturally gluten-free cornmeal dumplings perfectly complement the fall vegetables in this hearty stew, making it a complete meal in one pot.

INGREDIENTS | SERVES 6

1 teaspoon olive oil

3 russet potatoes, peeled and diced

3 carrots, cut into ½" chunks

2 stalks celery, diced

1 onion, diced

2 rutabagas or turnips, peeled and diced

1 cup cauliflower florets

2 quarts vegetable stock

1 tablespoon fresh thyme

1 tablespoon fresh parsley

⅔ cup water

2 tablespoons canola oil

½ cup cornmeal

2 teaspoons baking powder

½ teaspoon salt

1. Heat the olive oil in a nonstick skillet. Add all of the vegetables. Sauté until the onions are soft and translucent, about 3–5 minutes. Add to a 4-quart slow cooker.

2. Add the stock, thyme, and parsley. Stir. Cook for 4–6 hours on high or 8 hours on low until the vegetables are fork tender. Stir.

3. In a medium bowl, stir the water, oil, cornmeal, baking powder, and salt. Drop in ¼-cup mounds in a single layer on top of the stew. Cover and cook on high for 20 minutes without lifting the lid. The dumplings will look fluffy and light when fully cooked.

PER SERVING | Calories: 204 | Fat: 6 g | Protein: 4 g | Sodium: 436 mg | Fiber: 5.5 g | Carbohydrates: 35 g | Sugar: 6 g

Herbivore Versus Omnivore

To make this a nonvegetarian meal, use beef stock instead of vegetable broth and add 1 pound of diced, browned stew beef to the vegetables.

Sweet and Sour Red Cabbage

Cabbage is often overlooked when it comes to weekly meals, which is unfortunate considering how nutritious it is. The tart apples, sugar, and apple cider vinegar give the cabbage a tangy pickled flavor. Try this recipe as a side to roast pork.

INGREDIENTS | **SERVES 6**

1 large head red cabbage, sliced

2 medium onions, chopped

6 small tart apples, cored and quartered, and peeled (if preferred)

2 teaspoons salt

1 cup hot water

1 cup apple juice

⅓ cup sugar

⅔ cup apple cider vinegar

½ teaspoon caraway seeds

6 tablespoons butter, melted

1. Place cabbage, onions, apples, and salt into a greased 4-quart slow cooker.

2. In a bowl whisk together water, apple juice, sugar, vinegar, and caraway seeds. Pour over the cabbage.

3. Drizzle butter over everything and cover slow cooker. Cook on high for 3–4 hours or on low for 6–8 hours. Stir well before serving.

PER SERVING | Calories: 300 | Fat: 12 g | Protein: 3 g | Sodium: 793 mg | Fiber: 6.5 g | Carbohydrates: 49 g | Sugar: 38 g

Simple Garlic Mashed Potatoes

Everybody loves mashed potatoes! The only problem is you generally have to plan to make them right before dinner or they will get cold. Instead, you can put mashed potatoes in the slow cooker so you'll have them hot and ready whenever it's time for dinner!

INGREDIENTS | **SERVES 8**

5 pounds red potatoes, peeled and cut into cubes

½ cup butter, melted

3 tablespoons mayonnaise

2 teaspoons garlic powder

1½ teaspoons salt

1 teaspoon pepper

½ cup 2% milk

⅓ cup green onions, sliced

1. Cook potatoes in a large pot in salted water until very tender, about 15–20 minutes.

2. Drain potatoes. Place in a clean bowl or add back to the cooking pot. Mash potatoes with a potato masher. Stir in butter, mayonnaise, garlic powder, salt, pepper, and milk.

3. Spoon mashed potatoes into a greased 2.5- or 4-quart slow cooker. Cover and either keep on warm setting for up to 2 hours or on low for 2–4 hours. Before serving, sprinkle on green onions. If potatoes seem dry, stir in more milk before serving.

PER SERVING | Calories: 348 | Fat: 16.5 g | Protein: 6 g | Sodium: 497.5 mg | Fiber: 5 g | Carbohydrates: 46 g | Sugar: 4 g

CHAPTER 7

Soups, Stews, and Chilis

Hatteras Clam Chowder

This cozy, creamy chowder is thickened only by potatoes. Serve it with a fresh green salad and homemade gluten-free bread.

INGREDIENTS | SERVES 4

4 slices bacon, diced

1 small onion, diced

2 medium russet potatoes, peeled and diced

1 (8-ounce) bottle clam stock

2–3 cups water

½ teaspoon salt

½ teaspoon freshly ground pepper

2 (6.5-ounce) cans minced clams (do not drain)

1. In a 2-quart or larger saucepan, sauté bacon until crispy and browned. Add onion and sauté until translucent, about 3–5 minutes. Add cooked onions and bacon to a greased 2.5-quart slow cooker.

2. Add potatoes, clam stock, and enough water to cover (2–3 cups). Add salt and pepper.

3. Cover and cook on high for 3 hours until potatoes are very tender.

4. One hour prior to serving add in the clams along with broth from the cans and cook until heated through.

PER SERVING | Calories: 253 | Fat: 11.5 g | Protein: 12.5 g | Sodium: 601 mg | Fiber: 2 g | Carbohydrates: 25 g | Sugar: 3 g

Bacon Corn Chowder

This corn and potato chowder is given extra flavor with crunchy crumbled bacon.

INGREDIENTS | SERVES 4

4 slices bacon, diced

1 medium red onion, chopped

½ jalapeño chili, seeded and finely chopped

1 clove garlic, minced

2 tablespoons brown rice flour

½ teaspoon salt

¼ teaspoon pepper

2 (15-ounce) cans sweet corn kernels, drained, or 4 cups frozen sweet corn

3 red potatoes (about 1 pound), peeled and diced

4 cups gluten-free chicken broth

2 cups half-and-half

1 cup chopped cherry tomatoes

3 tablespoons sliced fresh basil leaves

1. In a large pan, sauté bacon until crispy and browned. Remove bacon and set aside. Cook onion in bacon grease and sauté until translucent, about 3–5 minutes.

2. Whisk in jalapeño, garlic, flour, salt, and pepper and cook for 1 minute more until flour is toasted.

3. Grease a 4- or 6-quart slow cooker with nonstick cooking spray. Add onion mixture to the slow cooker. Add corn, potatoes, and chicken broth. Stir ingredients together.

4. Cover and cook on high for 4 hours or on low for 8 hours.

5. One hour before serving stir in half-and-half. Add additional salt and pepper if desired. Serve chowder by ladling into large bowls and garnishing with bacon, chopped tomatoes, and fresh basil.

PER SERVING | Calories: 561.5 | Fat: 29.5 g | Protein: 17 g | Sodium: 1,929.5 mg | Fiber: 5 g | Carbohydrates: 62.5 g | Sugar: 6 g

Tuscan Potato, Kale, and Sausage Soup

An easy and delicious gluten-free version of a popular soup at a well-known Italian restaurant chain, this soup is so good you won't miss the breadsticks!

INGREDIENTS | SERVES 6

1 tablespoon olive oil

3 slices bacon, diced

1 pound Italian sausage, cut into bite-sized pieces

1 medium onion, chopped

2 cloves garlic, minced

3 tablespoons white wine

2 large russet potatoes, peeled and diced

4 cups gluten-free chicken broth

¼ teaspoon red pepper flakes

½ teaspoon salt

½ teaspoon ground black pepper

2 cups fresh kale, chopped

1 cup heavy cream

Instead of Kale . . .

If you aren't fond of kale, try adding 2 cups fresh baby spinach to the soup in the last hour of cooking.

1. In a large skillet heat olive oil and cook bacon and sausage until crisp and fat has been rendered, about 5 minutes. Remove bacon and sausage and add to a greased 4-quart slow cooker.

2. Sauté onion and garlic in the bacon fat until softened, 3–5 minutes.

3. Deglaze the pan with wine. Scrape the pan to remove all bits of vegetables and meat. Add all of the pan contents to the slow cooker.

4. Add potatoes, chicken broth, pepper flakes, salt, and ground pepper. Cover and cook on high for 4 hours or on low for 8 hours, until potatoes are very tender.

5. An hour before serving, stir in the kale and the cream. Continue to cook for 45 minutes to an hour until kale has softened and cream is warmed through. Be careful not to overcook at this point as the cream can curdle and separate if heated for too long.

PER SERVING | Calories: 358.5 | Fat: 25 g | Protein: 8 g | Sodium: 1,019 mg | Fiber: 2 g | Carbohydrates: 26 g | Sugar: 1.5 g

Simple Ground Turkey and Vegetable Soup

This soup is easy to throw together with pantry ingredients.

INGREDIENTS | SERVES 6

1 tablespoon olive oil
1 pound ground turkey
1 medium onion, diced
2 cloves garlic, minced
1 (16-ounce) package frozen mixed vegetables
4 cups gluten-free chicken broth
½ teaspoon pepper
½ teaspoon salt

1. In a large skillet over medium heat, add olive oil and heat until sizzling. Cook ground turkey until browned about 5–6 minutes, stirring to break up the meat. Add meat to a greased 4-quart slow cooker. Sauté onion and garlic until softened, about 3–5 minutes. Add to the slow cooker.

2. Add remaining ingredients. Cover and cook on high for 4 hours or on low for 8 hours. Serve with gluten-free crackers.

PER SERVING | Calories: 254 | Fat: 11.5 g | Protein: 19 g | Sodium: 1,001 mg | Fiber: 3.5 g | Carbohydrates: 20 g | Sugar: 1 g

Ham and Potato Soup

If you need a few shortcuts for this recipe, purchase peeled and diced potatoes in the freezer section of your grocery store, diced ham in the meat section, and precut celery and onions in the produce aisle!

INGREDIENTS | SERVES 6

½ cup diced celery
½ cup diced onion
1 tablespoon olive oil
3½ cups potatoes (about 2 large russet potatoes), peeled and diced
1¼ cups cooked ham, diced
5 cups gluten-free chicken broth
½ teaspoon salt
½ teaspoon ground white pepper
3 tablespoons sliced green onions
¼ cup shredded Cheddar cheese

1. In a large skillet, sauté celery and onion in olive oil until softened, about 3–4 minutes. Add to a greased 4-quart slow cooker.

2. Add potatoes, ham, broth, salt, and pepper to the slow cooker. Cover and cook on high for 4 hours or on low for 6–8 hours, until potatoes are very tender.

3. Ladle soup into bowls and garnish with green onions and Cheddar cheese.

PER SERVING | Calories: 238 | Fat: 9.5 g | Protein: 13 g | Sodium: 1,517 mg | Fiber: 2.5 g | Carbohydrates: 25 g | Sugar: 2 g

Creamy Potato Soup

This is a simple, comforting potato soup. For a unique flavor, stir in a few teaspoons of McCormick's Greek Seasoning about an hour before serving.

INGREDIENTS | SERVES 6

6 russet potatoes, peeled and diced

2 medium onions, diced

2 carrots, peeled and finely diced

2 celery stalks, washed and finely diced

6 cups gluten-free chicken broth

1 teaspoon dried basil

½ teaspoon salt

½ teaspoon ground white pepper

¼ cup brown rice flour

1½ cups half-and-half

1. Add potatoes, onions, carrots, celery, broth, basil, salt, and pepper to a greased 4–6-quart slow cooker. Cover and cook on high for 4 hours or on low for 8 hours.

2. One hour prior to serving, add the brown rice flour and the half-and-half to a medium bowl and whisk together. Set aside.

3. Using a potato masher, roughly mash potatoes in the slow cooker until they give the soup a creamy texture.

4. Stir half-and-half mixture into the potato soup.

5. Cover and continue to cook for 45 minutes to an hour until cream has been heated through and soup has thickened slightly.

PER SERVING | Calories: 387.5 g | Fat: 11 g | Protein: 12 g | Sodium: 1,208 mg | Fiber: 4.5 g | Carbohydrates: 64 g | Sugar: 4 g

African Peanut Soup

Peanut butter is an excellent source of protein. Feel free to play around with the seasonings in this unique soup. A small pinch of curry powder would be an excellent addition.

INGREDIENTS | SERVES 6

2 tablespoons olive oil

2 medium onions, chopped

2 large red bell peppers, seeded and chopped

4 cloves garlic, minced

1 (28-ounce) can crushed tomatoes, with liquid

8 cups gluten-free vegetable broth

¼ teaspoon ground black pepper

¼ teaspoon chili powder

½ cup uncooked brown rice

⅔ cup crunchy peanut butter

½ cup fresh chopped cilantro

Peanut Allergies and Intolerances

Peanut allergies are very serious and can be life-threatening. If you have a child or family member who has peanut allergies you can use almond butter or cashew butter in this recipe instead. Both can be found at specialty food stores, or you can make your own by grinding soaked almonds or cashews in a high-powered blender.

1. Heat olive oil in a large skillet. Cook onions and bell peppers until softened, usually 3–4 minutes.

2. Add garlic and cook for 1 minute more, stirring constantly. Add cooked vegetables to a greased 6-quart slow cooker.

3. Add tomatoes and their liquid, broth, ground pepper, chili powder, and brown rice to the slow cooker. Cover and cook on high for 4 hours or on low for 8 hours.

4. One hour prior to serving stir in the peanut butter. Heat for an additional 45 minutes to an hour until soup has been completely warmed through. Garnish with cilantro.

PER SERVING | Calories: 258 | Fat: 13 g | Protein: 10.5 g | Sodium: 1,121 mg | Fiber: 4.5 g | Carbohydrates: 27 g | Sugar: 8 g

Shortcut Albondigas Soup

Albondigas is a traditional Mexican soup with meatballs. This version uses prepared salsa in place of having to chop and prep a lot of vegetables and herbs for the soup.

INGREDIENTS | SERVES 6

5 cups gluten-free beef broth

2 large carrots, peeled and diced

⅓ cup uncooked white rice

1 medium onion, diced

1½ cups medium-hot salsa

2 slices gluten-free bread, crumbled

½ cup milk

1½ pounds ground beef

2 teaspoons dried mint

½ teaspoon salt

½ teaspoon ground pepper

1. Grease a 4–6-quart slow cooker. Add broth, carrots, rice, onion, and salsa.

2. In a small bowl soften crumbled gluten-free bread with milk. Stir in ground beef, mint, salt, and pepper.

3. Form 1"–2" meatballs with your hands and drop them in the soup. Cover and cook on high for 4 hours or on low for 8 hours.

PER SERVING | Calories: 329 | Fat: 13 g | Protein: 29 g | Sodium: 1,407 mg | Fiber: 2.5 g | Carbohydrates: 24 g | Sugar: 5 g

Minty Meatballs?

The flavor of these meatballs is distinctive because of the mint used. Some people also add additional mint into the soup itself, they enjoy the flavor so much. If you cannot find dried mint in the spices section of your grocery store, simply use a few teaspoons of dried mint from an herbal teabag. Alternatively, if your family isn't a fan of mint, use freshly chopped cilantro instead.

Chinese Congee (Simple Rice Porridge)

Congee is a very easy-to-digest rice porridge that's perfect for small children, those who are sick, or if you would simply enjoy a light meal.

INGREDIENTS | SERVES 8

¾ cup medium- or short-grain white rice

8 cups gluten-free chicken broth

1 teaspoon ground ginger, or 2 tablespoons fresh ginger, peeled and grated

4–6 dried shiitake mushrooms, reconstituted, thinly sliced (or fresh baby bella mushrooms, thinly sliced)

½ teaspoon salt

½ teaspoon ground white pepper

1 cup cooked pork, diced

2 hard-boiled eggs, peeled and chopped

4 green onions, thinly sliced

⅛ teaspoon sesame oil

1. In a fine mesh colander wash rice and drain until the water runs clear.

2. Add rice, chicken broth, ginger, mushrooms, salt, and white pepper to a 4–6-quart slow cooker. Cook on low for 12–16 hours or on high for 6–8 hours.

3. One hour prior to serving, add in the pork and chopped eggs.

4. To serve, ladle congee into bowls. Garnish with sliced green onions and a dash of sesame oil.

PER SERVING | Calories: 302 | Fat: 10 g | Protein: 24.5 g | Sodium: 1,237.5 mg | Fiber: 0.5 g | Carbohydrates: 27 g | Sugar: 1 g

Congee or Jook

A simple rice porridge that's usually flavored with pork and/or eggs and sometimes with duck meat, this porridge is popular in many Asian countries and is called by a variety of names including *congee* or *jook*. The porridge is made of rice that has been cooked thoroughly until the grains have broken down into starches, creating a creamy and comforting soup.

Comforting Chicken and Rice Soup

To keep the chicken in this soup extra moist, remove it from the slow cooker after 2 hours on high or 4 hours on low. Shred or cut the chicken, store it in the fridge, and then add it back to the soup an hour before serving.

INGREDIENTS | SERVES 8

1 tablespoon extra-virgin olive oil

1 medium onion, chopped

2 garlic cloves, minced

2 celery stalks, halved lengthwise, and cut into ½-inch-thick slices

2 medium carrots, cut diagonally into ½-inch-thick slices

4 fresh thyme sprigs

1 bay leaf

2 quarts (8 cups) gluten-free chicken broth

1 cup of water

1 cup long-grain white rice

4 large boneless, skinless chicken breasts

1 teaspoon salt

1 teaspoon ground pepper

1. In a large skillet heat olive oil. Add the onion, garlic, and celery. Cook and stir for about 6 minutes, until the vegetables are softened but not browned.

2. Add softened vegetables to a greased 6-quart slow cooker. Add remaining ingredients to the slow cooker.

3. Cover and cook on high for 4–6 hours or on low for 8–10 hours.

4. One hour prior to serving, use 2 forks to shred cooked chicken in the slow cooker and stir throughout the soup.

PER SERVING | Calories: 325 g | Fat: 8 g | Protein: 25 g | Sodium: 1,463 mg | Fiber: 2.5 g | Carbohydrates: 37 g | Sugar: 1.5 g

Greek Lemon-Chicken Soup

Lemon juice and egg yolks make this soup a lovely yellow color. It's a unique soup that's perfect for a spring luncheon.

INGREDIENTS | SERVES 4

4 cups gluten-free chicken broth

¼ cup fresh lemon juice

¼ cup shredded carrots

¼ cup chopped onion

¼ cup chopped celery

⅛ teaspoon ground white pepper

2 tablespoons butter

2 tablespoons brown rice flour

4 egg yolks

½ cup cooked white rice

½ cup diced, cooked boneless chicken breast

8 slices lemon

1. In a greased 4-quart slow cooker combine the chicken broth, lemon juice, carrots, onion, celery, and pepper. Cover and cook on high for 3–4 hours or on low for 6–8 hours.

2. One hour before serving, blend the butter and the flour together in a medium bowl with a fork. Remove 1 cup of hot broth from the slow cooker and whisk with the butter and flour. Add mixture back to the slow cooker.

3. In a small bowl, beat the egg yolks until light in color. Gradually add some of the hot soup to the egg yolks, stirring constantly. Return the egg mixture to the slow cooker.

4. Add the rice and cooked chicken. Cook on low for an additional hour. Ladle hot soup into bowls and garnish with lemon slices.

PER SERVING | Calories: 331 | Fat: 16 g | Protein: 21 g | Sodium: 1,136 mg | Fiber: 1 g | Carbohydrates: 27 g | Sugar: 2 g

Italian Wedding Soup

This is a delicious light soup with spinach and meatballs. When making the meatballs, use a light touch or they will become tough during cooking.

INGREDIENTS | SERVES 8

1 slice gluten-free bread, crumbled
¾ cup 1% milk
½ pound ground beef
1 cup grated Parmesan cheese, divided
1 large egg
½ small onion, finely minced
⅓ cup chopped fresh parsley
2 tablespoons chopped fresh basil
1 teaspoon dried oregano
1 teaspoon garlic powder
1 teaspoon salt
⅛ teaspoon red pepper flakes
1 cup chopped celery
1 cup chopped onion
8 cups gluten-free chicken broth
1 (10-ounce) package frozen spinach, defrosted and drained
3 cups cooked small gluten-free pasta

Gluten-Free Pasta

When choosing gluten-free pasta for the soup, look for small shapes such as ditalini or anelini. You can find these specialty pasta shapes from a gluten-free company called Le Veneziane and can order them through Amazon.com

1. Place bread in a medium bowl and pour milk over it. Let sit 10 minutes, then gently squeeze out excess liquid. Put bread in a large bowl; discard milk.

2. Add the ground beef, ½ cup Parmesan cheese, egg, minced onion, parsley, basil, oregano, garlic powder, salt, and red pepper flakes to bowl with bread. Gently toss to combine. Roll the meat mixture in your hands to create tiny meatballs.

3. Add celery, onion, chicken broth, meatballs, and spinach to a greased 6-quart slow cooker and cook on high for 4 hours or on low for 8 hours.

4. Add ½ cup cooked pasta to each bowl of hot soup and garnish with 1 tablespoon Parmesan cheese.

PER SERVING | Calories: 405 | Fat: 12 g | Protein: 24 g | Sodium: 1,635 mg | Fiber: 3 g | Carbohydrates: 49 g | Sugar: 4 g

Classic Minestrone

A traditional vegetarian Italian soup, minestrone can withstand long cooking periods and tastes even better on the second day.

INGREDIENTS | SERVES 12

3 tablespoons olive oil

1 cup minced white onion

3 stalks celery, chopped

4 cloves garlic, minced

1 small zucchini, chopped

4 cups gluten-free vegetable broth

2 (14-ounce) cans diced tomatoes, drained

2 (15-ounce) cans red kidney beans, drained

2 (15-ounce) cans cannellini (white) beans, drained

1 (28-ounce) can Italian-style green beans

½ cup julienned carrots

1 cup red wine (Chianti or Cabernet Sauvignon)

2 (6-ounce) cans tomato paste

2 tablespoons minced fresh parsley

1½ teaspoons dried oregano

2 teaspoons salt

½ teaspoon ground black pepper

1 teaspoon garlic powder

½ teaspoon Italian seasoning

4 cups fresh baby spinach

1 cup cooked small gluten-free pasta

1. In a large skillet heat the olive oil over medium heat. Sauté onion, celery, garlic, and zucchini in the oil 3–5 minutes until the onions are translucent.

2. Add sautéed vegetables and vegetable broth to a 6-quart slow cooker, along with tomatoes, red and white beans, green beans, carrots, wine, tomato paste, parsley, oregano, salt, pepper, garlic powder, and Italian seasoning.

3. Cover and cook on high for 8 hours.

4. One hour prior to serving, stir in spinach. Add 1 tablespoon of cooked gluten-free pasta to each cup of soup.

PER SERVING | Calories: 403 | Fat: 5 g | Protein: 19.5 g | Sodium: 1,216.5 mg | Fiber: 16 g | Carbohydrates: 69 g | Sugar: 10.5 g

Tuscan Tomato and Basil Soup

This taste is so fresh and delightful, you will want to serve it year-round. Garnish each serving with freshly grated Parmesan cheese and basil leaves.

INGREDIENTS | SERVES 4

4 tablespoons butter

¼ cup cornstarch

1½ cups whole milk

2 cups cherry or grape tomatoes

2 cups fresh basil leaves, stems removed

2 tablespoons chopped fresh oregano leaves

1 cup heavy cream

1 teaspoon salt

½ teaspoon ground black pepper

Make It a Meal

For a hearty vegetarian soup, add 2 cups of chopped fennel bulb and cook on high for 4 hours, or on low for 8 hours. For meat lovers, add 1 pound of cooked and drained sausage or ground beef to the ingredients and cook as directed. Alternately, for a cheesy tomato basil soup, whisk in 2 cups of shredded Cheddar cheese 30 minutes before serving.

1. In a saucepan over medium heat, melt the butter. Add the cornstarch and stir to combine. Cook for 5 minutes. Slowly whisk in milk and continue to cook for 3–5 minutes until mixture has thickened.

2. Process the tomatoes, basil, and oregano in a blender until smooth. Stir the tomato mixture into the hot roux mixture.

3. Pour the tomato mixture into a 4-quart slow cooker and cook on low for 4 hours or on high for 2 hours. In the last 30 minutes of cooking stir in cream, salt, and pepper.

PER SERVING | Calories: 453 | Fat: 37 g | Protein: 6 g | Sodium: 655 mg | Fiber: 3 g | Carbohydrates: 27 g | Sugar: 15 g

Tortilla Soup

This soup tastes even better the next day. Have it for dinner one day and lunch the next.

INGREDIENTS | SERVES 8

1 teaspoon cumin

1 teaspoon chili powder

1 teaspoon smoked paprika

⅛ teaspoon salt

25 ounces canned crushed tomatoes

14 ounces canned fire-roasted diced tomatoes

3 cups gluten-free chicken broth

2 cloves garlic, minced

1 medium onion, diced

4 ounces canned diced green chiles, drained

2 habanero peppers, seeded and diced

1 cup fresh corn kernels

2 cups cubed cooked boneless chicken breast

1. Place cumin, chili powder, paprika, salt, tomatoes, broth, garlic, onion, chiles, and peppers in a 4-quart slow cooker. Cover and cook on low for 6 hours.

2. Add the corn and cooked chicken. Cover and cook for an additional 45–60 minutes.

PER SERVING | Calories: 220.5 | Fat: 5 g | Protein: 28 g | Sodium: 826.5 mg | Fiber: 2.5 g | Carbohydrates: 17 g | Sugar: 5 g

Put the Tortilla in Tortilla Soup

Slice 4 corn tortillas in half, then into ¼" strips. Heat ½ teaspoon canola oil in a shallow skillet. Add the tortilla strips and cook, turning once, until they are crisp and golden. Drain on paper towel–lined plates. Blot dry. Divide evenly among the bowls of soup before serving.

Split Pea Soup

A comforting recipe for a creamy split pea, vegetable, and ham soup, this recipe can also be made vegetarian by using vegetable broth and leaving out the ham.

INGREDIENTS | SERVES 6

1 pound dried split green peas

1 large carrot, diced

1 large parsnip, diced

1 stalk celery, diced

1 medium onion, diced

2 shallots, minced

1½ cups cooked ham, diced into 1" cubes

½ teaspoon dried sage

¼ teaspoon celery seed

¼ teaspoon ground cayenne pepper

6 cups gluten-free chicken broth

3 tablespoons fresh lemon juice

1. Place all ingredients into a 4-quart slow cooker. Stir. Cook on low for 8–10 hours.

2. If the soup is thinner than desired, uncover and cook on high for 30 minutes before serving.

PER SERVING | Calories: 260 | Fat: 7 g | Protein: 17.5 g | Sodium: 1,556 mg | Fiber: 6 g | Carbohydrates: 32.5 g | Sugar: 7 g

Using Split Peas

Carefully pick over split peas to remove any stones or stems that might be present. Rinse them off and they are ready to use. Split peas are one of the few legumes that do not need to be pre-soaked or cooked before slow cooking.

Turkey and Wild Rice Soup

This is the perfect soup for leftover turkey after the holidays. Wild rice gives this soup an earthy, nutty flavor. A nice addition would be to garnish each serving with sautéed baby bella mushrooms.

INGREDIENTS | SERVES 6

6 cups gluten-free chicken broth
1 cup water
½ cup finely chopped green onions
½ cup uncooked wild rice
⅓ cup butter
¼ cup brown rice flour
½ teaspoon salt
¼ teaspoon poultry seasoning
⅛ teaspoon ground black pepper
2 cups half-and-half
8 slices bacon, cooked and crumbled
1½ cups diced cooked turkey breast
2 tablespoons dry sherry

Storing Cooked Bacon

You can buy precooked and crumbled bacon next to the salad dressings in the grocery store or you can make your own. Cooked and crumbled bacon will keep for several months in the freezer in a sealed zip-top bag.

1. In a greased 4–6-quart slow cooker combine chicken broth, water, green onions, and wild rice. Cover and cook on high for 4 hours or on low for 8 hours.

2. One hour prior to serving, melt the butter in a medium saucepan over medium-low heat. Whisk in flour, salt, poultry seasoning, and pepper all at once. Cook, stirring, until smooth and bubbly.

3. Stir the half-and-half into the saucepan and cook until thickened, about 2 minutes.

4. Add thickened cream to soup. Then stir in the bacon, turkey, and sherry. Cook on low for an additional hour and serve.

PER SERVING | Calories: 556 | Fat: 37.5 g | Protein: 22.5 g | Sodium: 1,550 mg | Fiber: 1 g | Carbohydrates: 31.5 g | Sugar: 1 g

Basic Beef Stew

Feel free to change the seasonings in this basic but delicious beef stew. You can also add red wine in addition to the beef broth for a richer taste.

INGREDIENTS | SERVES 6

4 tablespoons vegetable oil

⅓ cup brown rice flour

1 tablespoon garlic powder

1 teaspoon salt

1 teaspoon black pepper

2 pounds beef chuck, cubed

1 onion, diced

6 large potatoes, peeled and diced

6 carrots, sliced

3 stalks celery, sliced

4 cups gluten-free beef broth

1. Grease a 4- or 6-quart slow cooker with nonstick cooking spray. In a large skillet heat oil over medium high heat.

2. In a zip-top plastic bag, mix together the flour, garlic powder, salt, and pepper. Add a small handful of beef and shake until well coated. Repeat until all beef is coated in the flour mixture.

3. In batches, brown beef in hot oil, about 1 minute per side. Remove the browned meat and place in the slow cooker.

4. Lower heat under skillet to medium and add onions. Cook onion until softened, about 3–5 minutes then place on top of beef in slow cooker.

5. Add remaining ingredients to slow cooker. Cover and cook on high for 4 hours or on low for 6–8 hours.

PER SERVING | Calories: 810 | Fat: 40 g | Protein: 35 g | Sodium: 1,104 mg | Fiber: 12 g | Carbohydrates: 75 g | Sugar: 9 g

Beef and Sweet Potato Stew

This rich, deeply flavored beef stew with sweet potatoes, red wine, and cremini mushrooms is a crowd pleaser. Serve it over rice to absorb the delicious sauce.

INGREDIENTS | SERVES 8

¾ cup brown rice flour

1½ teaspoons salt, divided

1½ teaspoons ground black pepper, divided

1¼ pounds stew beef, cut into 1-inch chunks

¼ cup olive oil, divided

1 medium yellow onion, diced

2 cups carrots, peeled and diced

¾ pound cremini mushrooms, cleaned and cut in half

6 cloves of garlic, minced

3 tablespoons tomato paste

½ cup red wine

1 pound sweet potatoes, peeled and diced

4 cups beef broth

1 bay leaf

1½ teaspoons dried thyme

1 tablespoon gluten-free Worcestershire sauce

1 tablespoon sugar

1. In a large zip-top plastic bag, place flour, 1 teaspoon salt, and 1 teaspoon pepper. Add beef and close the bag. Shake lightly and open bag and make sure that all of the beef is coated in flour and seasoning. Set aside.

2. In a large skillet, heat 2 tablespoons of olive oil over medium heat. Cook beef in small batches until browned on all sides, about 1 minute per side. Add beef to a greased 4–6-quart slow cooker.

3. In the same skillet, heat the remaining 2 tablespoons of olive oil. Add onion and carrots and cook until onions are translucent, about 5 minutes.

4. Add mushrooms and garlic, and cook for another 2–3 minutes.

5. Add tomato paste and heat through. Deglaze the pan with the wine, scraping the stuck-on bits from the bottom of the pan. Add cooked vegetable mixture on top of the beef in the slow cooker.

6. Add the sweet potatoes, broth, bay leaf, thyme, and Worcestershire sauce. Cover and cook on low for 8 hours or on high for 4 hours.

7. Before serving, remove bay leaf and add sugar and remaining salt and pepper.

PER SERVING | Calories: 389 | Fat: 15 g | Protein: 20 g | Sodium: 1,104 mg | Fiber: 4.5 g | Carbohydrates: 34 g | Sugar: 7.5 g

Eastern North Carolina Brunswick Stew

Brunswick Stew is a traditional Southern vegetable stew with chicken and pork. Serve it with gluten-free cornbread and sliced tomatoes.

INGREDIENTS | SERVES 10

¼ cup unsalted butter

1 large yellow onion, diced

2 quarts (8 cups) water

1 pound boneless, skinless chicken breasts

1 pound boneless, skinless chicken thighs

2 cups pulled pork, chopped

1 (15-ounce) can green beans, undrained

2 (8-ounce) cans baby lima beans, undrained

2 (28-ounce) cans whole tomatoes, undrained and chopped

3 medium potatoes, peeled and diced

1 (15-ounce) can sweet corn

⅓ cup sugar

2 teaspoons salt

1 teaspoon pepper

2 teaspoons hot sauce

1. In a skillet heat butter until sizzling and cook onion until softened and fragrant, about 3–5 minutes. Add onion to a 6-quart slow cooker.

2. Add remaining ingredients. Cook on high for 4 hours or on low for 8 hours.

3. One hour before serving, remove chicken and shred using two forks. Return chicken to the soup. Add additional hot sauce, salt, and pepper as needed, to taste.

PER SERVING | Calories: 430.5 | Fat: 10 | Protein: 38 | Sodium: 1,240.5 mg | Fiber: 9 g | Carbohydrates: 49 g | Sugar: 14 g

Virginia, Georgia, or Maybe North Carolina?

The origins of "Brunswick Stew" have been debated for years. Some say the stew originates in Georgia; others say it began in Virginia. The stew is usually tomato-based with lima beans, corn, okra, and other vegetables. The meats used can vary. Many old recipes call for wild meats such as rabbit and squirrel. In Eastern North Carolina it's often served in restaurants with shredded pork barbecue, vinegary coleslaw, and cornbread.

Slow Cooker Pork Posole

Posole is a spicy, Mexican stew made from pork and hominy. For a milder version, simply use plain diced tomatoes instead of tomatoes with green chiles.

INGREDIENTS | SERVES 8

2 pounds of lean cubed pork

2 cans white or yellow hominy, drained and rinsed

1 can cubed potatoes, drained and rinsed

2 (15-ounce) cans diced tomatoes with green chiles (undrained)

2 cups warm water

1 cup carrots, chopped

4 garlic cloves, minced

1 medium onion, chopped

2 teaspoons cumin

2 teaspoons chili powder

1 teaspoon red pepper flakes

1 teaspoon dried oregano

1. Add all ingredients to a greased 4-quart slow cooker. Cook on low for 8 hours or on high for 4 hours.

2. Serve with shredded cheese, diced avocados, sliced black olives, pico de gallo, pickled jalapeño peppers, or sour cream, if desired.

PER SERVING | Calories: 412 | Fat: 5 g | Protein: 32 g | Sodium: 82 mg | Fiber: 6 g | Carbohydrates: 61 g | Sugar: 5 g

Corn by Any Other Name

Hominy is corn that has been soaked in a weak lye solution. This treatment gives the corn a creamy white texture and a distinctive taste, as it removes the germ and the bran of the grain. Hominy that has been roughly ground is known as hominy grits and is often served for breakfast.

Ham, Cabbage, and Carrot Stew

This cabbage stew, flavored with a meaty ham bone, is a very frugal recipe and makes enough for a crowd!

INGREDIENTS | SERVES 8

1 (2–3 pound) meaty ham bone

4 large carrots, sliced into 1" circles

½ head red or green cabbage, chopped

1 onion, finely chopped

8 cups gluten-free chicken broth

2 teaspoons salt

2 teaspoons pepper

2 cups cooked cubed ham

1. Add ham bone, carrots, cabbage, onion, chicken broth, salt, and pepper to a greased 4–6-quart slow cooker. Cover and cook on high for 4–6 hours or on low for 8–10 hours.

2. One hour before serving remove the ham bone and add in the cubed ham pieces. Cook for an additional hour and serve.

PER SERVING | Calories: 236 | Fat: 9 g | Protein: 18 g | Sodium: 2,100 mg | Fiber: 3 g | Carbohydrates: 21 g | Sugar: 4 g

Thick and Hearty Lancashire Lamb Stew

Make a double recipe and freeze half for another busy day. Cook beans the old-fashioned way or use canned cannellini beans instead.

INGREDIENTS | SERVES 6

¼ cup olive oil

½ cup brown rice flour

1 teaspoon salt

½ teaspoon ground black pepper

2 pounds lamb stew meat

2 slices bacon, chopped

4 cloves garlic

2 large onions

2 carrots, peeled and chopped

2 bay leaves

2 cups gluten-free chicken broth

1 cup dry white wine

½ bunch parsley

2 tablespoons dried rosemary

Juice and zest of ½ lemon

2 teaspoons gluten-free Worcestershire sauce

1 (1-pound) bag great northern beans, soaked overnight and then simmered for 5 hours, or 3 (13-ounce) cans white beans, drained

1. Heat the olive oil in a large skillet.

2. In a shallow bowl, combine the flour, salt, and pepper. Dredge the lamb in the flour mixture.

3. Brown the meat in the hot oil, about 1 minute on each side. Remove from pan and drain.

4. In the same pan, cook the bacon until crisp. Place lamb and bacon in a 6-quart slow cooker. Add remaining ingredients to the slow cooker.

5. Cover and cook on high for 4 hours or on low for 8 hours.

PER SERVING | Calories: 557 | Fat: 23 g | Protein: 39 g | Sodium: 973 mg | Fiber: 6 g | Carbohydrates: 40 g | Sugar: 4 g

Creamy Chicken Stew

This rich and creamy chicken stew is an excellent dish to serve with Buttermilk Gluten-Free Drop Biscuits (Chapter 14).

INGREDIENTS | SERVES 8

2 tablespoons olive oil

3 pounds boneless, skinless chicken breasts, cut into 1" cubes

1 teaspoon salt

1 teaspoon pepper

1 teaspoon paprika

2 cups white potatoes, peeled and cubed

3 large carrots, peeled and diced

2 cups frozen whole kernel corn

1 cup chopped green pepper

1 cup chopped sweet red pepper

1 cup diced celery

1 medium onion, diced

2 teaspoons dried basil

1 bay leaf

¼ teaspoon celery salt

7 cups gluten-free chicken broth

½ cup butter

⅓ cup brown rice flour

1. In a large skillet, heat olive oil. Sauté chicken pieces in small batches until they are browned, about 1–2 minutes per side. Add browned chicken to a greased 6-quart slow cooker.

2. Add salt, pepper, paprika, potatoes, carrots, corn, green and red peppers, celery, onion, basil, bay leaf, celery salt, and chicken broth to the slow cooker. Cover and cook on high for 4 hours or on low for 8 hours. One hour before serving remove bay leaf.

3. In a large saucepan, melt butter; whisk in flour until smooth. Cook and stir for 2 minutes. Gradually whisk in 2 cups of hot broth from the slow cooker. Bring to a boil; cook and stir for 2 minutes or until thickened. Whisk thickened sauce into stew in the slow cooker. Cook an additional hour.

PER SERVING | Calories: 558 | Fat: 25 g | Protein: 44 g | Sodium: 1,520 mg | Fiber: 7 g | Carbohydrates: 42 g | Sugar: 6 g

Leek, Potato, and Carrot Potage

Potage is a classic French home-style soup that is perfect for a blustery winter day.

INGREDIENTS | SERVES 6

4 cups sliced leeks

4 russet potatoes, peeled and cubed

2 carrots, diced

5 cups water

¼ teaspoon salt

½ teaspoon white pepper

1. Place all ingredients into a 4-quart slow cooker. Cook on low for 7 hours.

2. Purée using an immersion blender or purée in batches in a blender. Serve piping hot.

PER SERVING | Calories: 159 | Fat: 0.5 g | Protein: 4 g | Sodium: 140 mg | Fiber: 4 g | Carbohydrates: 36.5 g | Sugar: 4 g

Gumbo

Serve this Cajun classic over white or brown rice.

INGREDIENTS | SERVES 8

2 tablespoons butter

2 tablespoons brown rice flour

1 large green pepper, diced

4 cloves garlic, diced

1 onion, diced

2 carrots, diced

2 stalks celery, diced

1 quart gluten-free chicken stock

2 tablespoons Cajun seasoning

4 chicken andouille sausages, sliced

1½ cups diced fresh tomatoes

2 cups diced okra

1. In a nonstick skillet, melt the butter. Add the flour and stir until the flour is golden brown. Add the pepper, garlic, onion, carrots, and celery. Sauté for 3–5 minutes.

2. Add the mixture to a 4-quart slow cooker. Add the stock, seasoning, sausage, and tomatoes. Cook on low for 8–10 hours.

3. Add the okra for the last hour of cooking. Stir prior to serving.

PER SERVING | Calories: 146 | Fat: 5 g | Protein: 11 g | Sodium: 219 mg | Fiber: 2.5 g | Carbohydrates: 14 g | Sugar: 5 g

Hearty Beef Chili

The key to this hearty chili is keeping the ground beef in larger chunks (instead of breaking it up into very small pieces) when you are browning it for the slow cooker. If you prefer a spicier version add an additional tablespoon of chili powder, 1 teaspoon cumin, and ½ teaspoon cayenne pepper.

INGREDIENTS | SERVES 6

1 pound ground beef

1 cup chopped onion

¾ cup chopped green pepper

1 clove garlic, minced

1 (16-ounce) can diced tomatoes

1 (16-ounce) can pinto beans

1 (8-ounce) can tomato sauce

2 teaspoons chili powder

½ teaspoon crushed basil

1. Brown ground beef and onion in a large skillet, approximately 5–6 minutes. Leave the ground beef in larger chunks when cooking, instead of breaking it down into very small pieces. Add cooked beef and onion to a greased 4-quart slow cooker.

2. Add remaining ingredients. Cover and cook on high for 4 hours or on low for 8 hours.

PER SERVING | Calories: 235 | Fat: 8 g | Protein: 20 g | Sodium: 581 mg | Fiber: 6 g | Carbohydrates: 20 g | Sugar: 5 g

Where's the Beef?

Some people prefer to use all beef in their chili. For a full beef, bean-free chili, use 2 pounds of ground beef and leave out the pinto beans. Quartered button mushrooms can also add a meaty texture to this chili.

Black Bean and Butternut Squash Chili

This is a spicy and filling vegetarian chili. Feel free to use spinach for the greens in this recipe instead of kale.

INGREDIENTS | SERVES 8

2 tablespoons olive oil

1 medium sweet onion, chopped

3 cloves garlic, minced

3 tablespoons gluten-free chili powder

2 teaspoons cumin

2½ cups butternut squash, peeled, cooked, and cubed

2 (15-ounce) cans black beans, rinsed and drained

4 cups gluten-free vegetable broth

1 (14-ounce) can diced tomatoes in juice

2–3 cups fresh kale, washed, patted dry, chopped

1 teaspoon salt

½ teaspoon freshly ground pepper

1. In a skillet, heat olive oil. Sauté onion and garlic until soft, about 3–5 minutes. Add chili powder and cumin and cook for 1–2 minutes to release the aroma of the spices. Add onion mixture to a greased 4-quart slow cooker.

2. Add squash, beans, broth, and tomatoes to the slow cooker. Cover and cook on high for 4 hours or on low for 8 hours.

3. An hour prior to serving, stir in the chopped kale, salt, and pepper.

PER SERVING | Calories: 176 | Fat: 6 g | Protein: 15 g | Sodium: 435 mg | Fiber: 4 g | Carbohydrates: 15 g | Sugar: 4 g

Instead of Butternut

Any type of cubed winter squash (other than spaghetti squash), or even peeled and cubed sweet potatoes would work perfectly in this vegetarian stew.

Cincinnati Chili

This unusual regional favorite has a spicy sweet flavor that is wonderfully addictive! Serve over cooked gluten-free spaghetti with any combination of the following toppings: kidney beans, diced raw onion, and shredded Cheddar.

INGREDIENTS | SERVES 8

1 pound ground beef

15 ounces crushed tomatoes in juice

2 cloves garlic, minced

1 onion, diced

1 teaspoon cumin

1 teaspoon cocoa

2 teaspoons chili powder

½ teaspoon cloves

1 tablespoon apple cider vinegar

1 teaspoon allspice

½ teaspoon ground cayenne

½ teaspoon cinnamon

1 tablespoon gluten-free Worcestershire sauce

¼ teaspoon salt

1. In a nonstick skillet, quickly sauté the beef until it is no longer pink, about 5–6 minutes. Drain all fat and discard it.

2. Place beef and all other ingredients in a 4-quart slow cooker. Stir. Cook on low for 8–10 hours.

PER SERVING | Calories: 121 | Fat: 6 g | Protein: 12 g | Sodium: 68 mg | Fiber: 1 g | Carbohydrates: 5 g | Sugar: 2 g

Sauté the Meat When Making Chili

Even though it is not aesthetically necessary to brown the meat when making chili, sautéing meat before adding it to the slow cooker allows you to drain off any extra fat. Not only is it healthier to cook with less fat, your chili will be unappetizingly greasy if there is too much fat present in the meat during cooking.

Spicy Vegetarian Chili

Have a chili party and offer diners their choice of a hearty beef chili and this zesty and flavorful vegetarian chili.

INGREDIENTS | SERVES 8

2 tablespoons olive oil

1½ cups chopped yellow onion

1 cup chopped red bell pepper

2 tablespoons minced garlic

2 serrano peppers, seeded and minced

1 medium zucchini, diced

2 cups frozen corn

1½ pounds portobello mushrooms (about 5 large), stemmed, cleaned, and cubed

2 tablespoons chili powder

1 tablespoon ground cumin

1¼ teaspoons salt

¼ teaspoon cayenne pepper

2 (15-ounce) cans diced tomatoes

2 (15-ounce) cans black beans

1 (15-ounce) can tomato sauce

2 cups vegetable stock, or water

¼ cup chopped fresh cilantro leaves

1. In a large, heavy pot, heat the oil over medium-high heat. Add the onions, bell peppers, garlic, and serrano peppers, and cook, stirring, until soft, about 3 minutes.

2. Add softened vegetables to a greased 4–6-quart slow cooker. Add remaining ingredients, except for cilantro.

3. Cover and cook on high for 4–6 hours or on low for 8–10 hours. Stir in cilantro before serving.

PER SERVING | Calories: 236 | Fat: 5.5 g | Protein: 11 g | Sodium: 1,003 mg | Fiber: 11 g | Carbohydrates: 40 g | Sugar: 11 g

Pick Your Own Garnishes

A fun way to serve this chili is to prepare and chill bowls of chopped avocados, sour cream, shredded cheese, crushed tortilla chips, and salsa. Allow diners to garnish their own bowls of chili when it's time to eat.

Chicken Chili Verde

Enjoy this spicy chili over white or brown rice. You can also use a prepared gluten-free chili seasoning mix (such as Carroll Shelby's Chili Kit) in place of the spices in this recipe.

INGREDIENTS | SERVES 8

½ tablespoon olive oil

2 pounds skinless, boneless chicken breast, cubed

2 (28-ounce) cans whole peeled tomatoes, undrained

1 (16-ounce) can chili beans, drained and rinsed

1 (15-ounce) can kidney beans, drained and rinsed

1 (4-ounce) can diced green chile peppers, undrained

1 tablespoon Italian seasoning

1 tablespoon chili powder

2 teaspoons cumin

1 tablespoon sugar

1 onion, minced

3 cloves garlic, minced

½ cup water

1. Heat oil in a skillet over medium heat. Add the chicken. Cook, stirring frequently, until chicken is browned on all sides, about 1–2 minutes per side. Place browned chicken in a greased 4–6-quart slow cooker.

2. Add remaining ingredients over the chicken in the slow cooker.

3. Cover and cook on high for 3 hours or on low for 6 hours.

PER SERVING | Calories: 464 | Fat: 10 g | Protein: 41 g | Sodium: 445 mg | Fiber: 15 g | Carbohydrates: 53 g | Sugar: 13 g

Using Your Slow Cooker as a Rice Cooker

If you have a second slow cooker, you can use it to make rice while the chili is cooking. To make rice: grease a 2.5-quart or larger slow cooker with butter or nonstick spray. Add 1 cup of raw white rice, ½ teaspoon salt, and 2 cups of water. Cover and cook on high for 1½–2½ hours until rice is cooked through, has absorbed liquids, and is fluffy.

Lone Star State Chili

Texans prefer their chili without beans, but you can add a can or two of rinsed and drained kidney beans if you prefer it that way. Serve this dish with baked corn tortilla chips and a tossed salad with a sour cream dressing.

INGREDIENTS | SERVES 8

¼ pound bacon, diced

1 stalk celery, finely chopped

1 large carrot, peeled and finely chopped

1 (3-pound) chuck roast, cut into small cubes

2 large yellow onions, peeled and diced

6 cloves garlic, peeled and minced

6 jalapeño peppers, seeded and diced

1 teaspoon salt

½ teaspoon freshly ground pepper

4 tablespoons chili powder

1 teaspoon Mexican oregano

1 teaspoon ground cumin

1 teaspoon brown sugar

1 (28-ounce) can diced tomatoes

1 cup gluten-free beef broth

1. Add all of the ingredients to a 4–6 quart slow cooker in the order given, and stir to combine. The liquid in your slow cooker should completely cover the meat and vegetables. If additional liquid is needed add more crushed tomatoes, broth, or some water.

2. Cover and cook on low for 8 hours. Taste for seasoning, and add more chili powder if desired.

PER SERVING | Calories: 552 | Fat: 41 g | Protein: 32 g | Sodium: 677 mg | Fiber: 4 g | Carbohydrates: 12 g | Sugar: 6 g

Hot Pepper Precautions

Wear gloves or sandwich bags over your hands when you clean and dice hot peppers. It's important to avoid having the peppers come into contact with any of your skin, or especially your eyes. As an added precaution, wash your hands (and under your fingernails) thoroughly with hot soapy water after you remove the gloves or sandwich bags.

Easy Turkey and Rice Chili

This easy chili can be quickly put together in the slow cooker for a last-minute dinner since it's hot and ready in 2–3 hours.

INGREDIENTS | SERVES 4

1 pound ground turkey

¼ cup chopped onion

1 (14-ounce) can diced tomatoes

2–3 teaspoons chili powder

1 teaspoon cumin

1 teaspoon garlic

1 (27-ounce) can kidney beans, undrained

1½ cups water

1 cup cooked white rice

1. Brown ground turkey in a large skillet, for about 5–6 minutes until cooked through. Add onion and cook for 2–3 minutes until softened.

2. Place browned ground turkey and onions in a greased 4-quart slow cooker. Add tomatoes, chili powder, cumin, garlic, kidney beans, and water. Stir to combine. Cover and cook on high for 2–3 hours or on low for 5–6 hours.

3. An hour before serving stir in cooked rice.

PER SERVING | Calories: 416 | Fat: 10 g | Protein: 31 g | Sodium: 620 mg | Fiber: 12 g | Carbohydrates: 48 g | Sugar: 7 g

CHAPTER 8

Casseroles and Gluten-Free Pasta Dishes

Cottage Pie with Carrots, Parsnips, and Celery

Cottage Pie is similar to the more familiar Shepherd's Pie, but it uses beef instead of lamb. This version uses lots of vegetables and lean meat.

INGREDIENTS | SERVES 6

1 large onion, diced

3 cloves garlic, minced

1 carrot, diced

1 parsnip, diced

1 stalk celery, diced

1 pound lean ground beef

1½ cups gluten-free beef stock

½ teaspoon hot paprika

½ teaspoon crushed rosemary

1 tablespoon gluten-free Worcestershire sauce

½ teaspoon dried savory

⅛ teaspoon salt

¼ teaspoon freshly ground black pepper

1 tablespoon cornstarch and 1 tablespoon water, mixed (if necessary)

¼ cup minced fresh parsley

2¾ cups plain mashed potatoes

1. Sauté the onion, garlic, carrot, parsnip, celery, and beef in a large nonstick skillet until the ground beef is browned, about 5–6 minutes. Drain off any excess fat and discard it. Place the mixture into a greased 4-quart slow cooker.

2. Add the stock, paprika, rosemary, Worcestershire sauce, savory, salt, and pepper to the slow cooker. Stir.

3. Cook on low for 6–8 hours. If the meat mixture still looks very thin, create a slurry by mixing together 1 tablespoon cornstarch and 1 tablespoon water. Stir this into the meat mixture.

4. In a medium bowl, mash the parsley and potatoes using a potato masher. Spread on top of the ground beef mixture in the slow cooker. Cover and cook on high for 30–60 minutes or until the potatoes are warmed through.

PER SERVING | Calories: 229 | Fat: 5 g | Protein: 20 g | Sodium: 511 mg | Fiber: 1 g | Carbohydrates: 24 g | Sugar: 2 g

Save Time in the Morning

Take a few minutes the night before cooking to cut up any vegetables you need for a recipe. Place them in an airtight container or plastic bag and refrigerate until morning. Measure any dried spices and place them in a small container on the counter until needed.

Country Hamburger Casserole

Using similar ingredients to "Ground Beef Foil Packets" or "Hobo Meals," this beefy vegetable casserole is simmered in a creamy sauce.

INGREDIENTS | SERVES 8

4 potatoes, peeled and sliced

3 carrots, peeled and sliced

1 can peas, drained

2 stalks celery, diced

2 onions, sliced

2 pounds ground beef, browned

1 (15-ounce) can evaporated milk

1 cup gluten-free chicken broth

3 tablespoons brown rice flour

½ teaspoon salt

½ teaspoon pepper

1. Place potatoes in the bottom of a greased 4-quart slow cooker; top with carrots, peas, celery, and onion slices. Place ground beef on top.

2. In a medium bowl, whisk together milk, broth, flour, salt, and pepper and pour over ground beef.

3. Cover and cook on low for 6–8 hours. In the last 2 hours, vent slow cooker lid with a chopstick to allow excess water to escape.

PER SERVING | Calories: 417 | Fat: 16 g | Protein: 30 g | Sodium: 555 mg | Fiber: 6 g | Carbohydrates: 36 g | Sugar: 10 g

Instead of Ground Beef

Feel free to use ground turkey, ground pork, or ground sausage instead of ground beef. You can also make this a vegetarian casserole by using 2 cans of drained and rinsed navy beans instead of ground beef and substituting vegetable broth for the chicken broth.

Smoked Turkey Sausage and Vegetable Casserole

Prepared Italian dressing adds great flavor to the vegetables in this simple casserole. For a complete meal serve this with Gluten-Free Millet Bread (see Chapter 3).

INGREDIENTS | SERVES 4

5 tablespoons bottled zesty Italian salad dressing

2 tablespoons Dijon mustard

2 medium potatoes, cut into ½-inch slices

2 medium onions, sliced

2 medium carrots, cut into ½-inch slices

2 cups green cabbage, chopped

1 ring (1 pound) fully cooked smoked turkey sausage, cut into 1-inch slices

1 (14.5-ounce) can petite-diced tomatoes with Italian seasonings

Make Your Own Seasoned Tomatoes

Sometimes it can be hard to find canned petite-diced tomatoes with seasoning added to them. Instead you can use a can of plain petite-diced tomatoes and add 1 teaspoon Italian seasoning, ½ teaspoon of garlic powder, and ½ teaspoon of crushed basil.

1. In small bowl whisk together dressing and mustard.

2. In a 4-quart slow cooker, arrange potato slices on the bottom. Drizzle with one-third of the dressing mixture. Lay onion slices evenly over potatoes and drizzle with one-third of the dressing mixture. Top with carrots and cabbage; drizzle with remaining dressing.

3. Arrange sausage slices on top of vegetables. Pour diced tomatoes over the casserole.

4. Cover and cook on low for 8 hours or on high for 4 hours.

PER SERVING | Calories: 316 | Fat: 8 g | Protein: 30 g | Sodium: 501 mg | Fiber: 7 g | Carbohydrates: 33 g | Sugar: 10 g

Cabbage and Beef Casserole

A lower-carbohydrate beefy casserole using cabbage and tomato sauce.

INGREDIENTS | SERVES 6

2 pounds ground beef
1 small onion, chopped
1 head cabbage, shredded
1 (16-ounce) can tomatoes
½ teaspoon garlic salt
¼ teaspoon ground thyme
¼ teaspoon red pepper flakes
½ teaspoon oregano
1 (8-ounce) can tomato sauce

1. In a large skillet brown the ground beef for about 5–6 minutes. Remove ground beef to a bowl and set aside. In same skillet sauté onion until softened, about 3–5 minutes.

2. In a greased 4–6-quart slow cooker, layer cabbage, onion, tomatoes, garlic salt, thyme, pepper flakes, oregano, and beef. Repeat layers, ending with beef. Pour tomato sauce over casserole.

3. Cook on low for 8 hours or on high for 4 hours.

PER SERVING | Calories: 327 | Fat: 15 g | Protein: 33 g | Sodium: 625 mg | Fiber: 5 g | Carbohydrates: 15 g | Sugar: 9 g

Easy Italian Spaghetti

It doesn't get any easier than this. Because this meal cooks so quickly, you can put it together as soon as you get home from work.

INGREDIENTS | SERVES 4

1 pound ground beef, browned
1 (16-ounce) jar marinara sauce
1 cup water
8 ounces gluten-free pasta, uncooked
½ cup grated Parmesan cheese

Add browned ground beef, marinara sauce, and water to a greased 4-quart slow cooker. Cook on high for 2 hours or on low for 4 hours. 45 minutes prior to serving stir dry gluten-free pasta into meat sauce. The pasta will cook in the sauce. Serve with Parmesan cheese sprinkled on top of each serving.

PER SERVING | Calories: 623 | Fat: 22 g | Protein: 42 g | Sodium: 1,040 mg | Fiber: 5 g | Carbohydrates: 60 g | Sugar: 13 g

Lasagna with Spinach

There is no need to precook the gluten-free noodles in this recipe.

INGREDIENTS | SERVES 10

28 ounces low-fat ricotta cheese

1 cup defrosted and drained frozen cut spinach

1 egg

½ cup part-skim shredded mozzarella cheese

8 cups (about 2 jars) marinara sauce

½ pound uncooked gluten-free lasagna noodles

1. In a medium bowl, stir the ricotta, spinach, egg, and mozzarella.

2. Ladle a quarter of the marinara sauce along the bottom of a greased 6-quart slow cooker. The bottom should be thoroughly covered in sauce. Add a single layer of lasagna noodles on top of the sauce, breaking noodles if needed to fit in the sides.

3. Ladle an additional quarter of sauce over the noodles, covering all of the noodles. Top with half of the cheese mixture, pressing firmly with the back of a spoon to smooth. Add a single layer of lasagna noodles on top of the cheese, breaking noodles if needed to fit in the sides.

4. Ladle another quarter of the sauce on top of the noodles, and top with the remaining cheese. Press another layer of noodles onto the cheese and top with the remaining sauce. Take care that the noodles are entirely covered in sauce.

5. Cover and cook for 4–6 hours until cooked through.

PER SERVING | Calories: 393 | Fat: 13 g | Protein: 18 g | Sodium: 963 mg | Fiber: 6 g | Carbohydrates: 48 g | Sugar: 18 g

Biscuit-Topped Chicken Pie

Pure comfort food! This creamy chicken and vegetable pie is topped with homemade gluten-free buttermilk drop biscuits. To make the pie extra rich, drizzle a few tablespoons of melted butter over the biscuit topping right before cooking.

INGREDIENTS | SERVES 6

4 tablespoons brown rice flour

4 tablespoons butter

1 cup whole milk

1 cup gluten-free chicken broth

1 teaspoon salt

½ teaspoon ground black pepper

2 cups cooked chicken breast, cut or torn into bite-sized pieces

1 (12-ounce) can mixed vegetables, drained

1 prepared batch of dough for Buttermilk Gluten-Free Drop Biscuits (see Chapter 14)

Gluten-Free Baking Mixes

Instead of homemade biscuits, you can also use your favorite gluten-free biscuit baking mix. It must be an all-purpose mix that includes xanthan gum and a leavening ingredient such as baking powder or baking soda. Use a recipe on the package that will make 8–10 gluten-free biscuits as a topping for chicken pie.

1. In a small saucepan over medium heat, whisk together flour and butter. When butter has melted, slowly stir in milk, chicken broth, salt, and pepper. Cook on medium heat for 5–10 minutes, whisking constantly until mixture is thick, with a gravy consistency.

2. Add chicken and vegetables to a greased 4-quart slow cooker. Pour cream soup mixture into the slow cooker and mix with chicken and vegetables.

3. Using an ice cream scoop, drop biscuit dough over chicken, vegetables, and sauce.

4. Cover slow cooker and vent lid with a chopstick. Cook on high for 3–4 hours or on low for 6–8 hours until chicken sauce is bubbling up around the biscuits, and the biscuits are cooked through.

PER SERVING | Calories: 385 | Fat: 14 g | Protein: 21 g | Sodium: 1,079 mg | Fiber: 2 g | Carbohydrates: 40 g | Sugar: 3 g

Chicken Alfredo Pasta

Quartered artichokes add a tangy flavor to this easy pasta casserole.

INGREDIENTS | SERVES 4

1 pound boneless, skinless chicken thighs, cut into ¾-inch pieces

1 (14-ounce) can quartered artichokes, drained

1 (16-ounce) jar gluten-free Alfredo pasta sauce

1 cup water

½ cup sun-dried tomatoes, drained and chopped

8 ounces gluten-free pasta, uncooked

2 tablespoons shredded Parmesan cheese

1. In a greased 4-quart slow cooker, mix chicken, artichokes, Alfredo sauce, and water. Cover and cook on high for 3 hours or on low for 6 hours.

2. 45 minutes before serving, stir tomatoes and uncooked pasta into chicken mixture.

3. Cover lid and continue to cook until pasta is al dente. Sprinkle Parmesan cheese over individual servings.

PER SERVING | Calories: 490 | Fat: 9 g | Protein: 39 g | Sodium: 816 mg | Fiber: 9 g | Carbohydrates: 60 g | Sugar: 5.5 g

Make Your Own Alfredo Sauce

Most Alfredo sauces are naturally gluten-free: they're usually made with butter, cheese, cream, and spices. To make your own, whisk together over medium heat: ½ cup butter, 8 ounces of light cream cheese, 1 cup whole milk or half-and-half, ⅓ cup Parmesan cheese, and 1 tablespoon of garlic powder. Allow the mixture to cool. It will thicken as it cools.

Retro Tuna Pasta Casserole

The popular tuna casserole can now be made gluten-free! In this recipe the pasta is cooked separately, so it doesn't become overcooked in the casserole.

INGREDIENTS | SERVES 4

2 cans water-packed white tuna, drained and flaked

1 cup heavy cream

¾ cup mayonnaise

4 hard-boiled eggs, chopped

1 cup finely diced celery

½ cup finely minced onion

1 cup frozen garden peas

¼ teaspoon ground black pepper

1½ cups crushed potato chips, divided

2 cups gluten-free pasta, cooked

1. In a large bowl combine tuna, cream, mayonnaise, eggs, celery, onion, peas, ground pepper, and ¾ cup crushed potato chips.

2. Pour tuna mixture into a greased 4-quart slow cooker. Top with remaining potato chips. Cover and cook on low for 3 hours or on high for 1½ hours.

3. To serve: place tuna casserole on top of ½ cup of pasta per person.

PER SERVING | Calories: 973 | Fat: 73 g | Protein: 40 g | Sodium: 731 mg | Fiber: 4.5 g | Carbohydrates: 40 g | Sugar: 4 g

Spanish Chicken and Rice

Have Spanish extra-virgin olive oil at the table for those who wish to drizzle a little over the rice.
For more heat, sprinkle some additional dried red pepper flakes on top.

INGREDIENTS | SERVES 4

1 tablespoon olive or vegetable oil

4 bone-in chicken thighs

4 bone-in split chicken breasts

2 tablespoons lemon juice

4 ounces smoked ham, cubed

1 medium onion, peeled and diced

1 red bell pepper, seeded and diced

4 cloves of garlic, peeled and minced

2½ cups water

1¾ cups gluten-free chicken broth

1 teaspoon oregano

½ teaspoon salt

¼ teaspoon saffron threads, crushed

⅛ teaspoon dried red pepper flakes, crushed

2 cups converted long-grain rice

Adding a Vegetable to Spanish Chicken and Rice

After you've removed the chicken from the slow cooker in Step 4, stir in 1 cup (or more) of thawed baby peas. Stir into the mixture remaining in the cooker when you fluff the rice. The heat from the rice should be sufficient to warm the peas so you can serve immediately.

1. Bring the oil to temperature in a large nonstick skillet over medium-high heat. Put the chicken pieces in the skillet skin side down and fry for 5 minutes or until the skin is browned. Transfer the chicken to a plate and sprinkle the lemon juice over the chicken.

2. Pour off and discard all but 2 tablespoons of the fat in the skillet. Reduce the heat under the skillet to medium. Add the ham, onion, and bell pepper; sauté for 5 minutes or until the onion is transparent. Stir in the garlic and sauté for 30 seconds.

3. Grease a 6-quart slow cooker with nonstick spray. Pour the cooked ham and vegetables into the slow cooker. Add the water, broth, oregano, salt, saffron, red pepper flakes, and rice. Stir to combine.

4. Place the chicken thighs, skin side up, in the slow cooker and add the breast pieces on top of the thighs. Cover and cook on low for 6 hours or until the rice is tender and the chicken is cooked through. Place a split chicken breast and thigh on each serving plate. Stir and fluff the rice mixture and spoon it onto the plates.

PER SERVING | Calories: 807 | Fat: 13 g | Protein: 78 g | Sodium: 1,475 mg | Fiber: 2.5 g | Carbohydrates: 85 g | Sugar: 3 g

Classic Italian Risotto

Risotto should be very creamy on the outside, with just a bit of toothsome resistance on the inside of each grain of rice.

INGREDIENTS | SERVES 4

2 tablespoons butter

2 tablespoons olive oil

½ cup finely chopped sweet onion

2 stalks celery, finely chopped

¼ cup celery leaves, chopped

1½ cups arborio rice

1 teaspoon salt

5 cups gluten-free chicken or vegetable broth

¼ cup chopped parsley

½ teaspoon freshly ground black pepper

⅔ cup freshly grated Parmesan cheese

1. Place the butter and oil in a heavy-bottomed pot, melt butter, and add the onion, celery, and celery leaves. Cook for 3–5 minutes, until vegetables are softened.

2. Add the rice and stir to coat with butter and oil. Stir in salt. Add rice and softened vegetables to a greased 4-quart slow cooker.

3. Add remaining ingredients, except cheese, to the slow cooker. Cover and cook on high for 3 hours or on low for 6 hours.

4. Twenty minutes before serving, stir in Parmesan cheese.

PER SERVING | Calories: 1,120 | Fat: 38 g | Protein: 35 g | Sodium: 2,535 mg | Fiber: 3 g | Carbohydrates: 163 g | Sugar: 24 g

Shrimp Risotto

Shrimp-flavored broth gives this risotto a flavor boost. If you don't want to take the time to make it, substitute 1 cup of additional chicken broth and stir a pinch of crushed saffron threads directly into the slow cooker.

INGREDIENTS | SERVES 6

1 tablespoon olive oil

2 tablespoons butter, melted

2 medium white onions, peeled and diced

2 cups arborio rice

5 cups gluten-free chicken broth

½ cup dry white wine

1 cup Shrimp-Infused Broth (see sidebar)

1½ pounds shrimp, peeled and deveined

½ cup freshly grated Parmesan cheese

3 tablespoons fresh flat-leaf parsley, minced

½ teaspoon salt

Shrimp-Infused Broth

Add 1 cup of chicken broth and the shrimp shells from 1½ pounds of shrimp to a saucepan. Bring to a boil over medium-high heat; reduce the heat and maintain a simmer for 15 minutes or until the shells are pink. Strain; crush a pinch of saffron threads and stir it into the broth.

1. Add the oil, butter, and onions to the slow cooker. Stir to coat the onions in the oil. Cover and cook on high for 30 minutes or until the onion is transparent.

2. Stir in the rice; continue to stir for several minutes or until the rice turns translucent. Add the chicken broth and the shrimp-infused broth, along with the wine. Stir together well. Cover and cook on high for 2½ hours or until the rice is cooked al dente.

3. Add the shrimp to the slow cooker atop the risotto. Cover and cook on high for 20 minutes or until the shrimp is pink. Stir in the cheese, parsley, and salt. Serve immediately.

PER SERVING | Calories: 549 | Fat: 13 g | Protein: 34 g | Sodium: 1,497 mg | Fiber: 2.5 g | Carbohydrates: 67 g | Sugar: 2 g

Spicy Beans and Rice Casserole

Using salsa instead of tomatoes and added spices makes this casserole super easy to put together. It's delicious topped with a dollop of sour cream.

INGREDIENTS | SERVES 8

1 (15-ounce) can whole kernel corn, drained

1 (15-ounce) can black beans, rinsed and drained

1 (10-ounce) can diced tomatoes with green chiles

1 cup brown rice, uncooked

2¼ cups gluten-free chicken broth or water

1 cup salsa

1 cup Cheddar cheese, shredded

¼ cup chopped fresh cilantro

1. Grease a 4-quart slow cooker. Add corn, beans, tomatoes, rice, chicken broth or water, and salsa. Cover and cook on high for 3 hours or on low for 6 hours.

2. Once rice has absorbed water and is fully cooked stir in Cheddar cheese. Cook an additional 20 minutes on high to melt cheese and serve. Garnish with cilantro.

PER SERVING | Calories: 281 | Fat: 7 g | Protein: 12 g | Sodium: 737 mg | Fiber: 6 g | Carbohydrates: 44 g | Sugar: 5 g

Mediterranean Chicken Casserole

Raisins may seem like an odd ingredient to add to a main dish, but they provide a slightly sweet flavor that beautifully complements the tomatoes and spices.

INGREDIENTS | SERVES 4

1 medium butternut squash, peeled and cut into 2" cubes

1 medium bell pepper, seeded and diced

1 (14.5-ounce) can diced tomatoes, undrained

4 boneless, skinless chicken breast halves, cut into bite-sized pieces

½ cup mild salsa

¼ cup raisins

¼ teaspoon ground cinnamon

¼ teaspoon ground cumin

2 cups cooked rice, for serving

¼ cup chopped fresh parsley

1. Add squash and bell pepper to the bottom of a greased 4-quart slow cooker. Mix tomatoes, chicken, salsa, raisins, cinnamon, and cumin together and pour on top of squash and peppers.

2. Cover and cook on low for 6 hours or on high for 3 hours until squash is fork tender.

3. Remove chicken and vegetables from slow cooker with slotted spoon. Serve over cooked rice. Ladle remaining sauce from slow cooker over the vegetables. Garnish with parsley.

PER SERVING | Calories: 380 | Fat: 6 g | Protein: 40 g | Sodium: 396 mg | Fiber: 3 g | Carbohydrates: 41 g | Sugar: 9 g

Ham, Spinach, and Rice Casserole

Use leftover ingredients to create a tasty main dish. This casserole is also ideal for a brunch or breakfast.

INGREDIENTS | SERVES 4

2 tablespoons butter
½ onion, chopped
2 tablespoons brown rice flour
1 cup gluten-free chicken broth
½ teaspoon salt
½ teaspoon ground pepper
¼ teaspoon dried thyme
3 eggs, beaten
1 (10-ounce) package frozen spinach, defrosted and drained
1 cup cooked ham, chopped
1½ cups cooked rice
½ cup crushed gluten-free Rice Chex cereal

1. In a small saucepan over medium heat, heat the butter. Whisk in onion and flour. Cook for 2–3 minutes to toast the flour.

2. Slowly whisk in the chicken broth, salt, pepper, and thyme. Cook for 3–5 minutes until sauce has thickened, and set aside.

3. In a large bowl mix together the eggs, spinach, ham, and rice. Stir in the thickened chicken broth. Pour into a greased 4-quart slow cooker. Top with crushed Rice Chex.

4. Cover and vent lid with a chopstick. Cook on high for 3 hours or on low for 6 hours, or until casserole is set.

PER SERVING | Calories: 340 | Fat: 14 g | Protein: 17 g | Sodium: 1,111 mg | Fiber: 3 g | Carbohydrates: 36 g | Sugar: 1 g

Classic Polenta with Herbs and Parmesan

By using the slow cooker to make this creamy homemade polenta, you don't have to stand over the stove for nearly 2 hours stirring the pot.

INGREDIENTS | SERVES 6

7 cups water
2 tablespoons salt
2 cups yellow cornmeal
2–4 ounces unsalted butter
1 teaspoon dried basil
1 teaspoon dried parsley
1 teaspoon crushed rosemary
½ teaspoon freshly ground black pepper
½ cup freshly grated Parmesan cheese

1. Add all ingredients except cheese into a greased 4-quart slow cooker.

2. Whisk together thoroughly. Cover and cook on low for 6–7 hours or on high for 3–4 hours.

3. Thirty minutes prior to serving stir in Parmesan cheese.

PER SERVING | Calories: 327 | Fat: 17 g | Protein: 5 g | Sodium: 2,400 mg | Fiber: 2 g | Carbohydrates: 36 g | Sugar: 1 g

Sausage and Shrimp Jambalaya

This version of a "red" jambalaya originated in the French Quarter of New Orleans when saffron wasn't readily available. This Creole-type jambalaya contains tomatoes, whereas a rural Cajun jambalaya (also known as "brown jambalaya") does not.

INGREDIENTS | SERVES 8

2 tablespoons olive oil

1 large onion, chopped

2 medium celery stalks, chopped

1 medium green bell pepper, chopped

3 garlic cloves, minced

1 (28-ounce) can diced tomatoes, undrained

2 cups fully cooked smoked sausage, sliced into 1" pieces

1 tablespoon parsley flakes

½ teaspoon dried thyme leaves

½ teaspoon salt

¼ teaspoon pepper

¼ teaspoon red pepper sauce

2 teaspoons gluten-free Creole seasoning

¾ pound uncooked, peeled, deveined medium shrimp, thawed if frozen

4 cups hot cooked rice

¼ cup fresh parsley, chopped

1. In a large skillet, heat oil. Sauté onions, celery, and bell pepper until softened, about 3–5 minutes. Add garlic and cook 1 minute more.

2. Grease a 4-quart slow cooker and add sautéed vegetables and all remaining ingredients except shrimp, rice, and parsley.

3. Cover and cook on low for 6 hours or on high for 3 hours.

4. Add shrimp and continue to cook on low for 45 minutes to an hour until shrimp are bright pink. Serve jambalaya over a bed of rice and garnish with chopped fresh parsley.

PER SERVING | Calories: 296 | Fat: 9 g | Protein: 20 g | Sodium: 569 mg | Fiber: 1 g | Carbohydrates: 32 g | Sugar: 2 g

Instead of Shrimp

Use your favorite type of seafood instead of shrimp. Scallops, cod, or diced tilapia filets would also work well in this dish.

Chicken Pesto Polenta

This recipe uses precooked polenta that is cut and layered in a casserole lasagna-style. Most prepared polenta comes in tube form and is naturally gluten-free. Make sure to read the ingredients and call the manufacturer if you have any questions.

INGREDIENTS | SERVES 6

4 boneless, skinless chicken breasts, cut into bite-sized pieces

1 cup prepared pesto, divided

1 medium onion, finely diced

4 cloves garlic, minced

1½ teaspoon dried Italian seasoning

1 (16-ounce) tube prepared polenta, cut into ½" slices

2 cups chopped fresh spinach

1 (14.5-ounce) can diced tomatoes

1 (8-ounce) bag shredded low-fat Italian cheese blend

Make Your Own Pesto

Instead of using prepared pesto you can easily make your own: In a high-powered blender or food processor add 2 cups fresh basil leaves, ½ cup extra-virgin olive oil, ½ cup Parmesan cheese, ½ cup pine nuts, 3 garlic cloves, and salt and pepper to taste. Blend on high for a few minutes until mixture is creamy. You can use blanched almond flour in place of the Parmesan cheese, if you are intolerant to dairy.

1. In large bowl, combine chicken pieces with ½ cup pesto, onion, garlic, and Italian seasoning.

2. In a greased 4-quart slow cooker, layer half of chicken mixture, half the polenta, half the spinach, and half the tomatoes. Continue to layer, ending with tomatoes. Cover and cook on low for 4–6 hours or on high for 2–3 hours.

3. An hour before serving drizzle remaining pesto over casserole and top with shredded cheese. Cover and continue to cook for 45 minutes to an hour until cheese has melted.

PER SERVING | Calories: 636 | Fat: 39 g | Protein: 28 g | Sodium: 680 mg | Fiber: 5.5 g | Carbohydrates: 44 g | Sugar: 3.5 g

Cheddar Baked Hominy

Hominy is a wonderful, naturally gluten-free alternative to regular wheat pasta. Try it in this macaroni and cheese–inspired dish.

INGREDIENTS | SERVES 6

1½ cups whole milk

2 tablespoons cornstarch

1½ tablespoons butter

2 cups shredded Cheddar cheese, divided

1 (29-ounce) can white or yellow hominy, drained

1 egg, beaten

½ teaspoon sea salt

1 teaspoon freshly ground pepper

1 teaspoon garlic powder

¼ cup gluten-free bread crumbs or crushed tortilla chips

1. In a small bowl whisk together milk and cornstarch. Melt butter in a medium-sized saucepan and heat until sizzling. Add milk and cornstarch mixture. Whisk constantly until mixture thickens.

2. When thickened, add 1¼ cups cheese. Stir together until you have a thick cheesy sauce. Add drained hominy and mix thoroughly into sauce. Add beaten egg. Stir in salt, pepper, and garlic powder.

3. Pour mixture into a greased 4-quart slow cooker and sprinkle with bread crumbs or crushed tortilla chips. Cover and vent lid with a chopstick. Cook on low for 3–4 hours or on high for 2–2½ hours.

4. Thirty minutes prior to serving sprinkle remaining shredded cheese on top of casserole. Cover lid and cook for 25–30 minutes until cheese has melted.

PER SERVING | Calories: 723 | Fat: 20 g | Protein: 24 g | Sodium: 504 mg | Fiber: 6.5 g | Carbohydrates: 116 g | Sugar: 5 g

Thick and Creamy Corn and Lima Bean Casserole

This makes a satisfying meal and can be made with chopped ham for added flavor and a serving of protein. Simply add 1–2 cups of chopped ham into the slow cooker with the ingredients in step 2 and cook as directed.

INGREDIENTS | SERVES 4

2 tablespoons butter

½ sweet onion, finely chopped

½ cup minced celery

¼ cup minced roasted red pepper

½ cup gluten-free chicken broth

1 (10-ounce) package frozen lima beans

1 (10-ounce) package frozen corn kernels

2 eggs, well beaten

1½ cups heavy cream or evaporated milk

1 teaspoon salt

1 teaspoon paprika

1 teaspoon ground black pepper

1 teaspoon ground coriander

½ teaspoon ground allspice

1 cup gluten-free bread crumbs

1. Melt butter in a large skillet. Sauté onion and celery until softened, about 3–5 minutes.

2. Grease a 4-quart slow cooker. Add sautéed onions and celery. Add remaining ingredients to slow cooker, except for bread crumbs. Stir together and sprinkle bread crumbs on top.

3. Cover and vent the lid with a chopstick. Cook on low for 6 hours or on high for 3 hours.

PER SERVING | Calories: 671 | Fat: 45 g | Protein: 17 g | Sodium: 1,148 mg | Fiber: 8.5 g | Carbohydrates: 55 g | Sugar: 6 g

Better Than Canned

Stay away from canned creamed corn (as it contains wheat flour) and stick with fresh or frozen and make your own cream sauce. It's easy and gluten-free, and tastes so much better than the ones made with soups or mixes.

Corn Tortilla Casserole

Serve this casserole along with a tossed salad. Have some additional taco or enchilada sauce at the table along with an assortment of optional condiments, like chopped jalapeño peppers, diced green onions, sour cream, and guacamole.

INGREDIENTS | SERVES 8

2 tablespoons olive oil

2 pounds ground beef

1 small onion, peeled and diced

1 clove garlic, minced

1 envelope gluten-free taco seasoning

½ teaspoon salt

½ teaspoon freshly ground pepper

1 (15-ounce) can diced tomatoes

1 (6-ounce) can tomato paste

2 cups refried beans

9 corn tortillas

2 cups gluten-free enchilada sauce

2 cups (8 ounces) grated Cheddar cheese

1. In a large skillet, heat olive oil. Brown ground beef for approximately 5–6 minutes and set aside in a large bowl. In the same skillet sauté onions until softened, about 3–5 minutes. Add sautéed onions to ground beef.

2. Stir in the garlic, taco seasoning, salt, pepper, tomatoes, tomato paste, and refried beans into the ground beef and onions.

3. Grease a 4-quart slow cooker with nonstick spray. Add ⅓ of the ground beef mixture to cover the bottom of the slow cooker insert. Layer 3 tortillas on top of the ground beef mixture and cover with ⅓ of the enchilada sauce, then ⅓ of the shredded cheese. Repeat layers. Cover and cook on low for 6–8 hours. Cut into 8 wedges and serve.

PER SERVING | Calories: 520 | Fat: 26 g | Protein: 36 g | Sodium: 1,396 mg | Fiber: 7.5 g | Carbohydrates: 35 g | Sugar: 6 g

Zucchini and Sausage Casserole

Serve this casserole on a bed of mixed greens with a fruit salad on the side.

INGREDIENTS | SERVES 6

1 pound mild pork sausage

1¼ cups grated Parmesan cheese

½ teaspoon salt

½ teaspoon freshly ground pepper

2 teaspoons Greek seasoning or 1 teaspoon dried mint, ½ teaspoon dried oregano, and ½ teaspoon basil

2 eggs, beaten

1 cup whole milk

3 medium zucchini, sliced into ½" rounds

1 small onion, sliced

1. In a large skillet, brown ground sausage, drain the fat from the skillet, and set the sausage aside.

2. Grease a 4-quart slow cooker with nonstick spray. In a large bowl whisk together the Parmesan cheese, salt, pepper, and Greek seasoning. In another bowl whisk together the eggs and the milk.

3. Place ⅓ of the zucchini over the bottom of the slow cooker. Add ⅓ of the sliced onions over the zucchini. Add ⅓ of the cooked sausage over the onions. Add ⅓ of the milk/egg mixture over the sausage. Lastly add ⅓ of the Parmesan cheese mixture over everything. Repeat layers two more times, ending with the last of the Parmesan cheese mixture.

4. Cover, vent lid with a chopstick and cook on low for 6 hours or on high for 3 hours. Cut into squares to serve.

PER SERVING | Calories: 604 | Fat: 34 g | Protein: 60 g | Sodium: 1,866 mg | Fiber: 1 g | Carbohydrates: 13 g | Sugar: 5 g

Tamale Pie

A favorite of kids everywhere, this cornbread-topped ground beef and bean pie is a great weeknight dinner! To make this dish extra special, add 1 cup of shredded Cheddar cheese to the beef and bean filling.

INGREDIENTS | SERVES 6

1 pound ground beef
1 package gluten-free taco seasoning
½ cup warm water
1 (15-ounce) can pinto beans, drained and rinsed
1 (11-ounce) can corn, drained
1 (8-ounce) can tomato sauce
2 tablespoons melted butter
1 egg
1 tablespoon sugar
½ cup 2% milk
¾ cup gluten-free cornmeal
1 teaspoon baking powder
¼ teaspoon salt

1. In a large skillet brown ground beef until cooked through, approximately 5–6 minutes. Drain excess fat and add taco seasoning and water to the skillet. Stir to combine and then pour into a greased 4-quart slow cooker.

2. Add beans, corn, and tomato sauce to the seasoned ground beef. Stir to combine.

3. In a small bowl whisk together melted butter, egg, sugar, and milk. Add cornmeal, baking powder, and salt. Using a fork, whisk thoroughly to combine batter. Pour cornbread batter over the ingredients in the slow cooker.

4. Cover and vent the slow cooker with a chopstick or the handle of a wooden spoon. Cook on high for 3 hours or on low for 6 hours or until cornbread is golden brown on the edges.

PER SERVING | Calories: 372 | Fat: 14 g | Protein: 23 g | Sodium: 818 mg | Fiber: 5.4 g | Carbohydrates: 39 g | Sugar: 6.5 g

CHAPTER 9

Poultry

Rotisserie-Style Chicken

Here is a delicious alternative to buying rotisserie chicken in your grocery store. This flavorful roast chicken is incredibly easy to make in your slow cooker. For a fast weeknight meal, cook the chicken overnight in the slow cooker and serve for dinner the next day.

INGREDIENTS | SERVES 6

1 (4-pound) whole chicken
1½ teaspoons salt
2 teaspoons paprika
½ teaspoon onion powder
½ teaspoon dried thyme
½ teaspoon dried basil
½ teaspoon white pepper
½ teaspoon ground cayenne pepper
½ teaspoon black pepper
½ teaspoon garlic powder
2 tablespoons olive oil

Gravy

If you would like to make a gravy to go with the chicken, follow these directions: After removing the cooked chicken, turn slow cooker on high. Whisk ⅓ cup garbanzo bean flour or ⅓ cup brown rice flour into the cooking juices. Add salt and pepper to taste and cook for 10–15 minutes, whisking occasionally, until sauce has thickened. Spoon gravy over chicken.

1. Rinse chicken in cold water and pat dry with a paper towel.

2. In a small bowl mix together salt, paprika, onion powder, thyme, basil, white pepper, cayenne pepper, black pepper, and garlic powder.

3. Rub spice mixture over entire chicken. Rub part of the spice mixture underneath the skin, making sure to leave the skin intact.

4. Place the spice-rubbed chicken in a greased 6-quart slow cooker. Drizzle olive oil evenly over the chicken. Cook on high for 3–3½ hours or on low for 4–5 hours.

5. Remove chicken carefully from the slow cooker and place on a large plate or serving platter.

PER SERVING | Calories: 171 | Fat: 7.5 g | Protein: 23 g | Sodium: 474 mg | Fiber: 0 g | Carbohydrates: 0 g | Sugar: 0 g

Creamy Chicken in a Mushroom and White Wine Sauce

Many traditional slow cooker recipes call for using canned cream soups, which often contain wheat flour as an ingredient. For a gluten-free version, this recipe shows you how to make a simple homemade cream soup using cornstarch and milk.

INGREDIENTS | SERVES 4

4 boneless chicken breasts, cut into chunks

3 tablespoons cornstarch

1 cup 2% milk

½ cup white wine

½ teaspoon salt

½ teaspoon ground pepper

1½ teaspoons poultry seasoning

½ teaspoon garlic powder

½ teaspoon salt-free, all-purpose seasoning

2 (4-ounce) cans sliced mushrooms, drained and rinsed

1½ cups frozen peas

2 cups cooked gluten-free pasta

1. Grease a 4-quart slow cooker with nonstick cooking spray. Place chicken into the slow cooker.

2. In a saucepan whisk together the cornstarch, milk, and white wine. Whisk in salt, pepper, poultry seasoning, garlic powder, and salt-free seasoning. Cook over medium heat whisking constantly until sauce thickens. Pour sauce over chicken.

3. Add mushrooms on top of the chicken. Cook on low for 6 hours or on high for 3 hours.

4. One hour before serving stir in the frozen garden peas.

5. Serve over pasta.

PER SERVING | Calories: 619 | Fat: 25 g | Protein: 31 g | Sodium: 860 mg | Fiber: 6 g | Carbohydrates: 61 g | Sugar: 8 g

Tuscan Chicken and White Beans

Hearty white beans with warm Tuscan spices and tomatoes make this super easy slow-cooked chicken special enough for company!

INGREDIENTS | SERVES 4

3 large boneless, skinless chicken breasts

1 (15.5-ounce) can white beans, drained and rinsed

1 (14.5-ounce) can diced tomatoes

1 (4-ounce) can mushrooms, drained

¼ cup Spanish olives stuffed with pimientos, sliced in half

2 teaspoons onion powder

1 teaspoon garlic powder

1 teaspoon basil

1 teaspoon oregano

1 teaspoon ground pepper

½ teaspoon salt

2 teaspoons olive oil

White Beans

White beans, which are also called navy beans, Boston beans, or Yankee beans, are small, lightly colored beans that are very mild in taste and work well in a variety of recipes. If you don't have white beans available, cannellini beans or northern beans, which are slightly larger, are excellent substitutes.

1. Cut chicken breasts into large chunks and place in a greased 4-quart slow cooker.

2. Add beans, tomatoes (including the juice), mushrooms, and olives. Add onion powder, garlic powder, basil, oregano, ground pepper, and salt.

3. Mix all ingredients together in the slow cooker. Drizzle olive oil over the top of the chicken and vegetables.

4. Cook on high for 3½–4 hours or on low for 6 hours. Serve over cooked rice or gluten-free pasta, if desired.

PER SERVING | Calories: 365 | Fat: 20 g | Protein: 19 g | Sodium: 1,146 mg | Fiber: 5 g | Carbohydrates: 27 g | Sugar: 3 g

Chicken in Lemon Sauce

This recipe is for a one-pot meal. By completing a simple step at the end of the cooking time, you have meat, potatoes, vegetables, and sauce all ready to serve and eat.

INGREDIENTS | **SERVES 4**

1 (16-ounce) bag frozen cut green beans, thawed

1 small onion, peeled and cut into thin wedges

4 boneless, skinless chicken breast halves

4 medium potatoes, peeled and cut in quarters

2 cloves of garlic, peeled and minced

¼ teaspoon freshly ground black pepper

1 cup gluten-free chicken broth

4 ounces cream cheese, cut into cubes

1 teaspoon freshly grated lemon peel

Gluten-Free Chicken Broth

Reading food labels will become second nature when you are following a gluten-free diet. Remember to check the label on your canned chicken broth. Some brands add wheat starch or wheat flour as a thickener. Two readily available gluten-free brands are Swanson and Kitchen Basics.

1. Place green beans and onion in the slow cooker. Arrange the chicken and potatoes over the vegetables. Sprinkle with the garlic and pepper. Pour broth over all. Cover and cook on low for 5 or more hours or until chicken is cooked through and moist.

2. Evenly divide the chicken, potatoes, and vegetables between 4 serving plates or onto a serving platter; cover to keep warm.

3. To make the sauce, add the cream cheese cubes and grated lemon peel to the broth in the slow cooker. Stir until cheese melts into the sauce. Pour the sauce over the chicken, potatoes, and vegetables.

PER SERVING | Calories: 668 | Fat: 32 g | Protein: 28 g | Sodium: 1,190 mg | Fiber: 9.5 g | Carbohydrates: 65 g | Sugar: 5.5 g

Italian Turkey Sausage with Peppers and Onions

The colorful variety of peppers in this recipe makes a beautiful dinner presentation. Feel free to substitute chicken sausage for the turkey sausage if it is more readily available in your area. Also, this recipe has no added salt since processed sausage contains a lot of sodium.

INGREDIENTS | SERVES 4

1 large red pepper, sliced, with seeds removed

1 large yellow pepper, sliced, with seeds removed

1 sweet onion, sliced

2 tablespoons olive oil

2 teaspoons garlic powder

2 teaspoons oregano

20 ounces lean Italian turkey sausage

Sautéing Vegetables in the Microwave

One easy way to enhance the flavor of aromatic vegetables such as garlic, peppers, celery, and onions is to cook them in the microwave for just a few minutes before adding them to the slow cooker. This method softens the vegetables, releases their aroma, and begins the cooking process.

1. Mix peppers and onion in a large glass or microwave-safe bowl. Drizzle with olive oil, garlic powder, and oregano.

2. Microwave on high for 2–3 minutes, until vegetables are slightly softened and have become fragrant. Pour half of the onion/pepper mixture into the bottom of a greased 4-quart slow cooker.

3. Place the sausages side-by-side on top of the vegetables. Pour the remaining onion and pepper mixture on top of the sausages.

4. Cook on low for 6 hours or on high for 3 hours.

PER SERVING | Calories: 354 | Fat: 21 g | Protein: 29 g | Sodium: 837 mg | Fiber: 6 g | Carbohydrates: 15 g | Sugar: 3 g

Ground Turkey Joes

This easy, sweet and sour sandwich filling comes together quickly and is ready when you are. If you prefer, you can also use ground chicken or ground beef as a substitute for ground turkey.

INGREDIENTS | SERVES 4

2 teaspoons olive oil
1 pound lean ground turkey
½ cup onion, finely chopped
½ cup green pepper, finely chopped
1 teaspoon garlic powder
1 tablespoon prepared yellow mustard
¾ cup gluten-free ketchup
3 tablespoons brown sugar
1 tablespoon gluten-free Worcestershire sauce
¼ teaspoon salt
½ teaspoon ground pepper
4 gluten-free hamburger rolls

1. In a large skillet brown ground turkey, onion, and green pepper in olive oil for approximately 5–6 minutes. Drain off any grease.

2. Add turkey mixture to a greased 2.5-quart or 4-quart slow cooker. Add garlic powder, mustard, ketchup, brown sugar, Worcestershire sauce, salt, and pepper.

3. Mix ingredients together and cook on low for 4 hours or on high for 2 hours.

4. Serve on hamburger rolls.

PER SERVING | Calories: 365 | Fat: 13 g | Protein: 23 g | Sodium: 934 mg | Fiber: 1.5 g | Carbohydrates: 38 g | Sugar: 23 g

Multiple Meals

Instead of using this recipe as a sandwich filling you could also serve it over cooked rice, a baked potato, or gluten-free spaghetti noodles for a fun twist. For a Mexican-style variation, leave out the brown sugar and Worcestershire sauce and replace the ketchup with 1 cup of tomato sauce along with 1 packet of gluten-free taco seasoning.

Barbecue Chicken

Everyone loves barbecue chicken, especially in the summer. This homemade sauce is super easy to make and has great flavor. Serve the chicken with baked potatoes and coleslaw.

INGREDIENTS | SERVES 4

4 boneless, skinless chicken breasts
½ cup gluten-free ketchup
2 tablespoons apple cider vinegar
2 tablespoons molasses
2 tablespoons brown sugar
1 teaspoon liquid smoke flavoring
1½ tablespoons minced dried onions
¼ teaspoon cayenne pepper
2 teaspoons ground mustard

1. Place chicken in a greased 4-quart slow cooker.

2. In a bowl whisk together the ketchup, vinegar, molasses, brown sugar, smoke flavoring, dried onions, cayenne pepper, and mustard.

3. Pour the homemade barbecue sauce over the chicken.

4. Cook on low for 6 hours or on high for 3 hours.

PER SERVING | Calories: 282 | Fat: 4.5 g | Protein: 36 g | Sodium: 565 mg | Fiber: 0.5 g | Carbohydrates: 22 g | Sugar: 19 g

Orange Chicken

You can use light or dark brown sugar, depending on your preference. (Dark brown sugar will impart more molasses flavor to the dish.) Serve this dish over cooked rice or stir-fry vegetables, or with both.

INGREDIENTS | SERVES 8

3 pounds boneless, skinless chicken breasts
1 small onion, peeled and diced
½ cup orange juice
3 tablespoons orange marmalade
1 tablespoon brown sugar
1 tablespoon apple cider vinegar
1 tablespoon gluten-free Worcestershire sauce
1 teaspoon Dijon mustard
1 tablespoon cornstarch mixed with 2 tablespoons hot water
2 tablespoons grated orange zest

1. Grease the slow cooker with nonstick cooking spray. Cut the chicken breasts into bite-sized pieces. Add the chicken and the onion to the slow cooker.

2. In a small bowl, mix together the orange juice, marmalade, brown sugar, vinegar, Worcestershire sauce, and mustard. Pour over the chicken in the slow cooker.

3. Cover and cook on low for 5–6 hours, or until chicken is cooked through. About 10 minutes before serving whisk in the cornstarch slurry. Uncover the slow cooker, turn the temperature to high and continue to cook for 10 minutes to thicken the sauce. Serve with orange zest sprinkled on top.

PER SERVING | Calories: 235 | Fat: 4 g | Protein: 36 g | Sodium: 228 mg | Fiber: 0.5 g | Carbohydrates: 11 g | Sugar: 8 g

Chicken and Gluten-Free Dumplings

Fluffy gluten-free dumplings float on top of a savory chicken stew. You can make the biscuit topping from scratch use or your favorite all-purpose gluten-free baking mix.

INGREDIENTS | SERVES 4

4 chicken breasts, cut into chunks

4 cups gluten-free chicken broth

¾ teaspoon salt, divided

1 teaspoon ground pepper

2 celery stalks, thinly sliced

2 carrots, thinly sliced

½ onion, finely chopped

1 cup brown rice flour

1 cup arrowroot starch

1 teaspoon xanthan gum

1 tablespoon sugar

3 teaspoons baking powder

⅓ cup vegetable shortening

2 eggs, lightly beaten

1 cup 2% milk

Using a Gluten-Free All-Purpose Mix

If you prefer to use your favorite all-purpose gluten-free baking mix for the topping, simply follow the directions on the package for a batch that makes 6–8 biscuits. Then follow the directions, adding the uncooked dumplings to the slow cooker 30 minutes before you are ready to serve.

1. Place the chicken in a greased 4–6-quart slow cooker. Add chicken broth, ½ teaspoon salt, pepper, celery, carrots, and onion. Cook on high for 3–4 hours or on low for 6–8 hours.

2. In a mixing bowl whisk together the flour, arrowroot starch, xanthan gum, sugar, baking powder, and remaining ¼ teaspoon salt.

3. Cut the shortening into the dry ingredients with two knives or a pastry cutter until the mixture resembles small peas. Make a well in the center of the dry ingredients and add the eggs and milk. Gently mix the wet ingredients into the dry ingredients until you have a fluffy dough.

4. Thirty minutes before serving drop the dough in golf ball–sized spoonfuls into the hot chicken broth. Place the lid on the slow cooker and do not open it for 30 minutes so the dumplings will rise and cook through.

5. Serve dumplings with broth and chicken in large bowls.

PER SERVING | Calories: 890 | Fat: 32 g | Protein: 63 g | Sodium: 2,731 mg | Fiber: 4 g | Carbohydrates: 84 g | Sugar: 9 g

Roast Chicken with Lemon and Artichokes

This is an elegant twist on a simple roast chicken. Marinated artichoke hearts add a hint of zest while fresh lemons give the dish a bright flavor reminiscent of summer.

INGREDIENTS | SERVES 4

1 small onion, quartered

1 large carrot, sliced

1 large lemon

3 cloves garlic

1 (4-pound) whole chicken

½ teaspoon salt

½ teaspoon freshly ground pepper

2 tablespoons olive oil

1 (6-ounce) jar marinated artichoke hearts

Make a Quick Lemon Sauce

Make a sauce using the liquids from the cooked chicken by straining them into a saucepan. Whisk in 2 tablespoons of brown rice flour or garbanzo bean flour and cook on low heat until thickened. The resulting sauce will have a fragrant aroma of lemon, artichokes, and garlic. Serve over rice or gluten-free pasta with green beans or a salad.

1. Grease a large 6-quart slow cooker with nonstick cooking spray.

2. Place the onion and carrot in the slow cooker. Cut the lemon in half. Place half of the lemon, along with the garlic cloves, into the cavity of the chicken.

3. Cut the remainder of the lemon into 4–5 large slices.

4. Place the chicken on top of the onions and carrots. Place lemon slices on top of the chicken. Sprinkle salt and pepper over the chicken. Drizzle olive oil over chicken. Cook on low for 6–8 hours, or on high for 3–4 hours.

5. An hour before serving, place artichokes (discarding the oil) over the top of the chicken.

PER SERVING | Calories: 630 | Fat: 20 g | Protein: 97 g | Sodium: 692 mg | Fiber: 3 g | Carbohydrates: 9 g | Sugar: 2 g

Almond Chicken

The dried minced onion (sometimes sold as dried onion flakes) will absorb some of the chicken broth during the cooking process and naturally thicken the sauce. For a more subtle flavor, use freeze-dried shallots instead.

INGREDIENTS | SERVES 4

1 (14-ounce) can gluten-free chicken broth
4 strips bacon, cooked
2 pounds boneless, skinless chicken breasts
¼ cup dried minced onion
1 (4-ounce) can sliced mushrooms, drained
2 tablespoons gluten-free soy sauce
1½ cups sliced celery
2 cups cooked white rice
1 cup toasted slivered almonds

1. Add the chicken broth to a greased 4-quart slow cooker.

2. Cut the bacon and chicken into bite-sized pieces; add to the slow cooker along with the onion, mushrooms, soy sauce, and celery. Stir to combine.

3. Cover and cook on low for 6 hours.

4. Serve over rice and top with almonds.

PER SERVING | Calories: 956 | Fat: 31 g | Protein: 72 g | Sodium: 1,927 mg | Fiber: 6 g | Carbohydrates: 91 g | Sugar: 3 g

Toasting Almonds

You can toast slivered almonds by adding them to a dry skillet over medium heat. Stir frequently for about 5 minutes until the almonds begin to brown. Alternatively, you can bake them at 400°F for about 5 minutes, stirring them occasionally. Whichever method you use, watch the almonds carefully because they quickly go from toasted to burnt.

Hawaiian Chicken

Pineapple and green peppers give this chicken dish a distinctive and fruity flavor.

INGREDIENTS | SERVES 4

4 boneless, skinless chicken breasts

1 (15-ounce) can sliced pineapple, drained (reserve juice)

½ green pepper, sliced

½ red pepper, sliced

¼ teaspoon cinnamon

½ teaspoon Chinese five-spice powder

½ teaspoon crushed red pepper

Using Pineapple Juice

When buying canned fruit try to buy varieties that are canned in natural juices instead of corn syrup. The leftover juice can be saved in the refrigerator to use later as juice to drink, or even as a natural sweetener for a glass of iced tea or a bowl of warm oatmeal.

1. Place chicken breasts in a greased 4-quart slow cooker.

2. Add 2 slices of pineapple on top of each piece of chicken. If there are leftover pieces, simply set them alongside the chicken.

3. Place red and green pepper slices evenly over all the pieces of chicken. Sprinkle the cinnamon, Chinese five-spice powder, and crushed pepper evenly over the chicken.

4. Finally, pour ½ cup of the reserved pineapple juice over the chicken.

5. Cook on high for 2½–3 hours or on low for 5–6 hours.

PER SERVING | Calories: 336 | Fat: 6 g | Protein: 50 g | Sodium: 275 mg | Fiber: 2 g | Carbohydrates: 17 g | Sugar: 15 g

Honey-Glazed Chicken Drumsticks

It can be a challenge to eat at Chinese restaurants when you are avoiding gluten. But this Asian-inspired chicken is a great substitute for take-out! Serve with white rice, a salad, and egg drop soup.

INGREDIENTS | SERVES 4

2 pounds chicken drumsticks
1 tablespoon melted butter
¼ cup lemon juice
¾ cup honey
1 teaspoon sesame oil
3 cloves garlic, crushed
½ teaspoon ground ginger
½ teaspoon salt

Sesame Oil

Sesame oil is a highly flavored oil made from pressing either toasted or plain sesame seeds. It provides a unique nutty and earthy flavor to savory dishes. A little goes a long way and it's not very expensive. It can be found at most grocery stores in the Asian aisle.

1. Place chicken drumsticks in a greased 4-quart slow cooker.

2. In a glass measuring cup whisk together the melted butter, lemon juice, honey, sesame oil, garlic, ginger, and salt.

3. Pour the honey sauce over the drumsticks. Cook on high for 3–4 hours or on low for 6–8 hours.

PER SERVING | Calories: 596 | Fat: 233 g | Protein: 43 g | Sodium: 487 mg | Fiber: 0.5 g | Carbohydrates: 54 g | Sugar: 52 g

Mango Duck Breast

Slow-cooked mangoes soften and create their own sauce in this easy duck dish. If you prefer, you can use 1½ cups of frozen precut mango instead of fresh. Serve the duck with roasted winter vegetables and steamed asparagus.

INGREDIENTS | SERVES 4

2 boneless, skinless duck breasts
1 large mango, peeled and cubed
¼ cup gluten-free chicken stock
1 tablespoon finely grated fresh ginger
1 tablespoon minced hot pepper
1 tablespoon minced shallot

1. Place all ingredients into a 4-quart slow cooker.

2. Cook on low for 4 hours, or on high for 2 hours.

PER SERVING | Calories: 184 | Fat: 4 g | Protein: 17 g | Sodium: 71 mg | Fiber: 2 g | Carbs: 20 g | Sugar: 17 g

Turkey Drumsticks with Gluten-Free Stuffing

Turkey is too good to only be enjoyed on holidays! Surprise your family with the familiar and delicious aroma of turkey and stuffing.

INGREDIENTS | SERVES 4

1 onion, chopped

½ cup celery, chopped

2 tablespoons butter

2 teaspoons poultry seasoning

4 cups gluten-free bread, toasted and cubed

½ cup gluten-free chicken broth

¼ cup dried cranberries

2 large (about 3 pounds) turkey drumsticks

2 slices bacon

½ teaspoon salt

½ teaspoon ground pepper

Turkey Isn't Just for Thanksgiving

Turkey drumsticks can be found at many grocery stores year round and are an extremely budget-friendly protein. While many people prefer white turkey meat over dark, drumsticks and thighs can hold up well during long cooking periods. They stay moist and are a perfect meat for the slow cooker.

1. In a large glass bowl place onion, celery, butter, and poultry seasoning. Cook in microwave on high for 2 minutes until vegetables have softened.

2. Add bread cubes and broth to the softened vegetables. Stir in the dried cranberries. Pour stuffing into the bottom of a greased 4-quart slow cooker.

3. Place turkey drumsticks on top of stuffing. Place a piece of bacon on each drumstick. Sprinkle salt and pepper evenly over turkey.

4. Cook on high for 3 hours or on low for 6 hours. Each turkey drumstick makes 2 servings.

5. Cut turkey off of the bone and serve over stuffing.

PER SERVING | Calories: 368 | Fat: 14 g | Protein: 30 g | Sodium: 840 mg | Fiber: 2 g | Carbohydrates: 28 g | Sugar: 8 g

Spicy Olive Chicken

This recipe creates a delicious sauce underneath the roasted chicken.
The pan juices will add flavor to the sauce.

INGREDIENTS | SERVES 4

1 (3-pound) whole chicken, cut into 8 pieces

1 teaspoon salt

½ teaspoon ground black pepper

4 tablespoons unsalted butter

⅔ cup chopped sweet onion

2 tablespoons capers, drained and rinsed

24 green olives, pitted

½ cup gluten-free chicken broth

½ cup dry white wine

1 teaspoon prepared Dijon mustard

½ teaspoon hot sauce

2 cups cooked white rice

¼ cup fresh chopped parsley

Capers

Capers are flavorful berries. Picked green, they can be packed in salt or brine. Try to find the smallest—they seem to have more flavor than the big ones do. Capers are great on their own or incorporated into sauces. They are also good in salads and as a garnish on many dishes that would otherwise be dull.

1. Sprinkle the chicken pieces with salt and pepper and brown them in the butter in a large skillet for about 3 minutes on each side. Sauté the onion in the same skillet for an additional 3–5 minutes. Pour chicken, onions, capers, and olives into a greased 4-quart slow cooker.

2. In a small bowl whisk together the broth, wine, and mustard. Pour over chicken in the slow cooker. Add hot sauce. Cover and cook on high for 3–3½ hours or on low for 5½–6 hours.

3. When ready to serve, place chicken over rice. Ladle sauce and olives over each serving. Garnish with parsley.

PER SERVING | Calories: 934 | Fat: 25 g | Protein: 79 g | Sodium: 1,373 mg | Fiber: 3 g | Carbohydrates: 84 g | Sugar: 1.5 g

Easy Italian Chicken

To add vibrant color to this one-pot meal, use a red or orange pepper instead of green.

INGREDIENTS | SERVES 4

4 boneless, skinless chicken breasts

1 cup gluten-free Italian salad dressing

½ teaspoon salt

1 cup diced green peppers

1 cup diced onions

4 potatoes, peeled and quartered

1 (14.5-ounce) can green beans, drained and rinsed

1. Place chicken in a greased 4-quart slow cooker. Add Italian dressing, salt, green peppers, onions, and potatoes.

2. Cook on high for 3 hours or on low for 6 hours.

3. Add green beans during the last hour of cooking.

PER SERVING | Calories: 633 | Fat: 23 g | Protein: 55 g | Sodium: 1,822 mg | Fiber: 8 g | Carbohydrates: 49 g | Sugar: 11 g

Curried Coconut Chicken

Try a variation of this very mild curry—add a small chopped apple or ½ cup of golden raisins into the slow cooker with the other ingredients and cook as directed.

INGREDIENTS | SERVES 4

4 boneless, skinless chicken breasts

1 (14.5-ounce) can coconut milk

½ teaspoon salt

½ teaspoon ground pepper

2 teaspoons curry powder

½ teaspoon ground ginger

1 cup brown rice, uncooked

1. Place chicken breasts in a greased 4-quart slow cooker.

2. In a small bowl mix together coconut milk, salt, pepper, curry powder, and ginger. Pour over chicken in slow cooker.

3. Cook on high for 3 hours or on low for 6 hours. Stir in brown rice an hour before serving.

PER SERVING | Calories: 645 | Fat: 29 g | Protein: 55 g | Sodium: 584 mg | Fiber: 2 g | Carbohydrates: 39 g | Sugar: 0 g

Whole Grain Brown Rice

For weeknight meals many people shy away from cooking whole grain brown rice because it must be watched closely when cooked on the stove and can take a long time. With a slow cooker you simply stir in brown rice in the last hour of cooking. The rice will turn out light and fluffy with little effort.

Creole Chicken and Vegetables

This recipe is extremely quick to assemble, as none of the ingredients require chopping or slicing. The unique blend of spices in Creole seasoning gives this dish its signature flavor.

INGREDIENTS | SERVES 4

8 boneless, skinless chicken thighs

2 tablespoons Creole seasoning

1 (14-ounce) package of frozen mixed vegetables such as broccoli, cauliflower, and carrots

1 (15-ounce) can of diced tomatoes

½ teaspoon ground pepper

1 cup brown rice, uncooked

Checking Seasonings for Gluten

The Internet has become a valuable research tool to find out if processed foods are gluten-free. Spice mixes can often contain questionable ingredients and it's important to make sure they are safe for your diet. Many company websites have a "frequently asked questions" page that often lists their gluten-free products.

1. Place chicken thighs in the bottom of a 4-quart greased slow cooker.

2. Sprinkle Creole seasoning over chicken.

3. Add frozen vegetables, tomatoes, and pepper to the slow cooker.

4. Cook on high for 3 hours or on low for 6 hours. An hour before serving stir in the brown rice.

PER SERVING | Calories: 388 | Fat: 7 g | Protein: 33 g | Sodium: 174 mg | Fiber: 5 g | Carbohydrates: 47 g | Sugar: 6 g

Chicken Paprikash

If you prefer not to cook with wine, replace it with an equal amount of gluten-free chicken broth. You can also substitute an equal amount of drained plain yogurt or full-fat coconut milk for the sour cream.

INGREDIENTS | SERVES 8

1 tablespoon butter

1 tablespoon extra-virgin olive oil

1 large yellow onion, peeled and diced

2 cloves of garlic, peeled and minced

3 pounds boneless, skinless chicken thighs

½ teaspoon salt

¼ teaspoon freshly ground pepper

2 tablespoons Hungarian paprika

½ cup gluten-free chicken broth

¼ cup dry white wine

1 (16-ounce) container sour cream

4 cups cooked gluten-free pasta

Thickening or Thinning

If the resulting sauce for the chicken paprikash is too thin, add more sour cream. If it's too thick, slowly whisk in some milk.

1. Add the butter, oil, and onion to a microwave-safe bowl; cover and microwave on high for 1 minute. Stir, re-cover, and microwave on high for another minute or until the onions are transparent. Stir in the garlic; cover and microwave on high for 30 seconds. Add to the slow cooker.

2. Cut the chicken thighs into bite-sized pieces. Add the chicken to a greased 4–6-quart slow cooker. Stir in the salt, pepper, paprika, broth, and wine; cover and cook on low for 6 hours or on high for 3 hours.

3. Stir in the sour cream; cover and continue to cook long enough to bring the sour cream sauce to temperature, about 30 minutes. Serve over pasta. Sprinkle each serving with additional paprika if desired. Serve immediately.

PER SERVING | Calories: 1,100 | Fat: 44 g | Protein: 84 g | Sodium: 814 mg | Fiber: 5 g | Carbohydrates: 89 g | Sugar: 9 g

Turkey Meatballs with Tangy Apricot Sauce

These easy turkey meatballs are browned on the stovetop and then cooked in a mouthwatering sweet and sour sauce. For a simple variation try orange marmalade instead of apricot jam.

INGREDIENTS | SERVES 4

1 pound ground turkey
¾ cup almond flour
1 egg
¼ cup finely diced onions
¼ cup finely diced celery
½ teaspoon ground pepper
½ teaspoon salt
1 tablespoon olive oil
1 cup apricot preserves
¼ cup Dijon mustard

Are Meatballs Gluten-Free?

Meatloaf and meatballs are usually made with wheat bread crumbs. To make meatloaf or meatballs gluten-free, simply replace the bread crumbs called for in a recipe with almond flour, crushed tortilla chips, leftover gluten-free bread, or even potato flakes.

1. In a large bowl mix together the ground turkey, almond flour, egg, onions, celery, ground pepper, and salt. Roll into small meatballs. The meatball mixture will be slightly wet. Heat olive oil in a large skillet. Add meatballs to hot skillet and brown on all sides, about 1 minute per side.

2. Grease a 2.5-quart slow cooker. Add browned meatballs to the slow cooker.

3. In a small bowl mix together the preserves and mustard. Pour the sauce over the meatballs. Cook on high for 3 hours or on low for 6 hours.

4. If using meatballs as an appetizer instead of a main course, you can turn the slow cooker to the warm setting and leave them for up to 2 hours.

PER SERVING | Calories: 544 | Fat: 25 g | Protein: 27 g | Sodium: 633 mg | Fiber: 3 g | Carbohydrates: 58 g | Sugar: 36 g

Tarragon Chicken

This rich French dish can stand on its own when served with just a tossed salad and some crusty gluten-free bread.

INGREDIENTS | SERVES 4

½ cup plus 2 tablespoons brown rice flour or garbanzo bean flour

½ teaspoon salt

8 bone-in chicken thighs, skin removed

2 tablespoons butter

2 tablespoons olive oil

1 medium yellow onion, peeled and diced

1 cup dry white wine

1 cup gluten-free chicken broth

½–1 teaspoon dried tarragon

1 cup heavy cream

Tarragon Chicken Cooking Times

After 3 hours on high, the chicken will be cooked through and ready to eat. Yet, if you prefer to leave the chicken cooking for a longer period, after 7–8 hours on low the meat will be tender enough to fall away from the bone. You can then remove the bones before you stir in the cream.

1. Add ½ cup flour, salt, and the chicken thighs to a gallon-sized plastic bag; close and shake to coat the chicken.

2. Add the butter and oil to a large sauté pan and bring it to temperature over medium-high heat. Add the chicken thighs; brown the chicken by cooking the pieces on one side for 5 minutes, and then turning them over and frying them for another 5 minutes. Drain the chicken on paper towels and then place in a 4–6 quart slow cooker. Cover the slow cooker. Set temperature to low.

3. Add the onion to the sauté pan; sauté until the onion is transparent about 3–5 minutes. Stir in 2 tablespoons of brown rice flour, cooking until the onion just begins to brown. Slowly pour the wine into the pan, stirring to scrape the browned bits off of the bottom of the pan and into the sauce. Add the broth. Cook and stir for 15 minutes or until the sauce is thickened enough to coat the back of a spoon. Stir the tarragon into the sauce, and then pour the sauce over the chicken in the slow cooker. Cover and cook for 3 hours on high or 6 hours on low.

4. Pour the cream into the slow cooker; cover and cook for an additional 15 minutes or until the cream is heated through. Test for seasoning and add additional salt and tarragon if needed. Serve immediately.

PER SERVING | Calories: 656 | Fat: 41 g | Protein: 31 g | Sodium: 703 mg | Fiber: 2 g | Carbohydrates: 28 g | Sugar: 2 g

Sun-Dried Tomato and Feta Stuffed Chicken

Three Greek-inspired ingredients give these lovely chicken rolls an attractive appearance and exceptional flavor.

INGREDIENTS | SERVES 4

4 boneless, skinless chicken breasts

½ cup chopped oil-packed sun-dried tomatoes

⅓ cup crumbled feta cheese

¼ cup chopped pitted kalamata olives

1½ cups fresh baby spinach leaves

2 tablespoons olive oil

½ teaspoon salt

½ teaspoon freshly ground pepper

Sun-Dried Tomatoes

Sun-dried tomatoes are tomatoes that have been dried in the sun to remove moisture content. They have a distinct sweet, yet savory flavor. Most grocery stores carry them in the produce section. They are often preserved in oil, but can also be found dry. If not packed in oil, the tomatoes will need to be reconstituted in water before use.

1. Flatten chicken breasts on a wooden cutting board with the flat side of a meat mallet. Set chicken breasts aside.

2. In a small bowl mix together the tomatoes, cheese, and olives.

3. Place 3–4 spinach leaves in the middle of each flattened chicken breast. Place 2–3 tablespoons of the tomato filling on top the spinach leaves.

4. Fold one side of the flattened chicken breast over the filling and continue to roll into a cylinder and secure with 2–3 toothpicks per chicken breast. Place the chicken rolls seam side down in a greased 4-quart slow cooker.

5. Drizzle olive oil evenly over the top of the chicken rolls and sprinkle the chicken with salt and pepper. Cook on high for 3 hours or on low for 6 hours.

PER SERVING | Calories: 378 | Fat: 17 g | Protein: 52 g | Sodium: 791 mg | Fiber: 1 g | Carbohydrates: 3 g | Sugar: 1 g

Peruvian Roast Chicken with Red Potatoes

A traditional favorite from Latin American restaurants, this chicken dish has become popular in recent years, especially in cities along the East Coast.

INGREDIENTS | SERVES 4

1 (3–4 pound) whole chicken

2½ tablespoons garlic powder

2 tablespoons paprika

1½ tablespoons cumin

2 teaspoons black pepper

1 teaspoon salt

½ teaspoon oregano

1 lemon, cut into quarters

2 pounds red potatoes, washed and quartered

4 tablespoons white vinegar

4 tablespoons white wine

2 tablespoons olive oil

Lime Sauce

Peruvian chicken is often served with a dipping sauce on the side. You can make a homemade version by mixing together ½ cup mayonnaise with 2 tablespoons yellow mustard and 3 tablespoons lime juice.

1. Wash chicken with cold water and pat dry. Loosen skin over the breast meat if possible, being careful not to break the skin.

2. In a small bowl mix together the garlic powder, paprika, cumin, black pepper, salt, and oregano. Generously rub the chicken with the spice mixture. Rub the meat of the chicken under the skin with the spice mixture as well. Place the lemon quarters inside the chicken.

3. Place the potatoes in the bottom of a 6-quart slow cooker. Place the spice-rubbed chicken on top of the potatoes.

4. Drizzle the vinegar, wine, and olive oil over the chicken.

5. Cook on high for 4 hours or on low for 8 hours.

PER SERVING | Calories: 740 | Fat: 20 g | Protein: 90 g | Sodium: 914 mg | Fiber: 7 g | Carbohydrates: 44 g | Sugar: 3 g

Moroccan Chicken

This dish was inspired by traditional North African tagines and adapted for the slow cooker. Serve over cooked rice or mashed sweet potatoes

INGREDIENTS | SERVES 6

½ teaspoon coriander

½ teaspoon cinnamon

¼ teaspoon salt

1 teaspoon cumin

3 pounds (about 8) boneless, skinless chicken thighs, diced

1 onion, thinly sliced

4 cloves garlic, minced

2 tablespoons fresh ginger, minced or ½ teaspoon dried ginger

½ cup water

4 ounces dried apricots, halved

15 ounces canned chickpeas, drained and rinsed

1. In a large bowl, combine the coriander, cinnamon, salt, and cumin. Toss chicken in the spice mixture.

2. Place onion, garlic, ginger, and water into a 4-quart slow cooker. Place chicken on top of vegetables. Place dried apricots and chickpeas on top of chicken.

3. Cover and cook on low for 5–6 hours.

PER SERVING | Calories: 408 | Fat: 9 g | Protein: 48 g | Sodium: 504 mg | Fiber: 5 g | Carbohydrates: 30 g | Sugar: 10 g

Buffalo Chicken Sandwich Filling

Serve on toasted gluten-free bread with crumbled blue cheese or gluten-free ranch dressing on top of each sandwich.

INGREDIENTS | SERVES 4

6 boneless, skinless chicken thighs

¼ cup onion, diced

1 clove garlic, minced

½ teaspoon freshly ground black pepper

½ teaspoon salt

2 cups gluten-free buffalo wing sauce

1. Place all ingredients in a greased 4-quart slow cooker. Stir to combine. Cook on high for 2–3 hours or on low for 4–6 hours or until the chicken is easily shredded with a fork. If the sauce is very thin, continue to cook on high uncovered for 30 minutes or until thickened.

2. Shred the chicken and toss with the sauce.

PER SERVING | Calories: 316 | Fat: 4 g | Protein: 20 g | Sodium: 1,783 mg | Fiber: 1 g | Carbohydrates: 46 g | Sugar: 33 g

Chicken Piccata

Serve over mashed potatoes or gluten-free egg noodles.

INGREDIENTS | SERVES 4

2 large boneless, skinless chicken breasts, cut into very thin slices

1 cup brown rice flour

1 tablespoon olive oil

¼ cup lemon juice

3 tablespoons nonpareil capers

¾ cup gluten-free chicken stock

¼ teaspoon freshly ground black pepper

Dredge Details

Dredging is a process in which food is dragged through dry ingredients like corn-starch or gluten-free bread crumbs to coat it. Dredging can be a one-step process, but if a thicker crust or coating is desired the food is dredged in flour once, dipped in egg or milk, then dredged through flour, cornmeal, or gluten-free bread crumbs again. In slow cooking, dredging often has a dual purpose of coating the meat and thickening the sauce.

1. Dredge both sides of the sliced chicken breasts in the flour. Discard leftover flour.

2. Heat olive oil in a nonstick pan. Quickly sear the chicken on both sides to brown, approximately 1 minute per side.

3. Place the chicken, lemon juice, capers, stock, and pepper into a greased 4-quart slow cooker.

4. Cook on high for 2–3 hours or on low for 4–6 hours until the chicken is cooked through and the sauce has thickened.

PER SERVING | Calories: 330 | Fat: 7 g | Protein: 28 g | Sodium: 395 mg | Fiber: 1 g | Carbohydrates: 34 g | Sugar: 1 g

Chicken in Plum Sauce

For this rich, sweet entrée, you can use commercial gluten-free plum sauce or make your own Plum Sauce (see Chapter 5). Top each serving with toasted sesame oil and gluten-free soy sauce if desired.

INGREDIENTS | SERVES 4

1¾ cups plum sauce

2 tablespoons butter, melted

2 tablespoons orange juice concentrate, thawed

1 teaspoon Chinese five-spice powder

8 bone-in chicken thighs, skin removed

1. Grease a 4-quart slow cooker with nonstick cooking spray. Add the plum sauce, butter, juice concentrate, and five-spice powder to the slow cooker; stir to combine.

2. Add the chicken thighs. Cover and cook on low for 6 hours or on high for 3 hours.

PER SERVING | Calories: 252 | Fat: 11 g | Protein: 27 g | Sodium: 119 mg | Fiber: 1 g | Carbohydrates: 9 g | Sugar: 7 g

Butter Chicken

This dish is also called Chicken Makhani. The common name "Butter Chicken" is a bit of a misnomer as the dish traditionally only includes about a tablespoon of butter.

INGREDIENTS | SERVES 4

1 pound boneless, skinless chicken breasts

2 shallots, minced

2 cloves garlic, minced

½ knob of fresh ginger, peeled and minced

2 tablespoons lemon juice

2 teaspoons garam masala

2 teaspoons ground cumin

½ teaspoon cayenne

½ teaspoon fenugreek

¼ teaspoon salt

½ teaspoon freshly ground black pepper

1 tablespoon butter

1 tablespoon tomato paste

¾ cup plain low-fat Greek yogurt

1. Place the chicken, shallots, garlic, ginger, lemon juice, garam masala, cumin, cayenne, fenugreek, salt, pepper, butter, and tomato paste into a 4-quart slow cooker. Stir to combine. Cook on low for 5 hours or on high for 2½ hours.

2. About 10 minutes before serving stir in the yogurt.

PER SERVING | Calories: 254 | Fat: 8 g | Protein: 27 g | Sodium: 340 mg | Fiber: 3 g | Carbohydrates: 18 g | Sugar: 6 g

Do-It-Yourself Greek Yogurt

Greek yogurt is super thick and creamy, but is also low in fat. It is available in many grocery stores but can be tricky to find in some areas. A reasonable facsimile can be made by lining a colander with cheesecloth and straining low-fat plain yogurt over-night. Be sure to start with twice as much yogurt as the final product should be because the yogurt will reduce by half.

Chicken Cacciatore

If you prefer, you can remove the skin from a 3-pound chicken and cut it into 8 serving pieces and substitute that for the chicken thighs. Serve the chicken and sauce over cooked rice or gluten-free pasta.

INGREDIENTS | SERVES 4

¾ cup brown rice flour, divided

½ teaspoon salt

8 bone-in chicken thighs, skin removed (if using boneless reduce cooking time by 1 hour)

3 tablespoons olive oil

1 medium yellow onion, diced

4 cloves of garlic, minced

3 tablespoons coarsely chopped oil-packed sun-dried tomatoes

1 cup dry white wine

⅛ teaspoon dried sage

¼ teaspoon dried rosemary

Pinch dried red pepper flakes

½ teaspoon freshly ground black pepper

1. Add ½ cup of the flour, salt, and the chicken thighs to a gallon-sized plastic bag; close and shake to coat the chicken.

2. Add the oil to a large sauté pan and bring it to medium-high heat. Add the chicken thighs; brown the chicken by cooking the pieces on one side for 5 minutes, and then turning them over and frying them for another 5 minutes. Drain the chicken on paper towels and then place in a 4–6 quart slow cooker. Cover the slow cooker and set the temperature to low.

3. Add the onion to the sauté pan and cook until the onions begin to soften, about 3–5 minutes. Stir in the garlic and sauté for 30 seconds. Add the sun-dried tomatoes. Slowly pour the wine into the pan to deglaze (stirring to scrape the browned bits off the bottom of the pan.) Stir in the sage, rosemary, pepper flakes, and black pepper and then pour the sauce over the chicken in the slow cooker.

4. Cover and cook on high for 3–4 hours or on low for 6–7 hours.

PER SERVING | Calories: 428 | Fat: 16 g | Protein: 29 g | Sodium: 418 mg | Fiber: 1.5 g | Carbohydrates: 29 g | Sugar: 2 g

CHAPTER 10

Beef, Lamb, and Pork

Yankee Pot Roast

New England cooking is traditionally plain and straightforward. If your family prefers a heartier flavor, add a teaspoon of Mrs. Dash Garlic & Herb Seasoning Blend.

INGREDIENTS | SERVES 8

¼ pound salt pork, cut into cubes

2 stalks celery, diced

1 (4-pound) chuck or English roast

1 teaspoon salt

1 teaspoon freshly ground black pepper

2 large onions, peeled and quartered

1 (1-pound) bag of baby carrots

2 turnips, peeled and diced

8 medium potatoes, peeled

2 cups gluten-free beef broth

4 tablespoons butter

4 tablespoons brown rice flour

Mocking the Maillard Reaction

Contrary to myth, searing meat before it's braised doesn't seal in the juices, but it does—through a process known as the Maillard reaction—enhance the flavor of the meat through a caramelization process. Using beef broth (or, even better, a combination of brown stock and water) mimics that flavor and lets you skip the browning step.

1. Add the salt pork and the celery to the bottom of a 6-quart slow cooker. Place the roast on top of the pork; sprinkle with salt and pepper. Add the onions, carrots, turnips, and potatoes. Pour in the beef broth. Cover and cook on low for 8 hours.

2. Use a slotted spoon to move the meat and vegetables to a serving platter; cover and keep warm.

3. Mix the butter and flour together with ½ cup of the broth. Increase the slow cooker heat setting to high; cover and cook until the mixture begins to bubble around the edges. Whisk the flour mixture into the broth; cook, stirring constantly, for 10 minutes, or until the flour flavor is cooked out of the gravy and it's thickened enough to coat the back of a spoon. Taste the gravy for seasoning and stir in more salt and pepper if needed. Serve over or alongside the meat and vegetables.

PER SERVING | Calories: 930 | Fat: 62 g | Protein: 44 g | Sodium: 927 mg | Fiber: 8 | Carbohydrates: 47 g | Sugar: 8 g

New England Boiled Dinner

Cutting the meat into serving-sized pieces before you add it to the slow cooker will make the meat cook up more tender, but you can keep it in one piece if you prefer to carve it at the table.

INGREDIENTS | SERVES 8

1 (3-pound) boneless beef round rump roast

4 cups gluten-free beef broth

2 yellow onions, sliced

1 teaspoon prepared horseradish

1 bay leaf

1 clove of garlic, minced

6 large carrots, cut into 1" pieces

3 rutabagas, peeled and quartered

4 large potatoes, peeled and quartered

1 small head of cabbage, cut into 8 wedges

2 tablespoons butter

2 tablespoons brown rice flour

1 teaspoon salt, optional

½ teaspoon freshly ground black pepper, optional

Horseradish Gravy

If you prefer a more intense horseradish flavor with cooked beef, increase the amount to 1 tablespoon. Taste the pan juices before you thicken them with the butter and brown rice flour mixture, and add more horseradish at that time if you desire. Of course, you can have some horseradish or horseradish mayonnaise available as a condiment for those who want more.

1. Cut the beef into 8 serving-sized pieces and add it along with the broth, onions, horseradish, bay leaf, and garlic to a 6-quart slow cooker. Add the carrots, rutabagas, potatoes, and cabbage wedges. Cover and cook on low for 8 hours.

2. Remove meat and vegetables to a serving platter; cover and keep warm.

3. Increase the slow cooker setting to high; cover and cook until the pan juices begin to bubble around the edges. Mix the butter and flour in a bowl together with ½ cup of the pan juices; strain out any lumps and whisk the mixture into the simmering liquid in the slow cooker. Cook and stir for 15 minutes or until the flour flavor is cooked out and the gravy is thickened enough to coat the back of a spoon. Taste for seasoning and add salt and pepper if desired. Serve alongside or over the meat and potatoes.

PER SERVING | Calories: 543 | Fat: 15 g | Protein: 44 g | Sodium: 875 mg | Fiber: 13 g | Carbohydrates: 57 g | Sugar: 17 g

Beef and Cabbage

The longer cooking time helps the flavors develop. But because the meat is already cooked, this meal is done when the cabbage is tender, or in about 4 hours on low. Serve over cooked brown rice or mashed potatoes.

INGREDIENTS | SERVES 4

1 pound cooked stew beef
1 small head of cabbage, chopped
1 medium onion, peeled and diced
2 carrots, peeled and thinly sliced
2 stalks celery, sliced in ½-inch pieces
1 clove garlic, peeled and minced
2 cups gluten-free beef broth
1 (14½-ounce) can diced tomatoes
¼ teaspoon sugar
½ teaspoon salt
⅛ teaspoon freshly ground black pepper

1. Cut the cooked beef into bite-sized pieces and add it to a 4-quart slow cooker along with the cabbage, onion, carrots, and celery; stir to mix.

2. Add the garlic, broth, tomatoes, sugar, salt, and pepper to a bowl; mix well and pour over the beef. Set the slow cooker on high and cook for 1 hour or until the cabbage has begun to wilt.

3. Reduce heat to low and cook for 3–4 hours, or until cabbage is very tender. Adjust seasonings if necessary.

PER SERVING | Calories: 286 | Fat: 8 g | Protein: 29 g | Sodium: 974 mg | Fiber: 8 g | Carbohydrates: 24 g | Sugar: 13 g

Barbecue Western Ribs

At the end of the 8-hour cooking time, the meat will be tender and falling off of the bones. You can stretch this recipe to 8 servings if you serve barbecue beef sandwiches instead of 4 servings of beef. Add potato chips and coleslaw for a delicious, casual meal.

INGREDIENTS | SERVES 4

1 cup gluten-free hickory barbecue sauce
½ cup orange marmalade
½ cup water
3 pounds beef Western ribs

1. Add the barbecue sauce, marmalade, and water to greased 4–6-quart slow cooker. Stir to mix.

2. Add the ribs, ladling some of the sauce over the ribs. Cover and cook on low for 8 hours.

3. To thicken the sauce, use a slotted spoon to remove the meat and bones; cover and keep warm. Skim any fat from the sauce in the cooker; increase the heat setting to high and cook uncovered for 15 minutes or until the sauce is reduced and coats the back of a spoon.

PER SERVING | Calories: 709 | Fat: 23 g | Protein: 71 g | Sodium: 904 mg | Fiber: 0.5 g | Carbohydrates: 49 g | Sugar: 40 g

Swiss Steak

Minute steaks are usually tenderized pieces of round steak. You can instead buy 2½ pounds of round steak, trim it of fat, cut it into 6 portions, and pound each portion thin between 2 pieces of plastic wrap. Serve Swiss Steak over mashed potatoes.

INGREDIENTS | SERVES 6

½ cup brown rice flour or Bob's Red Mill All-Purpose Flour

1 teaspoon salt

¼ teaspoon freshly ground black pepper

6 (6-ounce) beef minute steaks

2 tablespoons vegetable oil

2 teaspoons butter

½ stalk celery, finely diced

1 large yellow onion, peeled and diced

1 cup beef broth

1 cup water

1 (1-pound) bag baby carrots

Swiss Steak and Pasta

If instead of mashed potatoes, you'd prefer to serve Swiss Steak over cooked gluten-free pasta, stir 2 tablespoons of tomato paste into the onions before you make the gravy in Step 3. Or, you can substitute 1 cup of diced tomatoes for the water.

1. Add the flour, salt, pepper, and steaks to a gallon-sized plastic bag; seal and shake to coat the meat.

2. Add the oil and butter to a large skillet and bring it to temperature over medium-high heat. Add the meat and brown it for 5 minutes on each side. Transfer the meat to a 4-quart slow cooker.

3. Add the celery to the skillet and sauté while you add the onion to the plastic bag; seal and shake to coat the onion in flour. Add the flour-coated onion to the skillet and, stirring constantly, sauté for 10 minutes or until the onions are lightly browned.

4. Add the broth to the skillet and stir to scrape up any browned bits clinging to the pan. Add the water and continue to cook until the liquid is thickened enough to lightly coat the back of a spoon. Pour into the slow cooker.

5. Add the carrots. Cover and cook on low for 8 hours.

6. Transfer the meat and carrots to a serving platter. Taste the gravy for seasoning, and add more salt and pepper if desired. Serve alongside or over the meat and carrots.

PER SERVING | Calories: 402 | Fat: 18 g | Protein: 37 g | Sodium: 670 mg | Fiber: 3 g | Carbohydrates: 20 g | Sugar: 4 g

Beef Biryani

Biryani is a one-dish meal that is well spiced but not spicy. Traditionally it is made using ghee, a type of clarified butter, but slow cooking brings out the flavor without adding fat.

INGREDIENTS | SERVES 6

1 pound top round, cut into strips
1 tablespoon minced fresh ginger
½ teaspoon ground cloves
½ teaspoon ground cardamom
½ teaspoon ground coriander
½ teaspoon freshly ground black pepper
½ teaspoon cinnamon
½ teaspoon cumin
¼ teaspoon salt
2 cloves garlic, minced
1 onion, minced
1 cup fat-free Greek yogurt
1 cup frozen peas
1½ cups cooked basmati or brown rice

1. Place the beef, spices, garlic, and onion into a 4-quart slow cooker. Stir. Cook for 5–6 hours on low.

2. About 30 minutes before serving, stir in the yogurt, peas, and rice. Cook for 30 minutes. Stir before serving.

PER SERVING | Calories: 346 | Fat: 8 g | Protein: 22 g | Sodium: 162 mg | Fiber: 3.5 g | Carbohydrates: 44 g | Sugar: 4 g

Roast Beef for Two

Couples deserve a good roast dinner just as much as larger families. So enjoy this one without having to eat leftovers for a week.

INGREDIENTS | SERVES 2

½ teaspoon freshly ground black pepper
½ teaspoon fennel seeds
½ teaspoon crushed rosemary
¼ teaspoon salt
½ teaspoon dried oregano
¾-pound bottom round roast, excess fat removed
¼ cup Caramelized Onions (see Chapter 3)
¼ cup gluten-free beef stock
1 clove garlic, sliced

1. In a small bowl, stir the pepper, fennel seeds, rosemary, salt, and oregano. Rub it onto all sides of the meat. Refrigerate for 15 minutes.

2. Place the roast in a 2-quart slow cooker. Add the onions, stock, and garlic. Cook on low for 6 hours, or on high for 3 hours. Remove roast and slice. Serve the slices topped with the Caramelized Onions. Discard any cooking juices.

PER SERVING | Calories: 277 | Fat: 12 g | Protein: 36 g | Sodium: 446 mg | Fiber: 1 g | Carbohydrates: 4 g | Sugar: 1 g

Ground Beef Ragout

Ragout is a term that generally refers to a slow-cooked stew with a variety of vegetables that can be made with or without meat. Ground beef is used in this version for a very economical main dish. Serve over cooked rice or prepared polenta.

INGREDIENTS | SERVES 4

1 pound ground beef

2 medium onions, finely chopped

1 large green pepper, diced with seeds removed

1 tablespoon olive oil

1 (14.5-ounce) can Italian-style stewed tomatoes

3 medium carrots, cut into ½" slices

½ cup gluten-free beef broth

½ teaspoon salt

½ teaspoon ground pepper

1 medium zucchini, halved lengthwise and cut into ½" slices

Not a Fan of Zucchini?

Instead of using zucchini, use yellow squash, precooked potatoes or sweet potatoes, parsnips, or even mushrooms. Use whatever vegetables you have on hand!

1. Brown ground beef in a skillet, discard grease, and spoon ground beef into a greased 4-quart slow cooker.

2. In the same pan, sauté onions and green pepper in olive oil for several minutes until softened. Add onions and green pepper to slow cooker.

3. Add tomatoes, carrots, broth, salt, and pepper to the slow cooker. Stir to combine all ingredients.

4. Cook for 4 hours on high or 8 hours on low.

5. An hour prior to serving stir in zucchini and allow to cook until fork tender.

PER SERVING | Calories: 304 | Fat: 15 g | Protein: 25 g | Sodium: 510 mg | Fiber: 4 g | Carbohydrates: 17 g | Sugar: 9 g

Slow Cooker Hamburgers

Here's another one of those "I didn't know you could make that in the slow cooker" recipes! By cooking hamburgers in the slow cooker you can prepare them as soon as you get home from work and they are ready to eat 60–90 minutes later with no mess or babysitting!

INGREDIENTS | SERVES 4

1 pound ground beef

1 egg

2 tablespoons onion, finely diced

½ teaspoon garlic powder

1 tablespoon gluten-free Worcestershire sauce

¼ teaspoon salt

¼ teaspoon ground pepper

Make Mine with Cheese Please!

If you would like to make cheeseburgers, or even bacon cheeseburgers, add the cheese and precooked bacon to each patty 20 minutes prior to serving. Serve burgers on gluten-free buns, over a fresh salad, or even on top of baked French fries!

1. Make a 2"–3" foil rack in the bottom of your 4-quart slow cooker by placing rolled strips of aluminum foil in the bottom of the greased stoneware insert. Make a grill pattern with the strips. This will allow the burgers to cook above the juices while sitting on the rack.

2. In a medium-sized bowl, mix together all ingredients. Shape mixture into 4 flat, round burger patties.

3. Place burgers on the foil rack.

4. Cook on high for 1–1½ hours or on low for 2–2½ hours, until the juices run clear when a knife or fork is inserted in the middle of each burger. Try not to overcook the burgers as they can quickly dry out.

PER SERVING | Calories: 221 | Fat: 12 g | Protein: 24 g | Sodium: 281 mg | Fiber: 0 g | Carbohydrates: 2 g | Sugar: 1 g

Meatloaf-Stuffed Green Peppers

This recipe is slightly different from traditional stuffed pepper recipes because it doesn't contain rice or potatoes to supplement the meat mixture. This is a great main dish option for those following low-carbohydrate food plans.

INGREDIENTS | SERVES 4

1 slice gluten-free bread, torn into very small pieces

¼ cup 2% milk

1 pound ground beef

½ teaspoon salt

½ teaspoon pepper

1½ teaspoons dried onion

1 egg

4 green peppers

Make It Grain-Free

To make this recipe completely grain-free and dairy-free (for those following a Paleo food plan or a GAPS food plan), use ¼ cup blanched almond flour in place of the gluten-free bread and use a nondairy substitute in place of the milk.

1. In a large bowl mix together the bread and milk. Set aside for 5 minutes.

2. Add ground beef, salt, pepper, dried onion, and egg to the softened bread. Mix meatloaf ingredients together well.

3. Carefully remove the tops, seeds, and membranes of the peppers. Fill each pepper with ¼ of the meatloaf mixture.

4. Place the stuffed peppers in a greased 4-quart slow cooker. Add ⅓ cup of water around the bottom of the stuffed peppers.

5. Cook on high for 3–4 hours or on low for 6–8 hours until green peppers are softened.

PER SERVING | Calories: 272 | Fat: 13 g | Protein: 26 g | Sodium: 448 mg | Fiber: 2 g | Carbohydrates: 11 g | Sugar: 4 g

Barbecue Meatloaf

The brown sugar sprinkled on top of the meatloaf helps to caramelize the sauce.

INGREDIENTS | SERVES 8

2 pounds lean ground beef

½ pound lean ground pork

2 large eggs

1 large yellow onion, finely diced

½ teaspoon salt

¼ teaspoon freshly ground pepper

1½ cups gluten-free quick-cooking oatmeal

1 teaspoon dried parsley

1½ cups barbecue sauce, divided

1 tablespoon brown sugar

1 teaspoon Mrs. Dash Extra Spicy Seasoning Blend

1. Add the ground beef, ground pork, eggs, onion, salt, pepper, oatmeal, parsley, and 1 cup barbecue sauce to a large bowl. Mix well with your hands. Form into a loaf that will fit into a 4–6-quart slow cooker.

2. Line the slow cooker with two pieces of heavy-duty aluminum foil long enough to reach up both sides of the slow cooker and over the edge. Grease the foil with nonstick cooking spray or olive oil.

3. Place the meatloaf on top of the foil in the slow cooker. Spread the remaining ½ cup of barbecue sauce over the top of the meatloaf. Sprinkle the brown sugar and Mrs. Dash Extra Spicy Seasoning blend over the top of the barbecue sauce. Cover and cook on low for 6–8 hours or on high for 3–4 hours or until the center of the meatloaf registers at least 165°F.

4. Slowly lift the meatloaf out of the slow cooker and place on a large platter. Allow the meat to rest for 15–20 minutes before serving.

PER SERVING | Calories: 387 | Fat: 14 g | Protein: 32 g | Sodium: 781 mg | Fiber: 2 g | Carbohydrates: 31 g | Sugar: 15 g

Easy Leg of Lamb

Although lamb can be an expensive cut of meat, you can often find it on sale during the holidays. Stock up on several cuts and freeze them when you find good prices.

INGREDIENTS | SERVES 6

1 (4-pound) bone-in leg of lamb

5 cloves garlic, skin removed, and cut into spears

2 tablespoons olive oil

1 tablespoon dried rosemary

½ teaspoon salt

½ teaspoon ground pepper

4 cups low-sodium, gluten-free chicken stock

¼ cup gluten-free soy sauce or red wine

1. Make small incisions evenly over the lamb. Place garlic spears into the slices in the lamb.

2. Rub olive oil, rosemary, salt, and pepper over the lamb. Place lamb into a greased 4- or 6-quart slow cooker.

3. Pour stock and soy sauce (or wine) around the leg of lamb. Cook on high for 4 hours or on low for 8 hours.

4. Serve the roast lamb in bowls. Ladle the sauce from the slow cooker over each serving.

PER SERVING | Calories: 536 | Fat: 24 g | Protein: 66 g | Sodium: 1,195 mg | Fiber: 1 g | Carbohydrates: 8 g | Sugar: 3 g

Lamb with Garlic, Lemon, and Rosemary

You can use the spice rub in this recipe as a marinade by applying it to the leg of lamb several hours (or up to one full day) before cooking. The red wine in this dish can be replaced with chicken or beef stock.

INGREDIENTS | SERVES 4

4 cloves of garlic, crushed

1 tablespoon fresh rosemary, chopped

1 tablespoon olive oil

½ teaspoon salt

1 teaspoon ground pepper

1 large lemon, cut into ¼" slices

1 (3-pound) leg of lamb

½ cup red wine

1. In a small bowl mix together garlic, rosemary, olive oil, salt, and pepper. Rub this mixture onto the leg of lamb.

2. Place a few lemon slices in the bottom of a greased 4-quart slow cooker. Place spice-rubbed lamb on top of lemon slices.

3. Add remaining lemon slices on top of lamb. Pour wine around the lamb.

4. Cook on low heat for 8–10 hours, or on high for 4–6 hours.

PER SERVING | Calories: 541 | Fat: 23 g | Protein: 70 g | Sodium: 511 mg | Fiber: 0 g | Carbohydrates: 2 g | Sugar: 0 g

Herbed Lamb Chops

This simple herb rub would make a fun Christmas gift to give to friends or family members who enjoy cooking! Include this recipe with a small jar of the rub.

INGREDIENTS | SERVES 4

1 medium onion, sliced
1 teaspoon dried oregano
½ teaspoon dried thyme
½ teaspoon garlic powder
¼ teaspoon salt
⅛ teaspoon ground pepper
2 pounds (about 8) lamb loin chops
1 tablespoon olive oil

1. Place onion on the bottom of a greased 4-quart slow cooker.

2. In a small bowl mix together oregano, thyme, garlic powder, salt, and pepper. Rub herb mixture over the lamb chops.

3. Place herb-rubbed lamb chops over the sliced onions. Drizzle olive oil over the lamb chops.

4. Cook on high for 3 hours or on low for 6 hours, until tender.

PER SERVING | Calories: 363 | Fat: 17 g | Protein: 46 g | Sodium: 292 mg | Fiber: 1 g | Carbohydrates: 3 g | Sugar: 1 g

Lamb and Root Vegetable Tagine

This exotic dish is a North African–inspired stew with curried root vegetables and apricots.

INGREDIENTS | SERVES 6

1 tablespoon olive oil
2 pounds leg of lamb, trimmed of fat and cut into bite-sized chunks
½ onion, chopped
1 clove garlic, minced
½ teaspoon pepper
½ teaspoon salt
1 cup gluten-free chicken stock
½ pound (about 2 medium) sweet potatoes, peeled and cut into 1" chunks
⅓ cup dried apricots, cut in half
1 teaspoon coriander
1 teaspoon cumin
¼ teaspoon cinnamon

1. In a large skillet, brown cubed lamb in olive oil, approximately 1–2 minutes per side. Add lamb to a greased 4-quart slow cooker. Cook onion and garlic in the same skillet for 3–4 minutes until soft and then add to slow cooker.

2. Add remaining ingredients to slow cooker. Cook on high for 4 hours or on low for 8 hours.

PER SERVING | Calories: 304 | Fat: 12 g | Protein: 32 g | Sodium: 371 mg | Fiber: 2 g | Carbohydrates: 15 g | Sugar: 6 g

Italian Pork with Cannellini Beans

This is an incredibly simple one-dish meal that is packed with flavor.

INGREDIENTS | SERVES 4

1½ pounds pork loin

28 ounces crushed tomatoes

1 head roasted garlic

1 onion, minced

2 tablespoons capers

2 teaspoons Italian seasoning

15 ounces canned cannellini beans, drained and rinsed

1. Place the pork loin into a 4-quart slow cooker. Add the tomatoes, garlic, onion, and capers. Cook on low for 7–8 hours.

2. One hour before serving, add the cannellini beans and continue to cook on low for the remaining time.

PER SERVING | Calories: 359 | Fat: 7 g | Protein: 45 g | Sodium: 532 mg | Fiber: 9 g | Carbohydrates: 28 g | Sugar: 8 g

How to Make Roasted Garlic

You can easily make your own roasted garlic in the oven. Simply cover a small baking sheet with aluminum foil and place 2–4 whole (unpeeled) heads of garlic on the pan. Drizzle 2 tablespoons of olive oil over the garlic and bake at 350°F for about 45 minutes. Allow to cool for 5–10 minutes and then gently squeeze garlic cloves out of the "paper" surrounding them. Alternately you could place the same ingredients in a 1.5-2.5-quart slow cooker. Cover and cook on high for 2 hours. Store roasted garlic cloves in the fridge for up to 2 weeks.

Mexican Pork Roast

Serve this pork over rice with Easy "Refried" Beans (see Chapter 6) on the side, or in burritos.

INGREDIENTS | SERVES 4

1 tablespoon olive oil

1 large sweet onion, peeled and sliced

1 medium carrot, peeled and finely diced

1 jalapeño pepper, seeded and minced

1 clove of garlic, peeled and minced

½ teaspoon salt

¼ teaspoon dried Mexican oregano

¼ teaspoon ground coriander

¼ teaspoon freshly ground black pepper

1 (3-pound) pork shoulder or butt roast

1 cup gluten-free chicken broth

Mexican Pork Roast Burritos

Warm 4 large brown rice flour tortillas (Food for Life brand tortillas can be found in the freezer section of some higher-end grocery stores). Spread refried beans on each tortilla. Divide the pork between the tortillas and top with salsa and, if desired, grated cheese, shredded lettuce, and sour cream. Roll and serve.

1. Add the olive oil, onion, carrot, and jalapeño to a 4–6 quart slow cooker. Stir to coat the vegetables in the oil. Cover and cook on high for 30 minutes or until the onions are softened. Stir in the garlic.

2. In a small bowl, combine the salt, oregano, coriander, and black pepper. Rub the spice mixture onto the pork roast.

3. Add the rubbed pork roast to the slow cooker. Add the chicken broth. Cover and cook on low for 6 hours or until the pork is tender and pulls apart easily.

4. Use a slotted spoon to remove the pork and vegetables to a serving platter. Cover and let rest for 10 minutes.

5. Increase the temperature of the slow cooker to high. Cook and reduce the pan juices by half.

6. Use 2 forks to shred the pork and mix it in with the cooked onion and jalapeño. Ladle the reduced pan juices over the pork.

PER SERVING | Calories: 576 | Fat: 28 g | Protein: 67 g | Sodium: 824 mg | Fiber: 1 g | Carbohydrates: 8 g | Sugar: 2 g

Polynesian Pork Chops

You can substitute pork steaks for the pork chops. (Because pork steaks tend to have more marbling, there's actually less chance of pork steaks drying out when prepared this way.)

INGREDIENTS | SERVES 6

6 (6-ounce) boneless pork chops

1 green bell pepper, seeded and diced

1 large onion, diced

2 cups converted rice

1 teaspoon sea salt

1 (20-ounce) can crushed pineapple

1 cup gluten-free honey-mustard barbecue sauce

3 cups water

½ teaspoon ground black pepper

1. Treat the slow cooker with nonstick cooking spray. Trim and discard any fat from the pork chops and then cut them into bite-sized pieces.

2. Arrange half of the pork on the bottom of the slow cooker. Top with the bell pepper, onion, and rice. Sprinkle with salt and place the remaining pork over the rice.

3. In a small bowl, combine the entire can of pineapple, barbecue sauce, water, and black pepper; stir to mix and then pour into the slow cooker. Cover and cook on low for 8 hours or until the pork is cooked through and the rice is tender.

4. Stir the mixture in the slow cooker to fluff the rice. Taste for seasoning and add additional salt, barbecue sauce, and pepper if needed.

PER SERVING | Calories: 576 | Fat: 6 g | Protein: 43 g | Sodium: 949 mg | Fiber: 4 g | Carbohydrates: 82 g | Sugar: 25 g

Tomato-Braised Pork

In this recipe pork is gently cooked in tomatoes to yield incredibly tender meat.

INGREDIENTS | SERVES 4

28 ounces canned crushed tomatoes

3 tablespoons tomato paste

1 cup loosely packed fresh basil

½ teaspoon freshly ground black pepper

½ teaspoon marjoram

1¼ pounds boneless pork roast

1. Place the tomatoes, tomato paste, basil, pepper, and marjoram into a greased 4-quart slow cooker. Stir to create a uniform sauce. Add the pork.

2. Cook on low for 7–8 hours or until the pork easily falls apart when poked with a fork. Serve pork and sauce over cooked rice or polenta with a salad on the side.

PER SERVING | Calories: 226 | Fat: 5 g | Protein: 34 g | Sodium: 176 mg | Fiber: 3 g | Carbohydrates: 10 g | Sugar: 7 g

Glazed Lean Pork Shoulder

Apples and apple cider form a glaze over a long cooking time that is both flavorful and light. Use crisp, in-season apples for best results.

INGREDIENTS | SERVES 8

3 pounds bone-in pork shoulder, excess fat removed

3 apples, thinly sliced

¼ cup apple cider

1 tablespoon brown sugar

1 teaspoon allspice

½ teaspoon cinnamon

¼ teaspoon nutmeg

Place the pork shoulder into a 4-quart slow cooker. Top with the remaining ingredients. Cook on low for 8 hours. Remove the lid and cook on high for 30 minutes or until the sauce thickens.

PER SERVING | Calories: 218 | Fat: 5 g | Protein: 31 g | Sodium: 69 mg | Fiber: 1 g | Carbohydrates: 10 g | Sugar: 8 g

Red Wine–Braised Pork Tenderloin Roast

This roast is simmered in red wine and beef broth for a tender and delicious meal. Serve with Simple Garlic Mashed Potatoes (see Chapter 6) and sautéed fennel or steamed broccoli.

INGREDIENTS | SERVES 6

2 pounds boneless pork tenderloin roast

1 tablespoon dried onion flakes

¼ teaspoon freshly ground black pepper

¼ teaspoon salt

2 teaspoons garlic powder

1 cup warm water

¾ cup red wine

1 teaspoon gluten-free beef bouillon granules or 1 cube of gluten-free beef bouillon

1. Place the pork roast into a greased 4-quart slow cooker.
2. In a large bowl whisk together the dried onion flakes, black pepper, salt, and garlic powder. Pour in the water, red wine, and bouillon and whisk everything together thoroughly.
3. Pour red wine mixture over the pork roast. Cover and cook on low for 4 hours or on high for 3 hours. Because pork tenderloin is such a lean cut you do not want to overcook this meat.

PER SERVING | Calories: 218 | Fat: 5 g | Protein: 33 g | Sodium: 174 mg | Fiber: 0 g | Carbohydrates: 2 g | Sugar: 0 g

Bubble and Squeak

Adding some ham and bacon to this traditional British dish makes it a complete meal, even if you choose to serve it without a salad.

INGREDIENTS | SERVES 6

6 strips bacon, cut into pieces

2 stalks celery, finely diced

3 large carrots, peeled and grated

1 medium yellow onion, peeled and diced

2 zucchini, grated and squeezed dry

3 large potatoes, peeled and diced

½ cup ham, chopped

3 cups coleslaw mix

1 teaspoon salt

½ teaspoon freshly ground black pepper

1. Place bacon, celery, carrots, onion, zucchini, potatoes, and ham into a 4-quart slow cooker. Cover and cook on high for 3 hours or until the potatoes are soft enough to mash down. Use the back of a large spoon or ladle to press the mixture down into the slow cooker to compress it.
2. Spread the coleslaw mix over the ham mixture. Cover and continue to cook on high for 30 minutes or until the cabbage is tender. If necessary, leave the pan over the heat until any excess moisture from the cabbage and zucchini evaporates. Season with salt and pepper. To serve, spoon portions directly from the slow cooker.

PER SERVING | Calories: 438 | Fat: 25 g | Protein: 13 g | Sodium: 1,061 mg | Fiber: 7 g | Carbohydrates: 37 g | Sugar: 6 g

Orange Honey–Glazed Ham

Many people are intimidated by making ham. Using the slow cooker makes it super easy and the homemade orange honey glaze is a breeze to mix up.

INGREDIENTS | SERVES 6

1 (4-pound) bone-in gluten-free ham (discard glaze or seasoning packet)

½ cup seltzer water

½ cup orange juice

¼ cup honey

1–2 tablespoons orange zest

1 teaspoon ground cloves

¼ teaspoon cinnamon

1. Place ham, seltzer water, and orange juice in a greased 4–6-quart slow cooker. Cook on low for 6–8 hours or on high for 3–4 hours.

2. In a small bowl mix together honey, orange zest, ground cloves, and cinnamon. Spread over ham. Cook for an additional 45 minutes to an hour, venting the slow cooker lid with a chopstick or spoon handle. The ham should become golden brown and glazed. If necessary, finish off ham in 350°F oven for 15–20 minutes to get a shiny glaze.

PER SERVING | Calories: 479 | Fat: 22 g | Protein: 47 g | Sodium: 2,345 mg | Fiber: 0.5 g | Carbohydrates: 20 g | Sugar: 14 g

Easy Brown Sugar Spiral-Sliced Ham

Making a holiday meal doesn't have to be hard or require a ton of ingredients! This super easy ham is simply rubbed with brown sugar, which beautifully caramelizes during slow cooking.

INGREDIENTS | SERVES 16

1 (8-pound) spiral sliced gluten-free ham (discard glaze packet)

1 cup brown sugar

Make Your Own Brown Sugar

Out of brown sugar? Simply cream together 1 cup of sugar with 2–3 tablespoons of dark molasses. Mix well with a fork until mixture has the appearance of regular brown sugar. Store in an airtight container.

Remove ham from packaging. Rub entire ham with the brown sugar. Place ham on the bottom of a greased 6-quart (or larger) oval slow cooker. Cook on low for 6–8 hours or on high for 3–4 hours.

PER SERVING | Calories: 446 | Fat: 21 g | Protein: 49.5 g | Sodium: 1,571 mg | Fiber: 0 g | Carbohydrates: 14.5 g | Sugar: 13 g

Holiday Recipes

Ham and Sweet Potatoes

Serve this dish with a tossed salad, some applesauce, a steamed vegetable, and some warm Buttermilk Gluten-Free Drop Biscuits (Chapter 14).

INGREDIENTS | SERVES 6

1 (20-ounce) can pineapple tidbits

1 (2-pound) boneless ham steak

3 large sweet potatoes, peeled and diced

1 large sweet onion, peeled and diced

½ cup orange marmalade

2 cloves of garlic, peeled and minced

¼ teaspoon freshly ground black pepper

½ teaspoon dried parsley

1 tablespoon brown sugar

1. Drain the pineapple, reserving 2 tablespoons of the juice.

2. Trim the ham of any fat and cut it into bite-sized pieces. Add the pineapple, 2 tablespoons pineapple juice, and ham to the slow cooker along with the sweet potatoes, onion, marmalade, garlic, black pepper, parsley, and brown sugar. Stir to combine.

3. Cover and cook on low for 6 hours.

PER SERVING | Calories: 451 | Fat: 14 g | Protein: 35 g | Sodium: 1,131 mg | Fiber: 4 g | Carbohydrates: 48 g | Sugar: 31 g

Spiced Apple Cider Turkey

This recipe makes candied sweet potatoes while it cooks the turkey in the brown sugar–cider sauce.

INGREDIENTS | SERVES 8

1 (3-pound) boneless turkey breast

½ teaspoon salt

½ teaspoon freshly ground black pepper

2 gala, fuji, or honeycrisp apples, peeled, cored, and sliced

4 large sweet potatoes, peeled and cut in half

½ cup apple cider or apple juice

½ teaspoon ground cinnamon

¼ teaspoon ground cloves

¼ teaspoon ground allspice

2 tablespoons brown sugar

1. Treat a 4–6 quart slow cooker with nonstick spray. Add turkey breast and season it with salt and pepper.

2. Arrange the apple slices over and around the turkey.

3. Add the sweet potato halves to the slow cooker.

4. In a small bowl combine the cider or juice, cinnamon, cloves, allspice, and brown sugar. Stir to combine and pour over the ingredients in the slow cooker.

5. Cover and cook on low for 5–6 hours or until the internal temperature of the turkey is 170°F.

PER SERVING | Calories: 282 | Fat: 1 g | Protein: 42 g | Sodium: 267 mg | Fiber: 3 g | Carbohydrates: 23 g | Sugar: 11 g

Pork Steaks in Apple and Prune Sauce

Serve this dish over mashed potatoes (available ready-made in most supermarket refrigerator or freezer cases: double check ingredients to make sure they are gluten-free) and alongside easy "steam-in-the-bag" green beans.

INGREDIENTS | SERVES 6

12 pitted prunes (dried plums)

3 pounds boneless pork steaks, trimmed of fat

2 Granny Smith apples, peeled, cored, and sliced

¾ cup dry white wine or apple juice

¾ cup heavy cream

1 teaspoon salt

½ teaspoon freshly ground pepper

1 tablespoon red currant jelly

1 tablespoon butter

1. Add the prunes, pork steak, apple slices, wine or apple juice, and cream to a 4-quart or larger slow cooker. Sprinkle with salt and pepper. Cover and cook on low for 6 hours.

2. Remove the pork from the slow cooker and keep warm. Skim the fat from the liquid in the slow cooker, and use an immersion blender to blend the fruit into the creamy broth.

3. Cook uncovered on high for 30 minutes or until the pan juices begin to bubble around the edges. Reduce the setting to low or simmer, and cook for 15 more minutes or until the mixture is reduced by half and thickened.

4. Whisk in the red currant jelly. Taste for seasoning and add more salt and pepper if needed. Whisk in the butter. Ladle the sauce over the meat or pour it into a heated gravy boat.

PER SERVING | Calories: 504 | Fat: 20 g | Protein: 51 g | Sodium: 516 mg | Fiber: 2 g | Carbohydrates: 21 g | Sugar: 14 g

Asian-Inspired Turkey Breast

A 3-pound turkey breast or roast will yield about 8 (4-ounce) servings. If you prefer larger portions, adjust the servings or increase the size of the roast. If you do the latter, you may need to increase the cooking time to ensure the poultry reaches the correct internal temperature.

INGREDIENTS | SERVES 8

½ cup orange marmalade

1 tablespoon fresh ginger, peeled and grated

1 clove of garlic, peeled and minced

½ teaspoon Chinese five-spice powder

1 teaspoon salt

½ teaspoon freshly ground black pepper

¼ cup orange juice

1 (3-pound) turkey breast or roast

1. Add the marmalade, ginger, garlic, five-spice powder, salt, pepper, and orange juice to a 4–6 quart slow cooker. Stir to mix.

2. Place the turkey breast or roast into the slow cooker. Spoon some of the sauce over the meat. Cover and cook on low for 8 hours or until the internal temperature of the meat is 170°F.

PER SERVING | Calories: 240 | Fat: 1 g | Protein: 41 g | Sodium: 388 mg | Fiber: 0 g | Carbohydrates: 14 g | Sugar: 12 g

Red Wine Pot Roast

A little bit of wine goes a long way in flavoring this simple one-crock meal. Using lean meat creates a light and delicate broth surrounding the vegetables.

INGREDIENTS | SERVES 6

⅓ cup red wine

½ cup water

4 red skin potatoes, quartered

3 carrots, cut into thirds

2 bulbs fennel, quartered

2 rutabagas, peeled and quartered

1 onion, sliced

4 cloves garlic, sliced

1½ pounds lean top round roast, excess fat removed

½ teaspoon salt

½ teaspoon freshly ground black pepper

1. Pour the wine and water into a greased 4-quart slow cooker. Add the potatoes, carrots, fennel, rutabagas, onion, and garlic. Stir.

2. Add the roast. Sprinkle with salt and pepper. Cook on low for 8 hours.

3. Remove and slice the beef. Use a slotted spoon to serve the vegetables. Discard the cooking liquid.

PER SERVING | Calories: 356 | Fat: 5 g | Protein: 31 g | Sodium: 366 mg | Fiber: 10 g | Carbohydrates: 44 g | Sugar: 11 g

Caribbean Chicken Curry

Traditional Jamaican curries are cooked for long periods of time on the stovetop, making them a logical fit for the slow cooker. The spices meld together and the chicken is very tender.

INGREDIENTS | SERVES 8

1 tablespoon Madras curry powder

1 teaspoon allspice

½ teaspoon ground cloves

½ teaspoon ground nutmeg

1 teaspoon ground ginger

2 pounds boneless, skinless chicken thighs, cubed

1 teaspoon canola oil

1 onion, chopped

2 cloves garlic, chopped

2 jalapeños, chopped, seeds removed

½ pound red skin potatoes, cubed

⅓ cup light coconut milk

1. In a medium bowl, whisk together the curry powder, allspice, cloves, nutmeg, and ginger. Add the chicken and toss to coat each piece evenly.

2. Place the chicken in a nonstick skillet and quickly sauté until the chicken starts to brown. Add to a 4-quart slow cooker along with the remaining spice mixture.

3. Heat the oil in a nonstick skillet and sauté the onion, garlic, and jalapeños until fragrant, about 3–5 minutes. Add to the slow cooker.

4. Add the potatoes and coconut milk to the slow cooker. Stir. Cook 7–8 hours on low.

PER SERVING | Calories: 189 | Fat: 7 g | Protein: 23 g | Sodium: 100 mg | Fiber: 1 g | Carbohydrates: 7 g | Sugar: 1 g

Bacon-Wrapped Leg of Lamb

Serve this holiday classic with steamed asparagus, cranberries, and mashed potatoes. Don't forget to make gravy (see sidebar) with the savory drippings from this delicious cut of meat.

INGREDIENTS | SERVES 4

1 (4-pound) bone-in leg of lamb

3 cloves of garlic, slivered into small spears

½ teaspoon salt

½ teaspoon pepper

8 slices bacon

1 tablespoon olive oil

Gluten-Free Lamb Gravy

Place 1 tablespoon of oil or butter in a small saucepan. Whisk in 2–3 tablespoons of brown rice flour. Cook the flour for a minute, whisking constantly so it doesn't burn. Add 1–2 cups of lamb drippings (and adding additional gluten-free chicken or beef broth if needed), and whisk over medium heat until gravy thickens. Add salt and pepper if needed. Keep gravy warm in a small 1½-quart slow cooker until dinner is served.

1. Make about 24 cuts about ½" deep evenly around the lamb. Place a garlic spear into each slit. Sprinkle salt and pepper over lamb.

2. Lay bacon evenly over and around the lamb. To keep the bacon in place, attach with toothpick halves. Drizzle lamb with olive oil.

3. Cook on high for 3–4 hours or low for 6–8 hours depending on how well done you prefer the lamb. Check the lamb after 2½ hours on high for a medium rare roast. You can also use a meat thermometer. For medium rare the internal temperature should reach 140–150°F; for well done the temperature should reach 160°F or above.

PER SERVING | Calories: 882 | Fat: 51 g | Protein: 97 g | Sodium: 959 mg | Fiber: 0 g | Carbohydrates: 1 g | Sugar: 0 g

Sweet Potato Casserole

This is a welcome side dish at almost any holiday buffet.

INGREDIENTS | SERVES 8

2 (29-ounce) cans sweet potatoes
⅓ cup plus 2 tablespoons butter, melted
2 tablespoons white sugar
2 tablespoons plus ⅓ cup brown sugar
1 tablespoon orange juice
2 large eggs, beaten
½ cup whole milk
⅓ cup chopped pecans
2 tablespoons brown rice flour

1. Drain the sweet potatoes, add to a bowl, and mash them together with ⅓ cup butter, white sugar, and 2 tablespoons brown sugar.

2. Stir in orange juice, eggs, and milk. Transfer the sweet potato mixture into a greased 4-quart slow cooker.

3. In a small bowl mix together 2 tablespoons butter, ⅓ cup brown sugar, pecans, and flour. Use a fork to thoroughly blend. Sprinkle over the sweet potatoes. Cover and cook on low for 6 hours.

PER SERVING | Calories: 396 | Fat: 15 g | Protein: 5 g | Sodium: 140 mg | Fiber: 7 g | Carbohydrates: 60 g | Sugar: 25 g

Creamed Corn

This recipe is definitely not for someone on a low-fat or low-carb diet. The cream cheese helps make the rich sauce for the corn.

INGREDIENTS | SERVES 12

4 cups frozen whole-kernel corn
1 (8-ounce) package cream cheese
½ cup butter
½ cup whole milk
1 tablespoon white sugar
½ teaspoon salt
½ teaspoon freshly ground black pepper

1. Add the corn to a 2.5–4-quart slow cooker. Cube the cream cheese and slice the butter; add them to the slow cooker along with the milk, sugar, salt, and pepper. Stir to combine.

2. Cover and cook on low for 4 hours. After 2 hours, stir the corn mixture and watch carefully.

3. Switch the slow cooker to the warm setting as soon as the cream sauce is thickened; keep warm until ready to serve. Otherwise, the corn can scorch and change flavor if the heat is left too high for too long.

PER SERVING | Calories: 195 | Fat: 14 g | Protein: 3 g | Sodium: 166 mg | Fiber: 1 g | Carbohydrates: 15 g | Sugar: 4 g

Hot German Potato Salad

Serve this with grilled brats and chilled mugs of ice cold gluten-free beer such as Red Bridge, Bard's Tale, or New Grist.

INGREDIENTS | SERVES 6

6 baking potatoes

1 small red onion, peeled and diced

3 stalks celery, diced

1 small green bell pepper, seeded and diced

¼ cup apple cider vinegar

½ cup water

¼ cup light olive or vegetable oil

2 tablespoons sugar

½ teaspoon celery seeds

¼ cup fresh flat-leaf parsley, minced

6 strips bacon, cooked until crisp, drained, and crumbled

1 teaspoon salt

½ teaspoon freshly ground black pepper

1. Scrub the potatoes; slice them into ¼-inch slices and add to a greased 6-quart slow cooker. Add the onion, celery, and bell pepper; stir to mix.

2. In a small bowl combine the vinegar, water, oil, sugar, and celery seeds. Whisk to mix and then pour into the slow cooker.

3. Cover and cook on low for 4 hours or until the potatoes are cooked through.

4. Stir in the parsley and crumbled bacon. Season with salt and pepper. Serve hot.

PER SERVING | Calories: 461 | Fat: 26 g | Protein: 12 g | Sodium: 937 mg | Fiber: 4 g | Carbohydrates: 45 g | Sugar: 7 g

Swap Bacon for Sausage

You can omit the oil and bacon and instead add 8 ounces of diced smoked sausage in Step 1. The fat that renders from the sausage should be sufficient to offset the vinegar; however, if you think it's too tart when you taste the dish for seasoning, you can stir in a little vegetable oil when you add the salt and pepper.

Hoppin' John

Hoppin' John is traditionally eaten on New Year's Day. Eating it with your first meal that day is supposed to ensure health and prosperity for the coming year.

INGREDIENTS | SERVES 8

1 cup dried black-eyed peas, rinsed and soaked for 8 hours or overnight

¾ cup water or Vegetable Stock (see Chapter 3)

1 teaspoon liquid smoke flavoring

1 teaspoon red pepper flakes

3 cups diced mustard or collard greens

14 ounces canned, diced tomatoes

½ teaspoon freshly ground black pepper

¼ teaspoon salt

1 teaspoon dried oregano

Place all ingredients into a 4-quart slow cooker. Stir. Cook on high for 5 hours. Serve this savory bean stew as a side-dish at your next New Year's Day party.

PER SERVING | Calories: 83 | Fat: 0 g | Protein: 6 g | Sodium: 150 mg | Fiber: 3 g | Carbohydrates: 15 g | Sugar: 3 g

Quick Prep for Black-Eyed Peas

Instead of soaking the black-eyed peas overnight, you can do a "quick soak." Place black-eyed peas in a large stockpot. Cover completely with water, and bring to a boil. Boil 2 minutes, reduce heat, and simmer for 1 hour.

Lemon-Garlic Green Beans

Lemon zest and sliced garlic add a fresh and bright flavor to these slow-cooked green beans.

INGREDIENTS | SERVES 4

1½ pounds fresh green beans, trimmed

3 tablespoons olive oil

3 large shallots, cut into thin wedges

6 cloves garlic, sliced

1 tablespoon grated lemon zest

½ teaspoon salt

½ teaspoon pepper

½ cup water

1. Place green beans in a greased 4-quart slow cooker. Add remaining ingredients over the top of the beans.

2. Cook on high for 4–6 hours, or on low for 8–10 hours. If you like your beans more crisp, check them on high after about 3½ hours or on low after about 6 hours. Fresh green beans are sturdy enough to withstand very long cooking temperatures without getting mushy.

PER SERVING | Calories: 182 | Fat: 10 g | Protein: 4 g | Sodium: 309 mg | Fiber: 6 g | Carbohydrates: 21 g | Sugar: 9 g

Slow Cooker Stuffing

Thanksgiving simply wouldn't be complete without stuffing on the table. The key to a really good gluten-free stuffing is to find or make a gluten-free bread that is very dry and somewhat dense.

INGREDIENTS | SERVES 6

6 cups toasted, cubed, and very dry gluten-free bread

½ cup butter

1 cup diced onion

1 cup diced celery

1½ teaspoons salt

1 teaspoon pepper

2 tablespoons poultry seasoning

1 pound gluten-free mild pork sausage

2½ cups gluten-free chicken broth

Gluten-Free Bread—Worth the Expense?

Store-bought gluten-free bread is expensive. It's less expensive to buy gluten-free baking ingredients, but either way you're spending more money than you would have for wheat bread. If you plan on keeping gluten-free bread in your diet (and sometimes that sandwich is just worth it!), make sure to save leftovers in a zip-top bag in your freezer for recipes like this.

1. Place bread cubes in a very large bowl and set aside. Melt butter in a large sauté pan over medium-high heat. When warm and sizzling, add onion and celery. Sauté until onion is translucent, about 3–5 minutes. Add salt, pepper, and poultry seasoning. Pour onion and butter mixture over bread cubes in bowl.

2. Add sausage to the sauté pan, breaking it up into small pieces. Brown sausage until completely cooked through. Pour sausage into stuffing mixture in bowl. Stir together thoroughly.

3. Pour stuffing into a greased 4-quart slow cooker. Slowly add chicken broth. If you prefer a moister dressing add additional chicken broth until desired consistency is reached.

4. Cook stuffing on high for 3–4 hours or on low for 6–8 hours. During the last hour and a half of cooking vent the lid of the slow cooker with a chopstick to let excess moisture escape.

PER SERVING | Calories: 367 | Fat: 20 g | Protein: 22 g | Sodium: 1,263 mg | Fiber: 2 g | Carbohydrates: 23 g | Sugar: 2 g

Honey-Ginger Carrots

Carrots and honey are a naturally delicious pair. Honey brings out the pure sweetness in baby carrots and fresh ginger gives this dish extra bite!

INGREDIENTS | SERVES 4

1 (16-ounce) package baby carrots, peeled
2 tablespoons orange juice
1 tablespoon honey
½ teaspoon freshly grated ginger
1 tablespoon orange zest
1 tablespoon fresh parsley

Storing Orange, Lemon, and Lime Zest

To keep fresh citrus zest on hand at all times, freeze it! Place zest in snack-sized zip-top bags and take out as much as you need when it's called for in a recipe. The zest should stay fresh for up to 6 months in the freezer.

1. Place baby carrots in a greased 2.5-quart slow cooker.

2. In a small bowl mix together orange juice, honey, ginger, and orange zest. Pour over carrots. Cook on high for 3–4 hours or on low for 6–7 hours until carrots are fork tender.

3. Serve carrots by spooning a little bit of the honey-orange sauce over them and then sprinkling a little bit of fresh parsley over each plate.

PER SERVING | Calories: 61 | Fat: 0 g | Protein: 1 g | Sodium: 88 mg | Fiber: 3 g | Carbohydrates: 15 g | Sugar: 10 g

Candied Butternut Squash

Butternut squash has a delicious natural sweetness and is an excellent replacement for sweet potatoes. Also, you can now buy ready-cut and peeled butternut squash in many grocery stores (in the produce section), making this recipe incredibly easy to assemble.

INGREDIENTS | SERVES 4

4–5 cups butternut squash, peeled, seeded, and cubed
⅓ cup brown sugar
2 tablespoons molasses
1 tablespoon orange zest
½ teaspoon ground cinnamon
½ teaspoon ground cloves

Add all ingredients to a greased 4-quart slow cooker. Cook on high for 3–4 hours or on low for 6–8 hours, until squash is fork tender.

PER SERVING | Calories: 181 | Fat: 0 g | Protein: 1 g | Sodium: 16 mg | Fiber: 4 g | Carbohydrates: 47 g | Sugar: 27 g

Butternut Squash Versus Sweet Potatoes

Wondering which might be better for you? Actually both are extremely healthy choices. Per cup, sweet potatoes have more fiber and protein than the squash, but one cup of butternut squash contains fewer calories, less overall carbohydrates, and the least amount of natural sugar. Both are high in vitamins A and C, and very low in sodium. In many recipes, they can be used interchangeably.

Sweet Citrus Cranberry Sauce

This combination of cranberries, brown sugar, orange and pineapple juice, simmered slowly during the day, will leave a wonderful aroma in your kitchen!

INGREDIENTS | SERVES 8

2 (12-ounce) packages fresh cranberries
Zest of 1 large orange
2 teaspoons cinnamon
1 cup pineapple juice
1 cup orange juice
1 cup brown sugar
1 cup sugar
1 cup water

1. Rinse cranberries through a strainer and toss out any bad ones. Pour cranberries into a greased 2.5-quart slow cooker.

2. Zest the orange with a microplane grater or citrus zester. Sprinkle zest over cranberries. Add cinnamon, pineapple juice, orange juice, brown sugar, sugar, and water to the cranberries.

3. Cook on high for 4 hours or on low for 8 hours. In the last 2 hours of cooking vent slow cooker with a chopstick or spoon handle to allow excess moisture to escape the slow cooker.

4. Serve hot or cold. If serving hot, the sauce will be thinner than most cranberry sauces, but is delicious on ham or turkey. To serve cold, refrigerate 8 hours or overnight. The sauce will thicken after cooling.

PER SERVING | Calories: 284 | Fat: 0 g | Protein: 0 g | Sodium: 12 mg | Fiber: 5 g | Carbohydrates: 73 g | Sugar: 63 g

Old-Fashioned Chocolate Cobbler

This chocolate dessert creates its own chocolate sauce underneath the thick, fudgy cake layer. Don't be alarmed if the appearance is not that of a normal cake. It's meant to be served with ice cream or whipped cream on top!

INGREDIENTS | SERVES 8

4 tablespoons butter, melted
1 cup brown rice flour
½ teaspoon baking powder
¼ teaspoon salt
½ cup plus ⅓ cup sugar, divided
2 tablespoons plus ¼ cup cocoa powder, divided
1 teaspoon vanilla
¾ cup 2% milk
1 egg
1¼ cups boiling water

1. Pour butter in the bottom of a greased 4-quart slow cooker.

2. In a small bowl whisk together the flour, baking powder, salt, ½ cup sugar, and 2 tablespoons cocoa powder. Stir in the vanilla, milk, and egg. Pour the batter into the slow cooker and spread it evenly. The butter will probably come up around the edges of the batter, this is okay.

3. Sprinkle ⅓ cup sugar and ¼ cup cocoa powder over the cake batter. Pour the boiling hot water over the entire cake.

4. Cook on low 2½–3 hours or on high for 1½–2 hours, or until a toothpick inserted in the middle of the cake portion comes out clean. Remove the slow cooker insert and set it on top of several pot holders or a heat-safe surface and allow to cool for 20–30 minutes. This will allow the "lava" or pudding underneath to thicken and set.

5. Serve warm with ice-cream or whipped cream.

PER SERVING | Calories: 238 | Fat: 8 g | Protein: 3 g | Sodium: 125 mg | Fiber: 2 g | Carbohydrates: 40 g | Sugar: 22 g

Pumpkin Custard

With this warm and spicy custard (which can be served hot or cold), you won't have to miss out just because you're gluten-free! Top each serving with whipped cream and chopped pecans.

INGREDIENTS | SERVES 8

¾ cup sugar

½ teaspoon salt

2 teaspoons cinnamon

1 teaspoon ginger

½ teaspoon cloves

½ cup sorghum flour or brown rice flour

½ teaspoon baking soda

3 large eggs, beaten

1 (14-ounce) can evaporated milk

1 (15-ounce) can pure pumpkin purée

2 tablespoons olive oil

Nuts about Coconut Milk

For those who are intolerant to dairy, coconut milk can be an excellent substitute in baked goods such as this pumpkin custard. You can use 1 (13.5-ounce) can of full-fat coconut milk in place of the evaporated milk called for; your guests will never know it's gluten *and* dairy free!

1. In a small bowl whisk together sugar, salt, cinnamon, ginger, cloves, flour, and baking soda.

2. Make a well in the center of the dry ingredients and add the eggs, evaporated milk, pumpkin purée, and olive oil. Whisk together ingredients thoroughly until you have a smooth batter.

3. Pour batter into a greased 4-quart slow cooker. Cover and vent the lid of the slow cooker with a chopstick or the handle of a spoon, to allow excess moisture to escape the slow cooker. Cook on high for 3–4 hours or on low for 6–8 hours.

4. Custard is done when a toothpick inserted in the middle comes out mostly clean. You can serve the custard warm or cold. (Most people prefer it cold.) Refrigerate the slow cooker insert for 8 hours or overnight before serving.

PER SERVING | Calories: 256 | Fat: 10 g | Protein: 8 g | Sodium: 308 mg | Fiber: 3 g | Carbohydrates: 37 g | Sugar: 25 g

Crustless Apple Pie

You may need to adjust the cooking time depending on the type of apples you use. A softer Golden Delicious should be cooked through and soft in the recommended cooking times, but a crisper Granny Smith, Roma, or Gala apple may take longer.

INGREDIENTS | SERVES 8

8 medium apples, cored, peeled, and sliced
3 tablespoons orange juice
3 tablespoons water
½ cup pecans, chopped
⅓ cup brown sugar
¼ cup butter, melted
½ teaspoon cinnamon
2 cups whipped heavy cream

1. Treat a 4-quart slow cooker with nonstick spray. Arrange apple slices on the bottom of the slow cooker.

2. In a small bowl combine the orange juice and water; stir to mix. Evenly drizzle over the apples.

3. In a separate bowl combine the pecans, brown sugar, butter, and cinnamon. Mix well. Evenly crumble the pecan mixture over the apples. Cover and cook on high for 2 hours or on low for 4 hours.

4. Serve warm or chilled, topped with whipped cream.

PER SERVING | Calories: 420 | Fat: 33 g | Protein: 2 g | Sodium: 26 mg | Fiber: 3 g | Carbohydrates: 32 g | Sugar: 26 g

Spiced Cider

The aroma of this warming cider will fill your whole house!

INGREDIENTS | SERVES 20

2 cinnamon sticks
1" chunk fresh ginger, peeled
1 tablespoon whole cloves
1 gallon apple cider
1 tablespoon dark brown sugar
½ teaspoon ground nutmeg

How to Make a Cheesecloth Packet

Place the items to be enclosed in the packet on a length of cheesecloth. Cut out a square about three times larger than the area the items take up. Pull all ends toward the middle and tie closed with kitchen twine.

1. Place the cinnamon sticks, ginger, and cloves into a cheesecloth packet. Place the packet, the cider, brown sugar, and nutmeg into a 6-quart slow cooker. Stir until the sugar dissolves.

2. Cook on high for 2–3 hours or until very hot. Reduce to low to keep hot until serving. Remove packet after cooking if desired.

PER SERVING | Calories: 114 | Fat: 1 g | Protein: 1 g | Sodium: 10 mg | Fiber: 1 g | Carbohydrates: 27 g | Sugar: 20 g

CHAPTER 12

Kid-Friendly Meals

Peachy Cinnamon Bread Pudding

Peaches, sugar, cinnamon and gluten-free toast are combined to make a delicious morning breakfast casserole.

INGREDIENTS | SERVES 4

4 cups gluten-free bread cubes, toasted

1 cup sugar

½ teaspoon cinnamon

4 large eggs, beaten

1½ cups 2% milk

1 tablespoon vanilla extract

1½ cups peeled and sliced fresh peaches

⅓ cup butter, melted

2 tablespoons sugar mixed with 1 teaspoon cinnamon

1. In a large bowl mix together bread cubes, sugar, cinnamon, eggs, milk, and vanilla. Fold in the peaches.

2. Pour ingredients into a greased 4-quart slow cooker. Drizzle butter over the casserole. Sprinkle cinnamon and sugar over the butter.

3. Cook on high for 3–4 hours or on low for 6–8 hours until eggs are set.

PER SERVING | Calories: 583 | Fat: 24 g | Protein: 13 g | Sodium: 294 mg | Fiber: 2 g | Carbohydrates: 80 g | Sugar: 64 g

Cheesy Toast Casserole

Try this hearty cheese-filled casserole with tomato soup for a warming winter lunch.

INGREDIENTS | SERVES 4

4 cups day-old toasted gluten-free bread

4 eggs, beaten

1½ cups 2% milk

1 tablespoon Dijon mustard

2½ cups shredded Cheddar cheese, divided

½ teaspoon salt

½ teaspoon pepper

1. In a large bowl mix together bread, eggs, milk, mustard, and 1¼ cups cheese.

2. Pour the mixture into a greased 4-quart slow cooker. Top with remaining cheese, salt, and pepper.

3. Cook on high for 3 hours or on low for 5 hours until eggs are set.

PER SERVING | Calories: 496 | Fat: 32 g | Protein: 30 g | Sodium: 1,069 mg | Fiber: 1 g | Carbohydrates: 21 g | Sugar: 6 g

Simple Tomato Soup

This healthy, but kid-friendly soup is made with canned tomatoes which are available year round at affordable prices. You can also make this soup with about 4 pounds of chopped fresh tomatoes if you prefer.

INGREDIENTS | SERVES 8

1 small sweet onion, finely diced

3 tablespoons butter

3 (14.5-ounce) cans low-sodium diced tomatoes

1 tablespoon honey

1 (15-ounce) can gluten-free chicken broth

½ teaspoon salt

1. In a small glass or microwave-safe bowl cook onions and butter in the microwave on high for 1 minute to soften them.

2. Add onions, butter, tomatoes, honey, and chicken broth to a greased 4-quart slow cooker. Cook on high for 4 hours or on low for 8 hours.

3. After cooking period is over, turn off slow cooker. Add salt to the soup. Allow soup to cool for about 20 minutes and then blend using an immersion blender or by pouring the soup (a little at a time) into a kitchen blender.

PER SERVING | Calories: 95 | Fat: 5 g | Protein: 2 g | Sodium: 378 mg | Fiber: 2 g | Carbohydrates: 10 g | Sugar: 6 g

Taco Chili

Note that you don't drain any of the canned ingredients used in this recipe. You include the entire contents of each can.

INGREDIENTS | SERVES 8

3 pounds lean ground beef

1 (1.2-ounce) package gluten-free taco seasoning mix

2 (15-ounce) cans chunky Mexican-style tomatoes

1 (15-ounce) can red kidney beans

1 (15-ounce) can whole kernel corn

1. Brown the ground beef in a large nonstick skillet over medium heat, for approximately 5–6 minutes, breaking apart the meat as you do so. Remove and discard any fat rendered from the meat before transferring it to a greased 4-quart slow cooker.

2. Add the taco seasoning mix, tomatoes, beans, and corn to the slow cooker and stir to combine. Cover and cook on low for 4–6 hours.

PER SERVING | Calories: 466 | Fat: 10 g | Protein: 50 g | Sodium: 298 mg | Fiber: 15 g | Carbohydrates: 45 g | Sugar: 5 g

Baked Potato Soup

This soup has the flavor of a loaded or stuffed baked potato but with much less fat.

INGREDIENTS | SERVES 6

1 onion, sliced

4 russet potatoes, peeled and cubed

5 cups water

¼ teaspoon salt

½ teaspoon white pepper

¼ cup shredded sharp Cheddar

3 tablespoons reduced-fat sour cream

2 strips turkey bacon, cooked and crumbled

⅓ cup diced green onion

1. Place the onion, potatoes, water, salt, and pepper into a 4-quart slow cooker. Cook on low for 7 hours.

2. Purée using an immersion blender or in batches in a blender.

3. Stir in the cheese, sour cream, bacon crumbles, and green onion.

PER SERVING | Calories: 164 | Fat: 3 g | Protein: 6 g | Sodium: 153 mg | Fiber: 2 g | Carbohydrates: 28 g | Sugar: 2 g

Southwestern Cheese Soup

Serve this soup with a tossed salad and gluten-free corn chips. Use hot or mild green chiles (or leave them out altogether), according to your personal preference.

INGREDIENTS | SERVES 8

2 pounds lean ground beef

1 package gluten-free taco seasoning mix

1 (15-ounce) can whole kernel corn, undrained

1 (15-ounce) can kidney beans, undrained

1 (15-ounce) can diced tomatoes, undrained

2 (15-ounce) cans stewed tomatoes, undrained

1 (7-ounce) can green chiles, minced and drained

2 pounds Velveeta cheese, cut into cubes

1. Fry the ground beef in a large nonstick skillet over medium-high heat, for approximately 5–6 minutes, breaking it apart as you do so. Drain and discard any fat rendered from the beef.

2. Transfer the ground beef to a greased 4-quart slow cooker and stir in the taco seasoning mix.

3. Add the corn, beans, tomatoes, and chiles to the slow cooker. Stir to combine. Cover and cook on low for 4 hours.

4. Stir the cheese into the soup. Cover, stirring occasionally; continue to cook on low until the cheese is melted and blended into the soup.

PER SERVING | Calories: 656 | Fat: 37 g | Protein: 46 g | Sodium: 1,475 mg | Fiber: 6 g | Carbohydrates: 37 g | Sugar: 15 g

Tuxedo Soup

This soup, which gets its name from the bowtie pasta, is one that kids will love. If you cannot find gluten-free bowtie pasta, simply use your favorite shape of gluten-free pasta. Serve this thick and hearty soup with a tossed salad and gluten-free garlic bread.

INGREDIENTS | SERVES 8

1 pound lean ground beef

1 medium onion, diced

1 small green pepper, seeded and diced

1 stalk celery, diced

1 medium carrot, diced

4 cloves garlic, peeled and minced

2 (15-ounce) cans diced tomatoes, undrained

1 cup water

1 (26-ounce) jar spaghetti sauce

1 tablespoon sugar

½ teaspoon Italian seasoning

2 cups cooked gluten-free bowtie pasta

1 teaspoon salt

½ teaspoon freshly ground black pepper

½ cup grated Parmesan cheese

¼ cup minced fresh flat-leaf parsley

Extra Vegetables

Thanks to the spaghetti sauce, you can hide more vegetables in Tuxedo Soup and the kids won't even notice. For example, dice a few more carrots and stir them in with the other ingredients in Step 1.

1. Add the ground beef, onion, green pepper, celery, and carrot to a nonstick skillet and sauté over medium heat for about 8 minutes or until the vegetables are tender and the meat is no longer pink.

2. Stir in the garlic and sauté for an additional 30 seconds. Drain and discard any excess fat. Transfer to a greased 4–6-quart slow cooker.

3. Stir in the undrained tomatoes, water, spaghetti sauce, sugar, and Italian seasoning. Cover and cook on low for 6–8 hours.

4. Stir pasta into the soup. Thin the soup with additional hot water if needed. Add salt and pepper. Ladle into soup bowls. Sprinkle cheese and flat-leaf parsley over each serving.

PER SERVING | Calories: 248 | Fat: 6 g | Protein: 16 g | Sodium: 866 mg | Fiber: 5 g | Carbohydrates: 32 g | Sugar: 13 g

One-Pot Spaghetti and Meatballs

Here's a classic comfort food the whole family will enjoy. It takes a little extra work to make the homemade gluten-free meatballs, but your family will agree it's well worth the effort when they taste this fabulous one-pot meal.

INGREDIENTS | SERVES 4

1 slice gluten-free bread, torn in very small pieces

¼ cup 2% milk

1 pound ground beef

½ teaspoon salt

½ teaspoon pepper

1½ teaspoons dried onion

1 egg

1 tablespoon olive oil

1½ cups prepared spaghetti sauce

⅓ cup water

4 ounces gluten-free spaghetti, uncooked and broken into small pieces

1. In a large bowl mix together bread and milk. Set aside for 5 minutes. Add ground beef, salt, pepper, dried onion, and egg. Mix well and roll into small meatballs.

2. In a skillet over medium heat, cook the meatballs in small batches in the olive oil until they are browned, approximately 5–6 minutes. Add meatballs to a greased 2.5-quart slow cooker.

3. Add spaghetti sauce and water to the slow cooker. Cook on high for 4 hours or on low for 8 hours.

4. An hour before serving add in the spaghetti pieces and stir into the sauce. Cook spaghetti for an hour. Try not to overcook the pasta, as it will become mushy.

PER SERVING | Calories: 464 | Fat: 19 g | Protein: 30 g | Sodium: 475 mg | Fiber: 3.5 g | Carbohydrates: 39 g | Sugar: 10 g

Apples-and-Onions Pork Chops

Try Gala apples in this sweet and savory dish; they are crisp and sweet.

INGREDIENTS | SERVES 4

4 crisp, sweet apples

2 large onions, sliced

4 thick-cut boneless pork chops (about 1 pound)

½ teaspoon ground cayenne

½ teaspoon ground cinnamon

¼ teaspoon allspice

¼ teaspoon ground fennel

Slow Cooking with Boneless Pork

Not only is there less waste associated with boneless pork chops or roasts, there is often less fat attached to the meat as well. Even without much fat, boneless pork is well suited to slow cooking. All of the moisture stays in the dish, ensuring tender pork.

1. Cut the apples into wedges. Place half of the wedges in the bottom of a greased 4-quart slow cooker along with half of the sliced onions. Top with a single layer of pork chops. Sprinkle with cayenne, cinnamon, allspice, and fennel and top with the remaining apples and onions.

2. Cook on low for 8 hours.

PER SERVING | Calories: 343 | Fat: 6.5 g | Protein: 42 g | Sodium: 93 mg | Fiber: 3.5 g | Carbohydrates: 28 g | Sugar: 19 g

Pizza Pasta

Kids + pizza = very happy kids! If you can't find diced pepperoni (in addition to the sliced pepperoni) brown ½ pound of ground beef to use instead.

INGREDIENTS | SERVES 6

3 (14-ounce) jars pizza sauce

1 cup water

1 (8-ounce) package sliced pepperoni

1 (8-ounce) package diced pepperoni

1 (4-ounce) can sliced mushrooms, drained

8 ounces uncooked gluten-free spiral or elbow pasta

2 cups shredded mozzarella cheese

1. Add pizza sauce, water, pepperoni, and mushrooms to a greased 4-quart slow cooker. Cook on high for 3–4 hours or on low for 6–8 hours.

2. Forty-five minutes prior to serving, add the pasta. Stir the pasta into the sauce and cover the casserole with cheese. Cook for 1 more hour and serve when the cheese has melted and the pasta is al dente.

PER SERVING | Calories: 794 | Fat: 47 g | Protein: 33 g | Sodium: 2,153 mg | Fiber: 6.5 g | Carbohydrates: 56 g | Sugar: 19 g

Tex-Mex Pork

Many kids enjoy the flavors of Mexican spices as long as you don't make a dish too hot. Feel free to add more or less of the spices depending on your family's spiciness preference.

INGREDIENTS | SERVES 6

3 pounds boneless pork roast

1 packet gluten-free taco seasoning mix, such as McCormick's Taco Seasoning

1 teaspoon garlic powder

1 teaspoon cumin

½ teaspoon cayenne pepper

2 tablespoons lime juice

2 tablespoons chopped green chiles with juice

¾ cup water

1. Place pork roast into a greased 4-quart slow cooker.

2. In a small bowl mix together taco seasoning, garlic powder, cumin, cayenne pepper, lime juice, chiles, and water. Pour seasoning mixture over pork roast.

3. Cook on high for 4 hours or cook on low for 8 hours until pork is very tender.

PER SERVING | Calories: 288 | Fat: 8 g | Protein: 50 g | Sodium: 146 mg | Fiber: 0 g | Carbohydrates: 1 g | Sugar: 0 g

Easy Mac and Cheese

This is a popular dish for a pot-luck supper or buffet.

INGREDIENTS | SERVES 8

2 cups 2% milk

1 (2-pound) box Velveeta cheese

½ teaspoon salt

¼ teaspoon freshly ground black pepper

4 cups uncooked gluten-free elbow macaroni

1. Grease a 4-quart slow cooker with nonstick spray. Pour the milk into the slow cooker.

2. Cut the cheese into small cubes. Stir into the milk. Season with salt and pepper. Cover and cook on low for 1–2 hours until cheese is melted.

3. Add dry gluten-free pasta. Cover and cook on low for another 45 minutes to an hour, or until the cheese is completely melted and the pasta is al dente. Stir together thoroughly and serve hot.

PER SERVING | Calories: 571 | Fat: 27 g | Protein: 27 g | Sodium: 1,755 mg | Fiber: 2 g | Carbohydrates: 53 g | Sugar: 13 g

Hawaiian-Style Rice with Pineapple, Mango, and Macadamia Nuts

This is perfect with grilled or roasted ham, pork chops, or pork tenderloin. You can also add crumbled crisp bacon as an interesting garnish.

INGREDIENTS | SERVES 6

1 cup water
1½ cups orange juice
1½ cups short-grained rice
Minced zest of 1 orange
1 teaspoon salt
⅛ teaspoon Tabasco sauce
½ cup chopped pineapple
1 ripe mango, peeled and diced
2 tablespoons butter
½ cup toasted macadamia nuts

1. Bring the water and juice to a boil in a saucepan. Stir in the rice and then add mixture to a greased 2.5-quart slow cooker. Cook on high for 2 hours or on low for 4 hours.

2. Add the rest of the ingredients on top of the rice and cook an additional 30 minutes until warmed through.

PER SERVING | Calories: 349 | Fat: 12 g | Protein: 5 g | Sodium: 397 mg | Fiber: 2.5 g | Carbohydrates: 55 g | Sugar: 12 g

Ground Beef Hash

This dish has great potential to create a variety of meals that your family will love. You could add mushrooms, garlic, or chopped carrots, use chili powder instead of Italian seasoning, or top each serving with shredded cheese.

INGREDIENTS | SERVES 6

2 pounds ground beef
2 medium onions, chopped
2 (15-ounce) cans diced tomatoes
1 large green pepper, chopped
1 cup uncooked white rice
1 tablespoon gluten-free Worcestershire sauce
2 teaspoons Italian seasoning
½ teaspoon salt
½ teaspoon pepper

1. Brown ground beef and onions in a skillet, for approximately 3–5 minutes. Pour into a greased 4-quart slow cooker. Add remaining ingredients and stir to combine.

2. Cook on high for 2–3 hours or on low for 4–6 hours until rice is cooked through.

PER SERVING | Calories: 425 | Fat: 15 g | Protein: 33 g | Sodium: 525 mg | Fiber: 3 g | Carbohydrates: 36 g | Sugar: 5 g

Cheesy Potato Wedges

Who doesn't like fries? Kids are especially fond of these salty, usually crispy treats. While these potatoes don't crisp up as much as fried ones, they are definitely a salty, cheesy, and delicious treat that's much healthier than fast food!

INGREDIENTS | SERVES 4

2 pounds red potatoes

2 teaspoons dried onions

1 teaspoon oregano

½ teaspoon garlic salt

½ teaspoon black pepper

2 tablespoons olive oil

¼ cup grated Parmesan cheese

1. Wash and scrub potatoes. Pat dry and cut into ½" wedges.

2. Place dried onions, oregano, garlic salt, and pepper in a gallon-sized zip-top bag. Add the potatoes to the bag and shake to coat the potatoes.

3. Pour the potatoes into a greased 4-quart slow cooker. Drizzle with olive oil.

4. Cover and cook on high for 4 hours or on low for 6–8 hours. Midway through the cooking process lift the lid of the slow cooker and carefully pour out any liquids that have collected on the bottom. Cover and resume cooking until potatoes are fork tender.

5. Place potatoes on a platter and sprinkle with Parmesan cheese and additional salt and pepper if needed.

PER SERVING | Calories: 244 | Fat: 8.5 g | Protein: 6.5 g | Sodium: 403 mg | Fiber: 4 g | Carbohydrates: 36 g | Sugar: 2 g

Classic Beans and Franks

Use your favorite gluten-free hot dogs in this recipe. All-beef hot dogs in particular have a wonderfully rich taste that pairs well with the salty sweet baked beans!

INGREDIENTS | SERVES 6

¼ cup onion, finely diced

2 teaspoons butter

1 (16-ounce) can baked beans

1 (16-ounce) package gluten-free hot dogs, cut into ½" slices

⅓ cup brown sugar

1 teaspoon ground mustard

1 teaspoon celery salt

1. In a small glass or microwave-safe bowl, cook onion and butter on high for about 1 minute until soft. Pour into a greased 2.5-quart slow cooker.

2. Add baked beans, hot dogs, brown sugar, mustard, and celery salt to the onions and mix well.

3. Bake for 4 hours on high or for 8 hours on low.

PER SERVING | Calories: 351 | Fat: 22 g | Protein: 12 g | Sodium: 1,263 mg | Fiber: 4 g | Carbohydrates: 24 g | Sugar: 13 g

Shortcut Chicken Parmesan

With a savory Italian sauce and lots of gooey mozzarella cheese, you'll never miss the breading in this recipe! Serve it with gluten-free garlic bread and steamed broccoli.

INGREDIENTS | SERVES 4

2 pounds boneless, skinless chicken breasts

1 (15-ounce) can tomato sauce

1 (4-ounce) can tomato paste

1 tablespoon Italian seasoning

½ teaspoon dried basil

½ teaspoon garlic powder

½ teaspoon salt

½ teaspoon ground pepper

2 cups shredded mozzarella

½ cup grated Parmesan cheese

1. Place chicken in the bottom of a greased 4-quart slow cooker.

2. In a large bowl mix together tomato sauce, tomato paste, Italian seasoning, basil, garlic powder, salt, and pepper. Pour sauce over chicken. Cook on high for 3–4 hours or on low for 5–6 hours.

3. An hour prior to serving sprinkle cheeses on top of the tomato sauce. Cook for 45 minutes to an hour until cheeses are melted and gooey.

PER SERVING | Calories: 525 | Fat: 22 g | Protein: 67 g | Sodium: 1,568 mg | Fiber: 2.5 g | Carbohydrates: 12.5 g | Sugar: 8.5 g

Everyday Hot Dogs

This recipe may seem a bit obvious, but many people don't realize you can use the slow cooker to cook simple foods like hot dogs. The food will stay hot for hours while not overcooking. Increase the amount of water and hot dogs depending on how many people you need to feed.

INGREDIENTS | SERVES 8

About 3 cups water

8 gluten-free hot dogs

8 gluten-free hot dog buns

Hot Dog Wraps

If you don't have gluten-free hot dog buns available, you can make hot dog wraps with washed and dried romaine lettuce leaves.

1. Fill a 2.5-quart slow cooker halfway full with water.

2. Place hot dogs in water and cook on high for 3 hours or on low for 6 hours. If you need to keep hot dogs warm for longer, place the heat setting on warm for up to 2 additional hours.

3. Using tongs, remove hot dogs carefully and place them in buns for serving.

PER SERVING | Calories: 223 | Fat: 12 g | Protein: 10 g | Sodium: 572 mg | Fiber: 2 g | Carbohydrates: 28 g | Sugar: 3 g

Saucy Brown Sugar Chicken

Kids will love the sweet and sour flavors of brown sugar and Dijon mustard in this super simple slow cooker chicken. Serve chicken over cooked gluten-free pasta, rice, or steamed zucchini strips.

INGREDIENTS | SERVES 4

4 skinless, boneless chicken breasts

1 (12-ounce) jar peach salsa

¼ cup brown sugar

1 tablespoon Dijon mustard

Slow Cooker Sundays

If you have multiple slow cookers you can make several main dishes at one time on Sunday afternoons. The ready-made meals can then be frozen or stored in the refrigerator for up to 5 days. You will save money and time by having homemade slow-cooked meals already prepared.

1. Place chicken breasts in a greased 4-quart slow cooker.

2. In small bowl mix together salsa, brown sugar, and mustard. Pour over chicken.

3. Cook chicken for 3–4 hours on high or 6–8 hours on low.

PER SERVING | Calories: 326 | Fat: 6.5 g | Protein: 48 g | Sodium: 725 mg | Fiber: 1.5 g | Carbohydrates: 18 g | Sugar: 16 g

French Fry Casserole

Another kid favorite that the whole family will love. Frozen French fries, ground beef, and a simple gluten-free cream sauce make a tasty weeknight meal. Serve with a salad or steamed green beans.

INGREDIENTS | SERVES 4

1 pound ground beef
1 tablespoon butter
½ onion, finely diced
1 cup mushrooms, sliced
½ green pepper, diced
2 tablespoons cornstarch
1⅓ cups whole milk
½ teaspoon salt
½ teaspoon pepper
3 cups frozen gluten-free shoestring-cut French fries
¾ cup shredded Cheddar cheese

Gluten-Free Shortcuts

You can make several batches of gluten-free cream sauce at the beginning of the week to make meals even easier to put together. Simply make a batch, pour in a glass jar with an airtight lid, and store in the refrigerator for up to 1 week.

1. Brown ground beef in a skillet on medium heat for approximately 3–5 minutes. Pour cooked ground beef into a greased 2.5-quart or larger slow cooker.

2. In a medium-sized saucepan, melt butter. Add onion, mushrooms, and green pepper. Cook for 3–5 minutes until softened. Mix cornstarch with milk and slowly add to cooked vegetables. Whisk together for 5–10 minutes over medium heat until thickened.

3. Pour cream sauce over ground beef in slow cooker. Sprinkle with salt and pepper. Top casserole with French fries. Vent the lid of the slow cooker with a chopstick to prevent extra condensation on the fries. Cook on high for 3–4 hours or on low for 4–6 hours.

4. One hour prior to serving sprinkle cheese on casserole. Cook an additional 45 minutes to an hour until cheese is melted.

PER SERVING | Calories: 632 | Fat: 31 g | Protein: 34 g | Sodium: 1,095 mg | Fiber: 3.5 g | Carbohydrates: 52 g | Sugar: 6 g

Honey Mustard Chicken Fingers

This recipe uses a "foil rack" technique in your slow cooker to create chicken fingers that stay relatively crunchy with the kick of sweet honey mustard sauce.

INGREDIENTS | SERVES 6

4 large boneless, skinless chicken breasts, patted dry and cut into strips

1 egg, beaten

1½ cups gluten-free bread crumbs or 1½ cups blanched almond flour

⅓ cup honey

⅓ cup Dijon mustard

1 teaspoon dried basil

1 teaspoon paprika

½ teaspoon salt

½ teaspoon pepper

½ teaspoon dried parsley

1. Dip chicken strips into the egg and dredge through the gluten-free bread crumbs or blanched almond flour.

2. Using nonstick spray or olive oil, brown chicken strips in a skillet in small batches just until they are golden brown, approximately 1 minute per side.

3. Make a 2"–3" foil rack in the bottom of your 4-quart slow cooker by placing rolled strips of aluminum foil in the bottom of the greased insert. Make a grill pattern with the strips. This will allow the chicken to cook above the juices while sitting on the rack.

4. In a small bowl mix together the honey, mustard, basil, paprika, salt, pepper, and parsley.

5. Place browned chicken fingers on the rack in the slow cooker. Drizzle half of the honey mustard sauce evenly over the chicken. Cook on high for 3 hours or on low for 6 hours. Serve the chicken tenders with remaining honey mustard sauce.

PER SERVING | Calories: 364 | Fat: 7 g | Protein: 38 g | Sodium: 746 mg | Fiber: 2 g | Carbohydrates: 35 g | Sugar: 17 g

Butterscotch-Caramel Sauce

This recipe lets you eliminate the tedious step of cooking sugar until it caramelizes, which involves bringing it to 310°F or higher. By using brown sugar, you end up with a rich sauce with less work.

INGREDIENTS | YIELDS 6 CUPS

½ cup (1 stick) butter

2 cups heavy cream

4 cups brown sugar

2 tablespoons fresh lemon juice

Pinch sea salt

1 tablespoon vanilla

1. Add the butter, cream, brown sugar, lemon juice, and salt to the slow cooker. Cover and cook on high for 1 hour or until the butter is melted and the cream begins to bubble around the edges of the crock. Uncover and stir.

2. Cover and cook on low for 2 hours, stirring occasionally. Uncover and cook on low for 1 more hour or until the mixture coats the back of the spoon or the sauce reaches its desired thickness. Stir in the vanilla.

PER SERVING (¼ CUP) | Calories: 122 | Fat: 5.5 g | Protein: 0 g | Sodium: 9 mg | Fiber: 0 g | Carbohydrates: 18 g | Sugar: 18 g

Slow-Cooked Pineapple

Slow cooking makes pineapple incredibly soft and tender. Serve as is or with vanilla bean ice cream.

INGREDIENTS | SERVES 8

1 whole pineapple, peeled

1 vanilla bean, split

3 tablespoons water or rum

Place all ingredients into a 4-quart slow cooker. Cook on low for 4 hours or until fork tender. Remove the vanilla bean before serving.

PER SERVING | Calories: 65 | Fat: 0 g | Protein: 0.5 g | Sodium: 1 mg | Fiber: 2 g | Carbohydrates: 14 g | Sugar: 11 g

Cooking with Vanilla Beans

Vanilla beans have a natural "seam" that can easily be split to release the flavorful seeds inside. After using a vanilla bean, wash it and allow it to dry. Then place it in a container with a few cups of sugar for a few weeks to make vanilla sugar. Use cup for cup in any recipe calling for sugar.

Peach Crisp

Serve with ice cream or with a dollop of whipped cream on top.

INGREDIENTS | SERVES 4

6 large peaches
¼ cup sugar
2 teaspoons ground cinnamon
¾ cup gluten-free rolled oats
¼ cup brown rice flour
½ cup brown sugar, packed
6 tablespoons butter
1 cup pecans, chopped

Quicker and Easier Fruit Crisp

Fruit crisp is a super versatile dessert. You don't have to limit yourself to fresh fruit. If you need to throw together a dessert in a hurry, you can thaw some frozen peaches or open a can of any pie filling and use that instead.

1. Wash and peel the peaches. Cut them in half, remove the pits, and slice the peaches. Toss together with sugar and cinnamon.

2. Grease a 4-quart slow cooker with nonstick cooking spray. Arrange the peaches on the bottom of the slow cooker.

3. To make the topping: in a medium bowl mix together the oats, flour, brown sugar, butter, and pecans using a fork until you have a crumbly topping mixture. Sprinkle the topping evenly over the fruit in the slow cooker.

4. Cover, vent the lid with a chopstick or the handle of a wooden spoon, and cook on high for 2 hours or on low for 4 hours or until the peaches are tender and the topping is crisp. The peach mixture may start to bubble up around the topping. Serve warm or chilled.

PER SERVING | Calories: 644 | Fat: 38 g | Protein: 7.5 g | Sodium: 11 mg | Fiber: 9 g | Carbohydrates: 74 g | Sugar: 49 g

Old-Fashioned Red Candy Apples

Everybody loves going to a county fair. But when you're following a gluten-free diet, the food is usually off-limits. But you can make fair-worthy crisp, red candy apples right in your own home using your slow cooker!

INGREDIENTS | SERVES 8

2 cups white sugar

1 cup light corn syrup

½ cup hot water

½ cup red cinnamon candies (Red Hots)

8 apples

8 wooden skewers or chopsticks

Cleaning Your Slow Cooker

Sugar that has been heated to the candy-making stage is hard to clean no matter what you're cooking in. To make cleaning a breeze after you've made candy apples, fill your slow cooker with warm water and add about a tablespoon of dish detergent. Cover and turn the slow cooker to the warm setting. Allow it to sit 8 hours or overnight. Pour out the water and then wash by hand. The sugary remnants will wash right off.

1. Place sugar, corn syrup, water, and cinnamon candies into a 2.5-quart slow cooker. Cover and cook on high for 1½–2 hours until the mixture is hot and starting to bubble on the sides of the slow cooker.

2. Line a large baking sheet with parchment paper or aluminum foil.

3. Wash apples thoroughly and pat dry with a paper towel. Stick a wooden skewer or chopstick firmly in the center of each apple.

4. Very carefully, dunk each apple and turn it over in the hot red candy liquid. You can use a spoon to help cover the apple if the top cannot be easily covered. Place each candy-coated apple on the lined baking sheet and allow to cool to room temperature. The candy coating will stay crisp on the apples for about 24 hours.

PER SERVING | Calories: 402 | Fat: 0.5 g | Protein: 0.5 g | Sodium: 26 mg | Fiber: 2 g | Carbohydrates: 112 g | Sugar: 83 g

CHAPTER 13

Five Ingredients or Fewer

Garlic and Artichoke Pasta

Artichoke hearts give this sauce a unique and savory flavor perfect for gluten-free pasta or rice.

INGREDIENTS | SERVES 6

2 (14.5-ounce) cans diced tomatoes with basil, oregano, and garlic

2 (14-ounce) cans artichoke hearts, drained and quartered

6 cloves garlic, minced

½ cup heavy cream

3 cups cooked gluten-free pasta

1. Pour tomatoes, artichokes, and garlic into a 4-quart slow cooker. Cook on high for 3–4 hours or on low for 6–8 hours.

2. Twenty minutes prior to serving, stir in cream.

3. Serve over hot pasta.

PER SERVING | Calories: 268 | Fat: 8 g | Protein: 10 g | Sodium: 325 mg | Fiber: 9 g | Carbohydrates: 42 g | Sugar: 5 g

Can't Find Seasoned Canned Tomatoes?

If you can't find diced tomatoes with herbs and spices in your grocery store, use regular diced tomatoes and add 2 teaspoons of Italian seasoning to your sauce.

Tuscan Chicken and Sausage Stew

You don't need a lot of ingredients to create a stew full of hearty and warm Tuscan flavors.

INGREDIENTS | SERVES 4

1 pound boneless, skinless chicken thighs

8 ounces turkey sausage, cut into ½" slices

1 (26-ounce) jar gluten-free pasta sauce

1 can green beans, drained

1 teaspoon dried oregano

1. Cut chicken thighs into bite-sized pieces. Place chicken into a greased 4-quart slow cooker.

2. Add remaining ingredients. Stir to combine and cook on high for 4 hours or on low for 8 hours.

PER SERVING | Calories: 416 | Fat: 15 g | Protein: 39 g | Sodium: 1,286 mg | Fiber: 6 g | Carbohydrates: 28 g | Sugar: 16 g

Change It Up

Don't like green beans or don't have them available in your pantry? Use navy beans, cannellini beans, or even black beans.

Chicken Corn Chowder

This incredibly easy chowder can be added to the slow cooker in less than 5 minutes. It doesn't get much easier than that! Feel free to vary the canned vegetables used or add additional seasonings.

INGREDIENTS | SERVES 4

1 pound boneless chicken breasts, cut into ½" pieces

2 (14.5-ounce) cans Mexican-style diced tomatoes

1 (10-ounce) can sweet whole kernel corn, drained

1 (8-ounce) package cream cheese

Make It Dairy-Free

In this recipe if you are not able to eat dairy you can replace the cream cheese with "Tofutti," a soy-based cream cheese substitute, or if you are intolerant to soy, you can use 6 ounces of full-fat coconut milk mixed with 2 tablespoons of lemon juice.

1. Add chicken breasts, diced tomatoes, and sweet corn to a greased 4-quart slow cooker. Cook on high for 4 hours or on low for 8 hours.

2. Twenty minutes prior to serving stir in cream cheese. If desired, serve with gluten-free corn chips and guacamole.

PER SERVING | Calories: 410 | Fat: 23 g | Protein: 30 g | Sodium: 826 mg | Fiber: 3.5 g | Carbohydrates: 23 g | Sugar: 8 g

Gluten-Free Cream of Mushroom Soup

Cream of mushroom soup is a simple and light main dish. It's also a perfect gluten-free base to use when a recipe calls for canned cream soup.

INGREDIENTS | SERVES 4

4 tablespoons butter

1 cup fresh mushrooms, finely diced

4 tablespoons cornstarch

2 cups whole milk

½ teaspoon each salt and pepper

Cream Soup Variations

You can make any number of homemade cream soups with this recipe. If you would rather have cream of celery soup, use 1 cup of finely diced celery instead of the mushrooms. For a cream of chicken soup use 1 cup finely diced chicken and 2 teaspoons of poultry seasoning. For a cheese sauce, add 1 cup of shredded sharp Cheddar cheese.

1. Heat butter in a deep saucepan until sizzling. Add diced mushrooms and cook until soft, approximately 4–5 minutes.

2. In a medium bowl whisk cornstarch into the milk. Slowly add to the mushrooms and butter. Cook on medium heat for 5–10 minutes, whisking constantly, until slightly thickened.

3. Carefully pour cream soup into a greased 2.5-quart slow cooker. Add salt, pepper, and any additional seasonings you would like. Cook on high for 2 hours or on low for 4 hours.

PER SERVING | Calories: 210 | Fat: 15 g | Protein: 4.5 g | Sodium: 350 mg | Fiber: 0.5 g | Carbohydrates: 13 g | Sugar: 6.5 g

Super Easy Chili

Everyone needs an easy chili recipe under their culinary belt. This recipe is very easy to put together and is perfect for lazy weekends. Serve with gluten-free tortilla chips and a dollop of sour cream.

INGREDIENTS | SERVES 4

1 pound ground beef, browned

1 (12-ounce) jar spicy salsa

1 (15.5-ounce) can diced tomatoes

1 (15.5-ounce) can chili beans or red beans (if using red beans, drain and rinse)

1. Add all ingredients to a greased 2.5-quart or larger slow cooker.

2. Cook on high for 4 hours or on low for 8 hours.

PER SERVING | Calories: 329 | Fat: 12 g | Protein: 30 g | Sodium: 1,056 mg | Fiber: 8 g | Carbohydrates: 25 g | Sugar: 7 g

Which Salsa Works Best for Chili?

Salsa is a great addition to chili recipes because it contains many traditional chili ingredients such as onions, peppers, and spices. If you want a hotter chili, use a very spicy salsa. If you want a milder or sweeter chili, use a chili with less heat or one that's made with fruit such as peaches.

Chicken Vegetable Soup

This soup is healthy and filling without a lot of calories. It's also a very frugal recipe, using ingredients you probably already have in your pantry right now. If you like, add some cooked white rice or gluten-free pasta to the soup before serving.

INGREDIENTS | SERVES 4

½ cup onions, chopped

1 (14.5-ounce) can Italian-seasoned diced tomatoes

1 (14.5-ounce) can low-sodium Veg-All mixed vegetables

1 (14.5-ounce) can low-sodium, gluten-free chicken broth

1 (10-ounce) can chunk chicken

1. Place onions in a small glass (or microwave-safe) bowl. Cover with plastic wrap and cook on high for 1–2 minutes until onions are soft.

2. Add softened onions, tomatoes, mixed vegetables, and chicken broth to a 2.5-quart or larger slow cooker. Cook on high for 4 hours or on low for 8 hours.

3. Thirty minutes prior to serving add chicken and pepper to the slow cooker. Stir to warm through. If needed, feel free to add salt and pepper.

PER SERVING | Calories: 245 | Fat: 7.5 g | Protein: 23 g | Sodium: 822 mg | Fiber: 4.5 g | Carbohydrates: 20 g | Sugar: 5.5 g

Pinto Bean–Stuffed Peppers

Stuffed peppers are most often filled with a ground meat mixture, but this recipe is an easy vegetarian option that will please the pickiest of diners.

INGREDIENTS | SERVES 4

1 cup cooked rice

1 (15-ounce) can pinto beans, drained and rinsed

1 (15-ounce) can tomato sauce

1 packet gluten-free taco seasoning (or use the recipe in Chapter 5)

4 medium red, yellow, or green peppers

1. In a large bowl mix together the rice, pinto beans, tomato sauce, and taco seasoning.

2. Carefully remove the tops, seeds, and membranes of the peppers. Fill each pepper with ¼ of the pinto bean mixture.

3. Place the stuffed peppers in a greased 4-quart slow cooker. Add ⅓ cup of water around the bottom of the stuffed peppers.

4. Cook on high for 3–4 hours or on low for 6–8 hours until peppers are softened.

PER SERVING | Calories: 319 | Fat: 3 g | Protein: 13 g | Sodium: 1,246 mg | Fiber: 21 g | Carbohydrates: 72 g | Sugar: 6 g

Barbecue Chicken and Beans

Barbecue sauce can make any meal taste like a cookout! Homemade gluten-free barbecue sauce can be used with any of your favorite barbecue recipes. It's cheaper than store-bought sauce, and you feel safe knowing it's gluten-free.

INGREDIENTS | SERVES 4

3–4 chicken breasts, cut into 1" pieces

1 (14.5-ounce) can red kidney beans, drained and rinsed

2 teaspoons gluten-free Worcestershire sauce

1 cup gluten-free homemade or store-bought barbecue sauce

2 cups cooked white rice

1. Add all ingredients except rice to a greased 2.5-quart or larger slow cooker.

2. Cook on high for 4 hours or on low for 8 hours. Serve over rice.

PER SERVING | Calories: 503 | Fat: 5 g | Protein: 45 g | Sodium: 1,094 mg | Fiber: 6 g | Carbohydrates: 65 g | Sugar: 18 g

Quick Homemade Barbecue Sauce

Mix together 1 cup gluten-free ketchup, ¼ cup apple cider vinegar, 2 tablespoons brown sugar or molasses, 1 tablespoon Dijon mustard, 1 tablespoon water, ½ teaspoon salt, ½ teaspoon black pepper. Cook over medium heat for 3–5 minutes and let cool. Use as you would any barbecue sauce. Store in an airtight container or a washed, recycled plastic bottle in the refrigerator for up to 1 month.

Black Bean and Cheese Tacos

No one will guess how fast and easy this vegetarian taco filling is to make. Serve with guacamole and sour cream.

INGREDIENTS | SERVES 4

1 (15-ounce) can black beans, drained and rinsed

¾ cup mild salsa

8 gluten-free corn taco shells

1 cup shredded Cheddar cheese

1 heart of romaine lettuce, shredded

1. Add black beans and salsa to a greased 2.5-quart slow cooker. Cook on high for 3–4 hours or on low for 6–8 hours.

2. Fill each taco shell with several tablespoons black bean filling, several tablespoons of shredded cheese, and a handful of shredded lettuce.

PER SERVING | Calories: 319 | Fat: 11 g | Protein: 16 g | Sodium: 782 mg | Fiber: 9 g | Carbohydrates: 40 g | Sugar: 3 g

Guacamole in a Minute

Halve and seed 2 large avocados. Scoop the avocado pulp into a bowl. Add 2–3 tablespoons of lime juice, a few halved grape tomatoes, 1 clove of garlic (minced), ½ teaspoon of salt, and ¼ teaspoon of Goya Adobo sin Pimiento (all-purpose Hispanic seasoning). Mash together and serve with chips or tacos.

Slow Cooker Cheeseburgers

This meal is reminiscent of "sloppy joes" but with a cheesy twist! Feel free to serve this cheesy ground beef not only in gluten-free buns, but over cooked rice or pasta, or even cooked spaghetti squash.

INGREDIENTS | SERVES 4

1 pound lean ground beef

¼ cup gluten-free ketchup

2 tablespoons yellow mustard

1 teaspoon dried basil

2 cups mild Cheddar cheese

1. Brown ground beef in a skillet over medium heat. Pour off grease, and add cooked ground beef to a greased 2.5-quart slow cooker.

2. Add ketchup, mustard, and basil to the slow cooker. Cook on high for 2–3 hours or on low for 4–5 hours.

3. Thirty minutes prior to serving add shredded Cheddar cheese to the ground beef mixture. When cheese is melted, spoon 3–4 tablespoons of cheeseburger mixture into each hamburger bun. Serve with lettuce, tomatoes, and any other hamburger toppings you desire.

PER SERVING | Calories: 480 | Fat: 20 g | Protein: 41 g | Sodium: 824 mg | Fiber: 3 g | Carbohydrates: 18 g | Sugar: 4 g

Reuben Casserole

If you were a fan of the distinct tangy flavors of a Reuben sandwich before you went gluten-free, you will love this zesty, sauerkraut-filled casserole dish!

INGREDIENTS | SERVES 6

8 ounces gluten-free corned beef, cut into ½" cubes

1 Granny Smith apple, peeled, cored, and chopped

1 (14-ounce) can sauerkraut, rinsed and drained

1¼ teaspoons caraway seeds

2 cups mashed potatoes

2 cups shredded Havarti or Swiss cheese, optional

¼ cup gluten-free Thousand Island dressing, optional

1. Grease a 2.5-quart or larger slow cooker. Add corned beef, apple, sauerkraut, and caraway seeds. Stir ingredients together.

2. Spoon mashed potatoes evenly over casserole ingredients. Cook on high for 3–4 hours or on low for 6–8 hours.

3. If desired, thirty minutes prior to serving, sprinkle cheese over mashed potatoes and cook until it is soft and melted. Drizzle a tablespoon of Thousand Island dressing over each serving.

PER SERVING | Calories: 372 | Fat: 21 g | Protein: 22 g | Sodium: 1,047 mg | Fiber: 3 g | Carbohydrates: 22 g | Sugar: 6 g

Beef Burrito Filling

London broil is a lean cut of meat that is perfect for the slow cooker. The longer it's cooked the more tender and succulent it becomes. With the addition of gluten-free taco seasoning it makes the perfect meaty filling for Mexican dishes, like burritos, enchiladas, and tacos.

INGREDIENTS | SERVES 6

1 package gluten-free taco seasoning

1 garlic clove, peeled and minced

2 pounds London broil

1 cup diced onion

2 tablespoons apple cider vinegar

1. In small bowl mix together the taco seasoning and garlic.

2. Rub London broil with the taco seasoning mixture. Place beef and onion in a greased 4-quart slow cooker. Drizzle apple cider vinegar over the meat and onions.

3. Cook on high for 4 hours or on low for 8 hours until meat can be shredded with a fork.

PER SERVING | Calories: 214 | Fat: 6 g | Protein: 34 g | Sodium: 128 mg | Fiber: 0.5 g | Carbohydrates: 3 g | Sugar: 1.5 g

Chorizo and Potato Casserole

If you don't have Mexican chorizo sausage available in your local grocery store, use mild breakfast sausage instead.

INGREDIENTS | SERVES 6

⅓ cup olive oil

1 small onion, diced

3 medium Yukon gold potatoes, peeled and cut into ½" cubes

8 ounces Mexican chorizo sausage, removed from casing

8 large eggs

1. In a heavy skillet, heat olive oil over medium heat until sizzling. Add onion and cook 3–5 minutes until soft.

2. Add potatoes and cook another 5–8 minutes until potatoes are fork tender. Using a large slotted spoon, remove potato mixture from skillet, place in a bowl, and set aside.

3. In the same skillet, brown chorizo over medium heat until cooked through.

4. Grease a 4-quart slow cooker. Layer the potato mixture with the cooked chorizo in the slow cooker.

5. In a large bowl mix together the eggs, salt, and pepper. Evenly pour over the layered ingredients.

6. Cook on high for 3–4 hours or on low for 6–8 hours until eggs are set. If necessary, add salt and pepper to taste, when serving.

PER SERVING | Calories: 449 | Fat: 33 g | Protein: 20 g | Sodium: 657 mg | Fiber: 3 g | Carbohydrates: 20 g | Sugar: 2 g

Corned Beef and Cabbage

This is a perfect meal for St. Patrick's Day or any day your family would enjoy the classic flavors of corned beef, cabbage, and potatoes.

INGREDIENTS | SERVES 8

½ small head of cabbage, cut into chunky wedges

4 medium carrots, cut into 2" pieces

1 medium onion, quartered

2 yellow potatoes, cut into 2" pieces

1 (4-pound) gluten-free corned beef brisket with spice packet

1. Place vegetables into the bottom of a greased 4-quart or larger slow cooker.

2. Place corned beef brisket over vegetables. Sprinkle seasoning packet over meat and vegetables.

3. Cook on high for 4–6 hours or on low for 8–10 hours.

PER SERVING | Calories: 631 | Fat: 33 g | Protein: 62 g | Sodium: 2,092 mg | Fiber: 4 g | Carbohydrates: 16 g | Sugar: 4.5 g

Root Vegetables

Root vegetables are great for the slow cooker because they become very tender, while retaining moisture over long cooking periods. Feel free to use different varieties of root vegetables in this recipe such as parsnips, turnips, or red onions.

Pesto Chicken

Pesto has such a unique nutty flavor from pine nuts and basil that it takes plain old chicken and makes it fabulous. This chicken also presents beautifully for a company dinner.

INGREDIENTS | SERVES 4

2 pounds boneless, skinless chicken thighs

3–4 red potatoes, diced

1 pint cherry tomatoes

½ cup prepared pesto

½ teaspoon pepper

½ teaspoon salt, optional

Place all ingredients in a greased 4-quart slow cooker. Cook on high for 3–4 hours or on low for 6–8 hours until chicken is tender. If desired, add salt to taste, per serving.

PER SERVING | Calories: 510 | Fat: 18 g | Protein: 39 g | Sodium: 506 mg | Fiber: 4 g | Carbohydrates: 37 g | Sugar: 4 g

Chicken with Mango-Lime Sauce

The citrusy flavors of orange juice, lime juice, and mangoes are combined to make a wonderful sweet and sour sauce.

INGREDIENTS | SERVES 4

4 boneless, skinless chicken breasts

⅓ cup lime juice

3 tablespoons orange juice

1 large mango, peeled and diced

2 cups gluten-free pasta, cooked

1. Add all ingredients to a greased 4-quart slow cooker. Cook on high for 3–4 hours or on low for 6–8 hours.

2. Serve chicken and sauce over gluten-free pasta.

PER SERVING | Calories: 399 | Fat: 6.5 g | Protein: 49 g | Sodium: 275 mg | Fiber: 2 g | Carbohydrates: 26 g | Sugar: 4 g

Don't Want to Cut a Mango?

Many grocery stores now carry precut mangoes either in the produce section or in the freezer section. Use 1 cup of prepared chopped mango in place of fresh mango if you'd like.

Salsa Chicken

This chicken is easy, versatile, and always delicious. Serve it any way you would like: in corn taco shells, over a salad, over cooked rice, or in a casserole.

INGREDIENTS | SERVES 4

4 boneless, skinless chicken breasts

1 (12-ounce) jar mild salsa

Add chicken and salsa to a greased 2.5- or 4-quart slow cooker. Cook on high for 3–4 hours, on low for 6–8 hours.

PER SERVING | Calories: 291 | Fat: 6 g | Protein: 51 g | Sodium: 777 mg | Fiber: 1 g | Carbohydrates: 5 g | Sugar: 3 g

No Salsa?

Use spaghetti sauce, taco sauce, pizza sauce, or jarred pesto in place of the salsa. Use whatever sauce you like to create a super easy chicken dish with flavors you love.

Pork Tenderloin with Nectarines

Pork combined with the flavor of ripe nectarines makes a lovely sweet and slightly tangy sauce. Serve sliced pork and sauce over cooked gluten-free pasta, rice, or steamed zucchini strips.

INGREDIENTS | SERVES 4

1¼ pounds pork tenderloin

1 tablespoon olive oil

4 ripe but firm nectarines, cut into 4 wedges

2 tablespoons white balsamic vinegar

1. Rub pork tenderloin with salt, pepper, and olive oil. Place in a greased 4-quart slow cooker.

2. Pour nectarines on top of and around the pork tenderloin. Drizzle balsamic vinegar over the pork and fruit. Cook on high for 3–4 hours or on low for 6–8 hours until pork is very tender.

3. Remove pork from slow cooker and slice before serving. If needed, add salt and pepper, to taste.

PER SERVING | Calories: 190 | Fat: 6 g | Protein: 29 g | Sodium: 370 mg | Fiber: 1 g | Carbohydrates: 1 g | Sugar: 1 g

Easy Applesauce Pork Chops

Kids and adults alike will love these tender pork chops covered in applesauce with just a hint of brown sugar. Serve with baked sweet potatoes and steamed broccoli.

INGREDIENTS | SERVES 4

4 large pork loin chops

1 cup naturally sweetened applesauce

¼ cup brown sugar

3 tablespoons apple cider vinegar

¼ teaspoon ground pepper

1. Place pork loin chops in the bottom of a greased 4-quart slow cooker.

2. Pour applesauce over the pork chops. Sprinkle brown sugar, vinegar, salt, and pepper evenly over the applesauce.

3. Cook on high for 4–5 hours, or on low for 8–9 hours until pork is tender. If necessary, add salt to taste, per serving.

PER SERVING | Calories: 261 | Fat: 6 g | Protein: 30 g | Sodium: 383 mg | Fiber: 1 g | Carbohydrates: 20 g | Sugar: 19 g

Turkey Cutlets with Red Onion Sauce

Turkey cutlets are 1" slices of uncooked turkey breast that can be purchased from many large grocery stores in the poultry section. It's a great way to prepare turkey for dinner without having to cook the whole bird.

INGREDIENTS | SERVES 4

1¼ pounds turkey cutlets

2 tablespoons olive oil

1 large red onion, thinly sliced

⅓ cup sweetened rice vinegar

Make It Chicken

If your family prefers the flavor of chicken to turkey, simply use 3–4 boneless chicken breasts instead of turkey cutlets.

1. Season turkey cutlets with salt and pepper and place in a greased 2.5-quart slow cooker.

2. In a small bowl mix together olive oil, red onion, and sweetened rice vinegar. Pour over the turkey cutlets. Cook on high for 3–4 hours or on low for 6–8 hours until turkey is cooked through. If necessary, add salt and pepper to taste, per serving.

PER SERVING | Calories: 230 | Fat: 9 g | Protein: 31 g | Sodium: 381 mg | Fiber: 1 g | Carbohydrates: 4 g | Sugar: 1.5 g

Pork Roast with Cranberry Sauce

This pairs wonderfully with the Wild Rice Pilaf in Chapter 6.

INGREDIENTS | SERVES 4

1 medium onion, thinly sliced

1¼ pounds pork loin

2 tablespoons sweetened dried cranberries

1 cup cranberry sauce

Cooking with Pork Loin

Pork loin is an exceptionally lean cut. If pork does have some excess fat it can be removed easily before cooking. Another lean cut is the tenderloin roast, which is as lean as skinless chicken breast.

1. Place the onion slices on the bottom of a greased 4-quart slow cooker. Top with the pork and the dried cranberries, and finally the cranberry sauce to cover the whole roast.

2. Cover and cook on low for 6 hours or on high for 3 hours. Remove the pork and slice it. Discard the cooking liquids.

PER SERVING | Calories: 305 | Fat: 5 g | Protein: 31 g | Sodium: 89 mg | Fiber: 1 g | Carbohydrates: 32 g | Sugar: 29 g

Quinoa with Chorizo

Try this quinoa side-dish as an alternative to rice. Chorizo has a savory, smoky, and garlicky flavor that adds zest to the mildness of quinoa. The sausage also adds a nice red color to this dish due to the paprika (also known as "pimenton") used to season it.

INGREDIENTS | SERVES 4

½ cup (or 1 link) Spanish-style chorizo
½ cup onions, diced
1 cup quinoa, rinsed
2 cups water or gluten-free chicken broth

Quinoa Basics

Although quinoa (pronounced "keen-wah") is treated like a grain, it is actually an edible seed. It is very high in protein and contains a balanced set of essential amino acids, making it a particularly complete source of protein. Quinoa is also high in fiber, iron, and magnesium.

1. Sauté the chorizo and onions in a small, nonstick skillet over medium heat until the onions are soft. Drain off any excess fat.

2. Add to a greased 2.5-quart or smaller slow cooker, along with quinoa and water or chicken broth.

3. Cover and cook on low for 2 hours or on high for 1 hour, until quinoa is soft and fluffy.

PER SERVING | Calories: 232 | Fat: 8 g | Protein: 10 g | Sodium: 191 mg | Fiber: 3 g | Carbohydrates: 29 g | Sugar: 1 g

Salmon with Lemon, Capers, and Rosemary

Salmon is very moist and tender when cooked in the slow cooker. This is a great meal for couples or when you just need to cook something small. Serve it with steamed kale and baked potatoes.

INGREDIENTS | SERVES 2

8 ounces salmon
2 tablespoons lemon juice
3 thin slices fresh lemon
1 tablespoon nonpareil capers
½ teaspoon minced, fresh rosemary

1. Place the salmon on the bottom of a 2.5-quart slow cooker. Pour ⅓ cup of water and lemon juice over the fish.

2. Arrange lemon slices in a single layer on top of the fish. Sprinkle with capers and rosemary.

3. Cook on low for 2 hours. Discard lemon slices prior to serving.

PER SERVING | Calories: 166 | Fat: 7 g | Protein: 22 g | Sodium: 181 mg | Fiber: 0.5 g | Carbohydrates: 2 g | Sugar: 1 g

Coconut Milk Yogurt

If you're intolerant to dairy proteins like casein or dairy sugar (lactose), this coconut milk yogurt is a perfect alternative and you can make it right in your slow cooker! Serve the yogurt plain or with any flavor jam or fresh fruit.

INGREDIENTS | SERVES 8

6 cups full-fat coconut milk

6 capsules of allergen-free probiotics or yogurt starter

3 tablespoons plain gelatin

½ cup sugar, optional

½ cup blackberry jam, optional

Using Probiotics to Make Yogurt

You will need to purchase a yogurt starter or probiotics that contain "live active cultures" for them to work properly to create this yogurt. Alternately, if you have a grocery store nearby that sells yogurt made from coconut milk, you can simply purchase a small container of plain coconut milk yogurt and use that as your starter instead of using probiotic capsules.

1. Pour the coconut milk into a 4-quart slow cooker. Turn the slow cooker on low and let it cook for 3 hours.

2. Turn the slow cooker off and let it sit for 3 hours. (Cooking the mixture first will help to kill off any bad bacteria that may be in the coconut milk.) Once the coconut milk has cooled after 3 hours, remove 1 cup of the warm coconut milk and mix it in a glass bowl with the contents of the probiotics capsules and the gelatin.

3. Return the probiotic/coconut milk mixture back to the slow cooker. Whisk thoroughly to distribute the probiotics and gelatin throughout the mixture. Place the lid back on the slow cooker.

4. Leave the slow cooker turned off, but wrap the slow cooker in several layers of bath towels to give the probiotics a warm environment to grow in. Leave the towel-wrapped slow cooker alone for 8–10 hours.

5. After 8 hours, stir in the sugar if desired and place the covered slow cooker insert into the fridge. Allow the yogurt to chill for 6–8 hours. This will allow the gelatin to thicken the yogurt, so it has the proper texture. Serve cold topped with blackberry jam.

PER SERVING | Calories: 447 | Fat: 36 g | Protein: 6 g | Sodium: 33 mg | Fiber: 0 g | Carbohydrates: 32 g | Sugar: 22 g

Ginger-Glazed Cornish Game Hen

The flavors of ginger and lime penetrate the meat, so you don't need to eat the skin to get the flavor.

INGREDIENTS | SERVES 2

1 large (4-pound) Cornish game hen or 2 small (2-pound) Cornish game hens

2 tablespoons ginger powder

2 tablespoons fresh lime juice

What Is a Cornish Game Hen?

The Cornish game hen first became available in the United States during the 1960s. Although the hen is often considered a separate kind of poultry, it is actually a small chicken. One large hen is perfect for two people, while a smaller 1–2 pound bird would be perfect for one.

1. Place the hen in a 2.5-quart slow cooker.

2. In a small bowl, whisk the ginger powder and lime juice. Pour over the hen.

3. Cook on low for 6 hours or on high for 3 hours. Discard skin before serving.

PER SERVING | Calories: 410 | Fat: 10 g | Protein: 70 g | Sodium: 255 mg | Fiber: 1 g | Carbohydrates: 4 g | Sugar: 0 g

CHAPTER 14

Gluten-Free Breads and Desserts

Gluten-Free Slow Cooker Yeast Bread

Did you know you can make gluten-free sandwich bread right in your slow cooker? If using the loaf pan for this bread, make sure to use the size recommended in the recipe. Otherwise, your bread can rise too high and then fall while baking.

INGREDIENTS | SERVES 12

⅓ cup arrowroot starch

⅓ cup blanched almond flour

3 tablespoons millet flour

1½ cups brown rice flour

1 teaspoon salt

1 tablespoon xanthan gum

2 teaspoons bread machine yeast
(try: Saf, Red Star, or Fleischmann's)

3 tablespoons sugar

1 egg, plus 2 egg whites, room temperature

1⅓ cups whole milk, heated to 110°F

3 tablespoons olive oil

Free-Form Oval Bread

If you don't have a large 6-quart slow cooker, simply line a 2.5-quart or a 4-quart slow cooker with parchment paper. Spray it with nonstick cooking spray. Coat your hands or a large spoon with cooking spray or olive oil and shape the dough into an oval loaf. Place loaf in the middle of the parchment paper and bake as directed. You will need to keep a close eye on the loaf as it can burn around the edges since it's closer to the heating element.

1. In a large bowl whisk together arrowroot starch, blanched almond flour, millet flour, brown rice flour, salt, xanthan gum, yeast, and sugar.

2. In a smaller bowl whisk together the egg, egg whites, milk, and oil.

3. Pour wet ingredients into whisked dry ingredients. Stir with a wooden spoon or a fork for several minutes until dough resembles a thick cake batter. First it will look like biscuit dough, but after a few minutes it will appear thick and sticky.

4. Line an 8½" × 4½" metal or glass loaf pan with parchment paper or spray with nonstick cooking spray. Pour bread dough into the pan. Using a spatula that's been dipped in water or coated with oil or nonstick cooking spray, spread the dough evenly in the pan. Continue to use the spatula to smooth out the top of the bread dough. Place the loaf pan in a 6-quart or larger oval slow cooker.

5. Cover the slow cooker and vent the lid with a chopstick or the handle of a wooden spoon. Cook on high for 3½–4 hours. The bread will rise and bake at the same time. The bread should be about double in size and the sides should be a light golden brown; the bread will not "brown" as much as it would in the oven.

6. Remove the bread from the pan and cool on a wire rack. Slice and keep in an airtight plastic bag on the counter for 2 days. Freeze any remaining bread.

PER SERVING | Calories: 164 | Fat: 6 g | Protein: 3 g | Sodium: 222 mg | Fiber: 1.5 g | Carbohydrates: 23 g | Sugar: 1.5 g

Slow Cooker Gluten-Free Yeast Rolls

This recipe proves how versatile gluten-free yeast dough can be, even in the slow cooker! You will need 2 (4-quart) slow cookers or 1 (6-quart) slow cooker for this recipe.

INGREDIENTS | SERVES 12

1 recipe Gluten-Free Slow Cooker Yeast Bread dough (see recipe in this chapter)

3 tablespoons olive oil or melted butter

½ teaspoon garlic powder

½ teaspoon toasted sesame seeds

½ teaspoon Italian seasoning

Drop Rolls

Instead of using cupcake liners you can simply line the slow cooker with parchment paper. Spray the parchment paper with nonstick cooking spray and drop the scoops of dough onto the parchment paper. Bake as directed.

1. Using an ice cream scoop, scoop dough into 12 balls and place each ball in a greased cupcake liner. Place the cupcake liners on the bottom of one large or two smaller slow cookers.

2. Brush rolls with melted butter and sprinkle garlic powder, sesame seeds, and/or Italian seasoning over the tops.

3. Cover and vent the lid with a chopstick or the handle of a wooden spoon. Cook on high for 1½–2½ hours until dough has almost doubled in size and the rolls are cooked through. You will need to watch the rolls at the end of the cooking period as they can get overdone on the edges since they are so close to the cooking element.

PER SERVING | Calories: 143 | Fat: 5 g | Protein: 2 g | Sodium: 204 mg | Fiber: 2 g | Carbohydrates: 21 g | Sugar: 0 g

Buttermilk Gluten-Free Drop Biscuits

Buttermilk adds a tangy flavor to these fluffy gluten-free biscuits.

INGREDIENTS | SERVES 12

2 cups brown rice flour

¼ cup sorghum flour

½ cup arrowroot starch

¼ cup potato starch or cornstarch

2 tablespoons sugar

4 teaspoons baking powder

1 teaspoon salt

1 teaspoon baking soda

1 teaspoon xanthan gum

½ cup chilled butter

1¼ cups buttermilk

1 egg

Dairy-Free "Buttermilk"

For a dairy-free buttermilk alternative mix 2 tablespoons of lemon juice or apple cider vinegar with 1¼ cups almond milk or coconut milk.

1. In a large bowl whisk together all dry ingredients. Cut butter into the dry ingredients with two knives or with a pastry cutter until it resembles small peas throughout the dry ingredients.

2. In a smaller bowl mix together buttermilk and egg. Pour buttermilk mixture into the dry ingredients and mix with a fork. Biscuit dough will be slightly stiff when thoroughly mixed.

3. Line a 6-quart slow cooker with parchment paper and spray it with nonstick cooking spray.

4. Using a ice cream scoop, scoop out 10–12 drop biscuits and place them on the parchment paper on the bottom of the slow cooker.

5. Cover and vent the lid of the slow cooker with a chopstick or the end of a wooden spoon. Cook on high for 2–2½ hours until the biscuits have risen by about half and are cooked through.

PER SERVING | Calories: 234 | Fat: 9 g | Protein: 3 g | Sodium: 502 mg | Fiber: 1 g | Carbohydrates: 35 g | Sugar: 3 g

Brazilian Cheese Bread

This cheesy, naturally gluten-free bread is made from tapioca starch, a flour often used in Brazilian cooking and baking.

INGREDIENTS | SERVES 12

1 teaspoon salt

2 cups tapioca starch

2 teaspoons garlic powder

⅔ cup freshly grated Parmesan cheese

½ cup olive oil

⅔ cup 2% milk

2 beaten eggs

Tapioca Starch or Tapioca Flour?

In America, tapioca starch and tapioca flour are the same thing. A common brand is Bob's Red Mill, which lists the product as "Tapioca Flour—also known as Tapioca Starch."

1. In a large bowl whisk together salt, tapioca starch, garlic powder, and Parmesan cheese.

2. Make a well in the center of the ingredients and add olive oil, milk, and eggs. Mix together until you have a sticky dough.

3. Line a 6-quart slow cooker with parchment paper and spray it with nonstick cooking spray.

4. Using a greased ice cream scoop, scoop out 10–12 balls of dough and place them on the parchment paper on the bottom of the slow cooker.

5. Cover and vent the lid of the slow cooker with a chopstick or the end of a wooden spoon. Cook on high for 2–2½ hours until the rolls have risen by about half and are cooked through.

PER SERVING | Calories: 198 | Fat: 10 g | Protein: 2 g | Sodium: 239 mg | Fiber: 0 g | Carbohydrates: 23 g | Sugar: 2 g

Creamy Hot Fudge Sauce

Try this sauce over frozen yogurt or ice cream.

INGREDIENTS | YIELDS 2 CUPS

12 ounces evaporated milk

10 ounces semisweet or bittersweet chocolate chips

1 teaspoon vanilla

½ teaspoon butter

⅛ teaspoon salt

1. Place all ingredients into a 1½- to 2-quart slow cooker. Cook on low, stirring occasionally, for 2 hours. The sauce will thicken as it cools.

2. Refrigerate leftovers. Reheat in the slow cooker for 1 hour on high or on the stovetop until warmed through, about 10 minutes.

PER SERVING (2 TABLESPOONS) | Calories: 240 | Fat: 12 g | Protein: 4 g | Sodium: 82 mg | Fiber: 2 g | Carbohydrates: 27 g | Sugar: 22 g

Vanilla Poached Pears

Slow poaching makes these pears meltingly tender and infuses them with a rich vanilla flavor.

INGREDIENTS | SERVES 4

4 Bosc pears, peeled

1 vanilla bean, split

2 tablespoons vanilla extract

2 cups water or apple juice

1. Stand the pears up in a 4-quart slow cooker. Add the remaining ingredients.

2. Cook on low for 2 hours or until the pears are tender. Discard all cooking liquid prior to serving.

PER SERVING | Calories: 115 | Fat: 0 g | Protein: 1 g | Sodium: 6 mg | Fiber: 5 g | Carbohydrates: 26 g | Sugar: 17 g

In a Pinch . . .

If you need an easy dessert, but don't have fresh fruit, use a large can of sliced or halved pears. Drain and rinse them thoroughly. Make the recipe as written, except use only ½ cup of water or apple juice.

Maple-Orange Pears

These pears, coated with the sweet flavors of maple, ginger, and orange, make a delicious fruit dessert.

INGREDIENTS | SERVES 6

6 pears
½ cup packed brown sugar
⅓ cup maple-flavored pancake syrup
1 tablespoon butter, melted
1 teaspoon grated orange zest
⅛ teaspoon ground ginger
1 tablespoon cornstarch
2 tablespoons orange juice

1. Peel pears and place them upright in 4-quart slow cooker.

2. In a small bowl mix the brown sugar, syrup, butter, zest, and ginger; pour over pears.

3. Cover and cook on high for 2–2½ hours or on low for 4 hours or until tender.

4. Using a slotted spoon, carefully remove pears from the slow cooker and place upright in a serving dish or individual dessert dishes.

5. In a small bowl mix cornstarch and orange juice together. Stir into sauce in cooker. Cover and cook on high for about 10 minutes or until sauce is thickened. Spoon orange sauce over pears.

PER SERVING | Calories: 237 | Fat: 2 g | Protein: 1 g | Sodium: 9 mg | Fiber: 5 g | Carbohydrates: 57 g | Sugar: 45 g

Baked Stuffed Apples

You can serve these baked apples as a warm dessert with some vanilla ice cream or along with some coffeecake for breakfast.

INGREDIENTS | SERVES 4

4 large tart baking apples
½ cup light brown sugar
4 teaspoons grated orange zest
1 teaspoon cinnamon
¼ cup golden seedless raisins
4 teaspoons frozen orange juice concentrate
4 teaspoons butter
½ cup apple cider or juice

1. Wash the apples and remove the core and the stem, but don't peel them.

2. Add the brown sugar, orange zest, and cinnamon to a small bowl; stir to mix.

3. Fill each apple with a tablespoon of raisins, a teaspoon of orange juice concentrate, and a generous tablespoon of the brown sugar mixture. Top the filling in each apple with a teaspoon of butter.

4. Pour the cider or juice into the slow cooker. Carefully place the apples upright in the slow cooker. Cover and cook on low for 5 hours or until the apples are cooked through and tender.

5. Use tongs and a spatula to remove the apples to dessert plates. Serve warm.

PER SERVING | Calories: 269 | Fat: 4 g | Protein: 1 g | Sodium: 10 mg | Fiber: 3 g | Carbohydrates: 61 g | Sugar: 53 g

Spiced Winter Fruit Compote

Warm fruit that's spiced with ginger, cardamom, and nutmeg. This would be perfect spooned over toasted gluten-free pound cake or even ice cream.

INGREDIENTS | SERVES 8

3 medium pears, peeled if desired, cored, and cubed

1 (15½-ounce) can pineapple chunks, undrained

1 cup dried apricots, quartered

½ cup dried cranberries

3 tablespoons frozen orange juice concentrate

2 tablespoons packed brown sugar

3 tablespoons tapioca starch

½ teaspoon ground ginger

¼ teaspoon cardamom

½ teaspoon freshly grated nutmeg

2 cups frozen unsweetened pitted dark sweet cherries

½ cup toasted flaked coconut

½ cup toasted pecans

1. In a greased 4-quart slow cooker combine pears, pineapple, apricots, and cranberries.

2. In a small bowl whisk together orange juice concentrate, brown sugar, tapioca starch, ginger, cardamom, and nutmeg. Pour orange juice mixture over fruit.

3. Cover and cook on low for 6–8 hours or on high for 3–4 hours. Stir in cherries 1 hour prior to serving.

4. To serve, spoon warm compote into dessert dishes. Top with coconut and nuts.

PER SERVING | Calories: 242 | Fat: 5 g | Protein: 2 g | Sodium: 4 mg | Fiber: 6 g | Carbohydrates: 51 g | Sugar: 39 g

Chocolate Bread Pudding

Fat-free evaporated milk gives this bread pudding a creamy texture, but it has several dozen fewer calories than heavy cream.

INGREDIENTS | SERVES 10

4 cups cubed gluten-free bread, day-old and toasted

2⅓ cups fat-free evaporated milk

2 eggs

⅓ cup light brown sugar

¼ cup cocoa

1 teaspoon vanilla extract

1. Grease a 4-quart slow cooker with nonstick cooking spray. Add the bread cubes.

2. In a medium bowl, whisk the evaporated milk, eggs, brown sugar, cocoa, and vanilla until the sugar and cocoa are dissolved. Pour over the bread cubes.

3. Cover and cook on low for 5 hours or until the pudding no longer looks wet.

PER SERVING | Calories: 116 | Fat: 1.5 g | Protein: 6 g | Sodium: 149 mg | Fiber: 1 g | Carbohydrates: 20 g | Sugar: 10 g

Old-Fashioned Rice Pudding

This creamy delicious rice pudding can be served hot or cold. Top it with sweetened whipped cream for a special treat.

INGREDIENTS | SERVES 6

¾ cup long-grain rice
3 cups whole milk
¾ cup granulated sugar
¾ teaspoon ground cinnamon
1 pinch salt
⅓ cup butter, melted

Long-Grain Versus Short-Grain

"Long-grain" is simply a classification for milled rice that is 3 times long as it is wide. Common varieties are basmati, jasmine, or Texmati. Short-grain and medium-grain rice are *less* than 3 times long as they are wide. Short grains are often more starchy and can be considered "sticky" rice. A common medium-grain rice is arborio, while a common short-grain rice is sushi rice.

1. In a colander, rinse rice with cold water, until water runs clear.

2. Pour rice into a greased 4-quart slow cooker. Add remaining ingredients and stir to combine.

3. Cover and cook on high for 2½–3 hours, until rice has absorbed the liquid.

4. Serve warm or refrigerate until cold.

PER SERVING | Calories: 347 | Fat: 14 g | Protein: 6 g | Sodium: 251 mg | Fiber: 0.5 g | Carbohydrates: 49 g | Sugar: 31 g

Cinnamon-Vanilla Tapioca Pudding

Tapioca pudding is a favorite among children. This dessert can be made overnight and placed in the refrigerator to serve as a cold afternoon snack.

INGREDIENTS | SERVES 4

4 cups whole milk
⅔ cup white sugar
2 eggs, lightly beaten
½ cup small pearl tapioca
½ teaspoon cinnamon
1 tablespoon vanilla

1. In a greased 2.5-quart or 4-quart slow cooker whisk together milk, sugar, eggs, tapioca, cinnamon, and vanilla.

2. Cover and cook on high for 2½–3 hours or on low for 6 hours, stirring occasionally.

3. Serve warm or cold.

PER SERVING | Calories: 392 | Fat: 10 g | Protein: 10 g | Sodium: 140 mg | Fiber: 0 g | Carbohydrates: 62 g | Sugar: 47 g

Gingerbread Pudding Cake

This cake may not be the prettiest cake you'll ever make, but the warm spices paired with vanilla bean ice cream is excellent.

INGREDIENTS | SERVES 6

½ cup brown rice flour
½ cup arrowroot starch
½ cup sugar
1 teaspoon baking powder
¼ teaspoon baking soda
1¼ teaspoons ground ginger
½ teaspoon ground cinnamon
¾ cup 2% milk
1 egg
½ cup raisins
2¼ cups water
¾ cup packed brown sugar
½ cup butter

1. Grease a 4-quart slow cooker with nonstick cooking spray. In a medium bowl, whisk together flour, arrowroot starch, sugar, baking powder, baking soda, ginger and cinnamon.

2. Stir milk and egg into dry ingredients. Stir in raisins (batter will be thick). Spread gingerbread batter evenly in the bottom of the prepared cooker.

3. In a medium saucepan, combine the water, brown sugar, and butter. Bring to a boil; reduce heat. Boil gently, uncovered, for 2 minutes. Carefully pour water/brown sugar mixture over the gingerbread batter.

4. Cover and vent lid with chopstick or the end of a wooden spoon. Cook on high for 2–2½ hours until cake is cooked through and a toothpick inserted about ½" into the cake comes out clean. (It may not look like it's all the way cooked through.)

5. Remove slow cooker insert from the metal cooker. Allow to cool for 45 minutes to an hour to allow "pudding" to set beneath the cake.

6. To serve, spoon warm cake into dessert dishes and spoon "pudding sauce" over the warm cake.

PER SERVING | Calories: 460 | Fat: 17 g | Protein: 3 g | Sodium: 170 mg | Fiber: 1 g | Carbohydrates: 75 g | Sugar: 52

Applesauce Cake

A lightly spiced cake that can be frosted with whipped vanilla icing or eaten plain, this cake would also be delicious with Spiced Winter Fruit Compote (see recipe in this chapter) spooned over each serving.

INGREDIENTS | SERVES 9

½ cup brown rice flour

½ cup plus 2 tablespoons arrowroot starch

½ cup sugar

1 teaspoon baking powder

½ teaspoon baking soda

½ teaspoon xanthan gum

¼ teaspoon salt

1 teaspoon cinnamon

½ teaspoon ground nutmeg

¼ teaspoon ground cloves

2 tablespoons canola oil

1 cup applesauce

2 eggs

Make a Round or Oval Cake

If you can't find any aluminum cans to use for this recipe, you can pour the batter into the bottom of a 4-quart slow cooker that's been lined with parchment paper. Cover, vent the lid and cook on high for 2–2½ hours or until cake is cooked through in the middle. You'll have to watch the cake carefully as it could burn on the edges and the bottom.

1. In a large bowl whisk together flour, arrowroot starch, sugar, baking powder, baking soda, xanthan gum, salt, cinnamon, nutmeg, and cloves. Mix together thoroughly.

2. In a smaller bowl mix together the oil, applesauce, and eggs.

3. Mix wet ingredients into dry ingredients with a fork, until you have a thick batter.

4. Grease 3 emptied and cleaned (15-ounce) aluminum cans and place ⅓ of the cake batter into each can. Place the cans into a 4-quart slow cooker.

5. Cover the slow cooker and vent the lid with a chopstick. Cook on high for 3–3½ hours or on low for 6–7 hours. Cakes should rise and become a golden brown on top when done.

6. Remove cans of cake carefully from slow cooker and allow to cool before removing from cans. Slice each canned cake into 3 round pieces of cake. These pieces can be placed in cupcake liners and served as cupcakes.

PER SERVING | Calories: 163 | Fat: 4 g | Protein: 2 g | Sodium: 207 mg | Fiber: 1 g | Carbohydrates: 29 g | Sugar: 14 g

Easy Chocolate Cake

This chocolate cake is easy to mix together to make a batch of cupcakes. To make your own chocolate cake mix simply whisk together all dry ingredients and place in a sanitized glass jar with a tight-fitting lid. Little jars of gluten-free cake mix make a nice homemade gift.

INGREDIENTS | SERVES 9

⅓ cup brown rice flour

⅓ cup arrowroot starch

⅓ cup sorghum flour

½ teaspoon xanthan gum

¾ cup sugar

¼ cup unsweetened baking cocoa

1 teaspoon baking powder

¼ teaspoon baking soda

¼ cup oil

¾ cup almond milk

½ teaspoon vanilla extract

2 eggs, slightly beaten

Everybody Loves Chocolate Chips

Mini chocolate chips make a nice addition to this cake. The Enjoy Life company makes gluten-free and dairy-free mini chocolate chips.

1. In a large bowl whisk together brown rice flour, arrowroot starch, sorghum flour, xanthan gum, sugar, cocoa, baking powder, and baking soda. Mix together thoroughly.

2. In a smaller bowl whisk together the oil, almond milk, vanilla, and eggs.

3. Mix wet ingredients into dry ingredients with a fork until you have a thick cake batter.

4. Grease 3 emptied and cleaned (15-ounce) aluminum cans and place ⅓ of the cake batter into each can. Place the cans in a 4-quart slow cooker.

5. Cover the slow cooker and vent the lid with a chopstick. Cook on high for 3–3½ hours or on low for 6–7 hours. Cakes should rise and about double in size and become a dark brown on top when done.

6. Remove cans of cake carefully from slow cooker and allow to cool before removing from cans. Slice each canned cake into 3 round pieces of cake. These pieces can be placed in cupcake liners and served as cupcakes. Eat plain or frost with your favorite icing.

PER SERVING | Calories: 249 | Fat: 11 g | Protein: 5 g | Sodium: 107 mg | Fiber: 3 g | Carbohydrates: 34 g | Sugar: 17 g

Crustless Lemon Cheesecake

Cheesecake bakes perfectly in the slow cooker. In this recipe, the slow cooker is lined with parchment paper, which makes for a very easy clean up!

INGREDIENTS | SERVES 8

16 ounces cream cheese, softened
⅔ cup sugar
2 large eggs
1 tablespoon cornstarch
1 teaspoon fresh lemon zest
2 tablespoons fresh lemon juice

1. In a large bowl beat cream cheese and sugar together until smooth.

2. Beat in eggs and continue beating on medium speed of a hand-held electric mixer for about 3 minutes.

3. Beat in remaining ingredients and continue beating for about 1 minute.

4. Line a 4-quart slow cooker with parchment paper. Pour batter onto the parchment paper.

5. Cover and cook on high for 2½–3 hours or until cheesecake is set. Remove slow cooker insert and place in fridge to chill for 2–6 hours. Slice to serve.

PER SERVING | Calories: 279 | Fat: 20 g | Protein: 5 g | Sodium: 198 mg | Fiber: 0 g | Carbohydrates: 20 g | Sugar: 18 g

Right-Side-Up Pineapple Cake

This is a fun and pretty cake to make, and it turns out beautifully in the slow cooker!

INGREDIENTS | SERVES 9

½ cup plus 1 tablespoon fine brown rice flour

½ cup arrowroot starch

½ cup sugar

1 teaspoon baking powder

½ teaspoon baking soda

½ teaspoon xanthan gum

¼ teaspoon salt

¼ cup oil

¾ cup 2% milk

2 eggs

1 teaspoon vanilla extract

6 pineapple rings

6 maraschino cherries

¼ cup pecans, chopped

¼ cup brown sugar, lightly packed

2 tablespoons butter, melted

1. In a large bowl whisk together flour, arrowroot starch, sugar, baking powder, baking soda, xanthan gum, and salt. Mix together thoroughly.

2. In a smaller bowl whisk together the oil, milk, eggs, and vanilla.

3. Mix wet ingredients into dry ingredients with a fork until you have a thick cake batter.

4. Line a 4-quart slow cooker with parchment paper. Spray with nonstick cooking spray. Pour cake batter onto the parchment paper and spread evenly.

5. Gently place the pineapple rings on top of cake. Add a cherry to the middle of each slice. Sprinkle pecans and brown sugar over cake. Drizzle melted butter over cake.

6. Cover the slow cooker and vent the lid with a chopstick. Cook on high for 2½–3 hours. Cake should rise and become a golden brown when done.

PER SERVING | Calories: 277 | Fat: 12 g | Protein: 3 g | Sodium: 218 mg | Fiber: 1.5 g | Carbohydrates: 38 g | Sugar: 22 g

Blueberry Cobbler

An old-fashioned cobbler with sweetened fruit on the bottom and a crunchy, biscuity topping, this dessert can be served plain or with ice cream.

INGREDIENTS | SERVES 6

¾ cup water
⅔ cup plus 2 tablespoons sugar
2 tablespoons cornstarch
3 cups fresh or frozen blueberries
½ cup brown rice flour
½ cup arrowroot starch
1 teaspoon baking powder
¼ teaspoon xanthan gum
⅓ cup 2% milk
1 tablespoon melted butter
½ teaspoon cinnamon mixed with 2 teaspoons sugar
2 tablespoons cold butter, cut into small pieces

Make It Easier

If you don't want to go to the trouble of making your own fruit filling, use a can of cherry pie filling, apple pie filling, or even a can of whole cranberry jelly. Make the cobbler even easier by replacing the brown rice flour, arrowroot starch, baking powder and xanthan gum with 1 cup of Gluten-Free Bisquick.

1. Grease a 4-quart slow cooker.

2. In a small saucepan add water, ⅔ cup sugar, and cornstarch. Whisk together and cook over high heat, stirring constantly until boiling. Allow to boil for 1 minute. The mixture will turn translucent and thicken. Remove from heat and add blueberries. Pour blueberry filling into the greased slow cooker.

3. In a small bowl whisk together flour, arrowroot starch, baking powder, 2 tablespoons sugar, and xanthan gum. Make a well in the center of the dry ingredients and add milk and melted butter. Mix until you have a thick batter.

4. Drop batter by tablespoons on top of the blueberry filling and use a fork to spread evenly over the casserole.

5. Sprinkle cinnamon and sugar mixture over the top of the casserole. Dot with butter.

6. Cover and vent slow cooker lid with a chopstick or the end of a wooden spoon. Cook on high for 2½–3 hours or until fruit filling is bubbling on the sides of the topping and the biscuit topping is cooked through.

PER SERVING | Calories: 307 | Fat: 7 g | Protein: 2 g | Sodium: 91 mg | Fiber: 3 g | Carbohydrates: 62 g | Sugar: 36 g

CHAPTER 15

Beverages

Spiced Cherry Punch

The apple and orange juices add natural sweetness to this refreshing punch, but you can also stir in some sugar to taste if you prefer a sweeter punch. Have dark rum or other adult beverage available for those who wish to add it to the punch.

INGREDIENTS | SERVES 14

8 cups (2 quarts) apple cider or apple juice

½ cup tart cherry juice concentrate

3 cups water

2 cups orange juice

1½ teaspoons whole allspice berries

1½ teaspoons whole cloves

2 (3-inch) cinnamon sticks

1 tablespoon aromatic bitters (optional)

Tart Cherry Juice Concentrate

Tart cherry juice concentrate is available at most natural food stores or online through Michigan producers like Brownwood Acres Foods, Inc. (*www.brownwoodacres.com*) and King Orchards (*www.kingorchards.com*).

1. Add the apple cider or apple juice, cherry juice concentrate, water, and orange juice to a 4-quart slow cooker.

2. Add the allspice berries and whole cloves to a muslin spice bag or a piece of cheesecloth that has been rinsed and wrung dry; secure with a piece of kitchen twine and add to the juices in the cooker.

3. Add the cinnamon sticks. Stir in the aromatic bitters if using. Cover and cook until very hot but not boiling, about 2 hours on high or 4 hours on low.

4. Remove the spices in the muslin bag or cheesecloth and cinnamon sticks from the cooker. The punch can be kept at serving temperature by setting the slow cooker on low, keeping in mind that the flavors will become more concentrated the longer the punch is uncovered and on the heat. Serve in punch glasses or mugs garnished with cinnamon sticks if desired.

PER SERVING | Calories: 83 | Fat: 0 g | Protein: 0 g | Sodium: 9 mg | Fiber: 0.5 g | Carbohydrates: 20 g | Sugar: 16 g

Hot Cranberry-Pineapple Punch

If you prefer, you can omit the brown sugar and water and sweeten the punch with 2 cups of apple juice instead.

INGREDIENTS | SERVES 20

8 cups cranberry juice

8 cups unsweetened pineapple juice

2 cups brown sugar, packed

2 cups water

2 (3-inch) cinnamon sticks

2 teaspoons whole cloves

Chilled Cranberry-Pineapple Punch

After slow cooking, allow the punch to cool to room temperature and then chill until needed. Add 3–4 cups lemon-lime soda or Mountain Dew. Serve in punch cups or in tall glasses over ice, garnished with a maraschino cherry.

1. Add the cranberry juice, pineapple juice, brown sugar, and water to a 6-quart slow cooker.

2. Break the cinnamon sticks into smaller pieces and add them along with the whole cloves to a muslin spice bag or wrap them in cheesecloth tied shut with cotton string or kitchen twine. Add to the slow cooker. Cover and cook on low for 1 hour.

3. Uncover and stir until the brown sugar is dissolved into the juice. Cover and cook for another 7–8 hours.

4. Uncover the cooker and lift out the spice bag or cheesecloth. Holding it over the slow cooker, squeeze it to extract the seasoned juice. To serve, ladle into heatproof mugs.

PER SERVING | Calories: 185 | Fat: 0 g | Protein: 1 g | Sodium: 11 mg | Fiber: 1 g | Carbohydrates: 47 g | Sugar: 43 g

Cinnamon Apple Tea

This recipe uses instant tea mix, which already contains sugar. However, if you would prefer to simply use 2 family-sized tea bags, you can do that as well and then sweeten each individual serving as desired.

INGREDIENTS | SERVES 12

3 quarts (12 cups) water
12 ounces frozen apple juice concentrate
½ cup instant tea mix
6 whole cloves
3 cinnamon sticks
1 orange, thinly sliced

1. Place water, juice concentrate, tea mix, cloves, and cinnamon sticks in 4-quart or larger slow cooker, stir to combine. Cover and cook on high for 2 hours.

2. Reduce to low heat. Remove cloves and cinnamon sticks and add orange slices to tea.

PER SERVING | Calories: 26 | Fat: 0 g | Protein: 0 g | Sodium: 15 g | Fiber: 1 g | Carbohydrates: 7 g | Sugar: 4 g

Citrus Cider

With three different types of juice, this cider packs a serious punch of vitamin C. It's perfect for sipping when you have a cold or are feeling a bit under the weather.

INGREDIENTS | SERVES 10

2 quarts apple cider or apple juice
1 cup orange juice
½ cup lemon juice
⅓ cup honey
2 sticks cinnamon
8 whole cloves
½ teaspoon ground ginger

Place all ingredients in a 4–6-quart slow cooker. Cover and cook on high for 2 hours or on low for 4 hours. While serving, place slow cooker on the warm or low setting.

PER SERVING | Calories: 144 | Fat: 0 g | Protein: 0.5 g | Sodium: 11 mg | Fiber: 1 g | Carbohydrates: 36 g | Sugar: 30 g

Mulled Cranberry Punch

The tart-sweet flavors of this punch simmered with warm spices make it a perfect drink to serve during the fall.

INGREDIENTS | SERVES 10

1 (11.5-ounce) can frozen white grape–raspberry juice concentrate

1 (32-ounce) bottle cranberry juice

4 cups water

1 orange

2 cinnamon sticks, broken

8 whole cloves

4 whole allspice

No Cheesecloth?

Instead of using cheesecloth to create the spice bag in this mulled punch, you can simply use a large metal or plastic tea ball to place all the spices in while the tea is simmering. When you've finished using it, discard the spices and rinse out the tea ball to use again.

1. In a 4–6-quart slow cooker, place juice concentrate, cranberry juice, and water.

2. Using a vegetable peeler, remove a long peel from the orange. Juice orange and strain out the seeds. Add strained orange juice to the slow cooker.

3. Using a double-thickness square of cheesecloth, place the orange peel, cinnamon sticks, cloves, and allspice in the center. Close up the cheesecloth and tie up using cotton kitchen string. Add the spice bag to the slow cooker.

4. Cover and cook on low for 6 hours or on high for 3 hours. Discard the spice bag and serve with the slow cooker turned to the warm setting.

PER SERVING | Calories: 50 | Fat: 0 g | Protein: 0 g | Sodium: 5 mg | Fiber: 1 g | Carbohydrates: 13 g | Sugar: 12 g

Creamy Hot Chocolate

You can easily make this recipe dairy-free by using your favorite nondairy milk to replace the milk and half-and-half. If you like the flavor of coconut milk, it has a super creamy texture for hot chocolate.

INGREDIENTS | SERVES 6

⅓ cup unsweetened cocoa powder
½ cup sugar
¼ teaspoon salt
⅓ cup hot water
3½ cups whole milk
1 tablespoon vanilla extract
½ cup half-and-half

1. In the bottom of a 2.5–4-quart slow cooker, whisk together the cocoa powder, sugar, and salt. Slowly whisk in the hot water, milk, and vanilla. Cover the slow cooker and cook on high for 1½ hours or on low for 3 hours.

2. Right before serving whisk in the half-and-half, and heat another 5–10 minutes, just long enough to heat through.

PER SERVING | Calories: 195 | Fat: 7 g | Protein: 6 g | Sodium: 169 mg | Fiber: 2 g | Carbohydrates: 27 g | Sugar: 24 g

Maple Pumpkin Spice Lattes

This warm latte is reminiscent of a drink you would pay big bucks for at a local coffee chain. By making your own you're not only saving money, but you'll have enough for a whole week's worth of breakfasts or after-dinner coffees. Try it with a whipped cream topping.

INGREDIENTS | SERVES 8

2 cups very strong coffee or espresso
4 cups whole milk
¾ cup plain pumpkin purée
⅓ cup maple syrup
1 tablespoon vanilla
2 teaspoons of pumpkin pie spice

In a 4-quart slow cooker whisk together all ingredients. Cover and cook on high for 1½ hours or on low for 3 hours. When serving, turn slow cooker to the warm setting for up to 2 hours. Serve warm.

PER SERVING | Calories: 118 | Fat: 4 g | Protein: 4 g | Sodium: 62 mg | Fiber: 0 g | Carbohydrates: 15 g | Sugar: 14 g

Make Your Own Pumpkin Pie Spice

If you don't have pumpkin pie spice, mix together 3 tablespoons ground cinnamon, 2 tablespoons ground ginger, 2 teaspoons ground nutmeg, 1½ teaspoons ground allspice, and 1½ teaspoons ground cloves. Store in an airtight container.

German Mulled Wine

To add a touch of sweetness to this drink, sprinkle a few pieces of cinnamon red hot candies into each serving.

INGREDIENTS | SERVES 12

5 cups apple cider
5 cups burgundy wine
½ cup honey
1 teaspoon whole cloves
12 whole allspice berries
Zest of 1 lemon
2 (3-inch) pieces cinnamon sticks

1. Add the cider, wine, and honey to a 4-quart slow cooker.

2. Put cloves, allspice berries, and lemon zest in a double square of cheesecloth. Pull up corners of cheesecloth and tie securely with cotton kitchen string. Add to the slow cooker along with the cinnamon sticks.

3. Cover and cook on low for 3–4 hours. When serving, turn slow cooker to the warm setting for no longer than 2 hours.

PER SERVING | Calories: 176 | Fat: 0 g | Protein: 0 g | Sodium: 9 mg | Fiber: 0 g | Carbohydrates: 26 g | Sugar: 22 g

Warm Spiced Turmeric Tea

A soothing tea with a peppery kick made purely from spices, this tea is delicious served with several tablespoons of coconut milk or half-and-half stirred in right before drinking.

INGREDIENTS | SERVES 4

4 cups water
⅓ cup honey
2 tablespoons ground cinnamon
1½ tablespoons ground turmeric
1 tablespoon ginger
2 teaspoons nutmeg
1 teaspoon cloves

1. Add water, honey, and all spices to a 2.5-quart slow cooker. Whisk together thoroughly to combine spices into the water.

2. Cover and cook on high for 2–3 hours or on low for 5–6 hours. Occasionally remove the lid and whisk tea. Serve warm.

PER SERVING | Calories: 105 | Fat: 0.5 g | Protein: 0 g | Sodium: 2 mg | Fiber: 2 g | Carbohydrates: 27 g | Sugar: 23 g

A Note on Turmeric

Turmeric has been used for centuries in Chinese and Indian medicine because of its natural anti-inflammatory properties. It's a deep yellow-orange in color and is often used in Indian curries. Turmeric is also a good source of manganese, iron, vitamin B_6, and potassium.

Slow Cooker Chai Tea

Feel free to leave the cardamom pods out of this warm tea if you don't have them readily available. Alternately, you can purchase ground cardamom and sprinkle a little on each mug of tea.

INGREDIENTS | SERVES 8

8 cups water

2 family-sized tea bags (or 8 individual-sized tea bags)

½ cup sugar

16 whole cloves

16 whole cardamom seeds, removed from pods

5 cinnamon sticks

1 (2-inch) knob of ginger, peeled

1 cup 2% milk

1. Add water, tea bags, sugar, cloves, cardamom, cinnamon sticks, and ginger to a 4-quart slow cooker.

2. Cover and cook on high for 3 hours or on low for 6 hours. Before serving use a metal or plastic sieve to remove the spices, ginger, and tea bags from the tea.

3. Slowly stir in the milk and turn the slow cooker to the warm setting for serving. Leave the tea in the slow cooker for no more than 2 hours on the warm setting. Tea can be refrigerated and reheated for later use.

PER SERVING | Calories: 95 | Fat: 1 g | Protein: 2 g | Sodium: 22 mg | Fiber: 2 g | Carbohydrates: 20 g | Sugar: 14 g

Salted Caramel Mocha Lattes

The slight hint of salt in this warm, creamy drink balances out the sweetness of the caramel. When serving this sweet drink offer whipped cream, additional caramel sauce, chocolate syrup, or sea salt for toppings.

INGREDIENTS | SERVES 6

3 cups whole milk

3 cups strongly brewed coffee

2 tablespoons unsweetened cocoa

⅓ cup sugar

¼ teaspoon salt

1 teaspoon vanilla extract

⅓ cup caramel sauce

1. Place all ingredients a 4-quart slow cooker. Use a whisk to combine ingredients thoroughly.

2. Cover slow cooker and cook on high for 1–2 hours or on low for 2–3 hours, until mixture is hot and simmering.

PER SERVING | Calories: 172 | Fat: 4 g | Protein: 4.5 g | Sodium: 163 mg | Fiber: 1 g | Carbohydrates: 29 g | Sugar: 26 g

Strongly Brewed Coffee

To get a very strong coffee flavor in this drink use about 3–4 tablespoons of ground coffee per cup of water. The coffee will be diluted when combined with the milk in this recipe and will be creamy and delicious.

Vanilla Bean White Hot Chocolate

Children love this creamy, rich, warm vanilla-y drink made with white chocolate baking pieces.

INGREDIENTS | SERVES 8

8 cups whole milk

1 (12-ounce) package white chocolate chips

2 tablespoons vanilla extract

⅛ teaspoon salt

1 vanilla bean

2 cups whipped heavy cream

1. Add milk, white chocolate chips, vanilla, and salt to a 4-quart slow cooker. Use a whisk to combine ingredients thoroughly.

2. Using a sharp knife, cut the vanilla bean in half and scrape out the tiny seeds and add them to the milk mixture.

3. Cover slow cooker and cook on high for 1–2 hours or on low for 2–3 hours, until mixture is hot and simmering.

4. Serve in large mugs or coffee cups with whipped cream on top.

PER SERVING | Calories: 566 | Fat: 42 g | Protein: 10 g | Sodium: 159 mg | Fiber: 2.5 g | Carbohydrates: 40 g | Sugar: 36 g

Peppermint Mocha Lattes

A refreshing coffee drink made right in your slow cooker. You could also make a chilled peppermint mocha latte by refrigerating the leftovers and serving the drink over ice the next day!

INGREDIENTS | SERVES 6

3 cups whole milk

3 cups strongly brewed coffee

¼ cup unsweetened cocoa

⅓ cup sugar

½ teaspoon peppermint extract

⅛ teaspoon salt

2 cups whipped heavy cream

1. Add milk, coffee, cocoa, sugar, peppermint extract, and salt to a 4-quart slow cooker. Use a whisk to combine ingredients thoroughly.

2. Cover slow cooker and cook on high for 1–2 hours or on low for 2–3 hours, until mixture is hot and simmering.

3. Serve in large mugs or coffee cups with whipped cream.

PER SERVING | Calories: 401 | Fat: 34 g | Protein: 6 g | Sodium: 132 mg | Fiber: 1 g | Carbohydrates: 21 g | Sugar: 17 g

Gluten-Free Ingredient Resources

Amazon.com

Nearly all of the specialty gluten-free ingredients used in this cookbook can be purchased from Amazon.com.

www.amazon.com

Better Than Bouillon

This company makes gluten-free chicken, beef, and vegetable soup bases that are in a paste form. They should be stored in the refrigerator upon opening. The ORGANIC variety of soup bases are gluten-free (the "regular" ones are NOT!), so make sure to look for the organic label. This gluten-free stock is a really helpful pantry staple to have because you can make as much or as little as you need according to the recipe you are using. Nearly all the recipes in this book were tested using Better Than Bouillon Organic Soup Bases.

http://www.superiortouch.com/retail/products/better-than-bouillon/organic-bases

Betty Crocker

Betty Crocker now offers gluten-free products such as gluten-free cake, brownie, and cookie mixes, along with Gluten-Free Bisquick. These products can now be found in many grocery stores.

www.bettycrocker.com/products

Blue Diamond Almond Breeze

This preferred brand of casein-free, soy-free, nondairy milk can be purchased at many grocery stores or online in shelf-stable packaging.

www.bluediamond.com

Bob's Red Mill

For the gluten-free flours used in this cookbook (brown rice flour, sorghum flour, millet flour, arrowroot starch, garbanzo bean flour, and tapioca starch/flour) along with gluten-free cornmeal, grits, all-purpose gluten-free flour, pancake mix, xanthan gum, guar gum, SAF instant yeast, and gluten-free baking powder.

www.bobsredmill.com

Glutino

A gluten-free food producer of crackers, breads, and cookies.

www.glutino.com

Honeyville Blanched Almond Flour

Blanched almond flour is a high-protein flour that's used in several recipes in this cookbook. This brand is preferred over others as the quality is consistently high.

http://store.honeyvillegrain.com

Kikkoman

Primarily a producer of gluten-free/wheat-free soy sauce.
www.kikkomanusa.com/homecooks/products

Kinnikinnick

A gluten-free food producer of cookies, breads, and dry cake and pancake mixes.
http://consumer.kinnikinnick.com

Le Veneziane

Le Veneziane produces gluten-free corn pasta in very unique shapes as called for in some recipes such as small gluten-free pasta in the Italian Wedding Soup in Chapter 7. These pastas can be purchased from Amazon.com.
www.amazon.com/Veneziane-Italian-Gluten-Pasta-Rigate

Native Forest Organic Coconut Milk

A nondairy alternative for milk, which can be used in numerous applications in gluten-free cooking and baking.
http://edwardandsons.com

Premier Japan

Producers of gluten-free Asian sauce products such as soy sauce, hoisin sauce, and oyster sauce.
www.edwardandsons.com

San J

Producers of gluten-free Asian sauce products such as soy sauce, hoisin sauce, oyster sauce, fish sauce, etc.
www.san-j.com

Tinkyáda

A prominent producer of gluten-free pasta. This product can be found in many local grocery stores.
www.tinkyada.com

Celiac Disease/Gluten Sensitivity and Gluten-Free Support Group Resources

Celiac.com

Founded by Scott Adams in 1995, one of the oldest online resources for all information gluten-free, including *The Journal of Gluten Sensitivity*, an online gluten-free mall, and a host of gluten-free forums.
www.celiac.com

Celiac Disease Foundation

A very active gluten-free and celiac disease awareness organization that's been in operation since 1990.
www.celiac.org

Celiac Sprue Association (CSA)

A great resource for finding local gluten-free support groups, along with basic information on starting the gluten-free diet.
www.csaceliacs.info

Gluten Sensitivity Group (GIG)

Another resource for finding local gluten-free support groups, as well as information on safe foods that are certified gluten-free by GIG programs.
www.gluten.net

The National Foundation for Celiac Awareness

A not-for-profit organization that supports raising awareness for celiac disease and gluten sensitivity.
www.celiaccentral.org

Helpful Slow Cooker Equipment Sources

Hamilton Beach

Slow cookers

www.hamiltonbeach.com

Reynolds Consumer Products Company

Reynolds Slow Cooker Liners, Reynolds Aluminum Foil, Reynolds Parchment Paper

www.reynoldskitchens.com

Rival

Slow cookers

www.crock-pot.com

Taylor Products

Cooking, oven, and food thermometers

www.taylorusa.com

WestBend

Slow cookers

westbend.com

Index

Note: Page numbers in **bold** indicate recipe category lists.

We Have
EVERYTHING®
on Anything!

With more than 19 million copies sold, the Everything® series has become one of America's favorite resources for solving problems, learning new skills, and organizing lives. Our brand is not only recognizable—it's also welcomed.

The series is a hand-in-hand partner for people who are ready to tackle new subjects—like you!

For more information on the Everything® series, please visit *www.adamsmedia.com*

The Everything® list spans a wide range of subjects, with more than 500 titles covering 25 different categories:

Business	History	Reference
Careers	Home Improvement	Religion
Children's Storybooks	Everything Kids	Self-Help
Computers	Languages	Sports & Fitness
Cooking	Music	Travel
Crafts and Hobbies	New Age	Wedding
Education/Schools	Parenting	Writing
Games and Puzzles	Personal Finance	
Health	Pets	